Richard Renstrom Great Motorcycle Legends

Richard Renstrom Great Motorcycle Legends

HAESSNER
PUBLISHING, INC.

Revised edition: 1st edition published in 1972
under the title "The Great Motorcycles"

Cover design by John M. Peckham

ISBN 0-87799-057-3

Library of Congress Catalog Card No: 77-74638

Printed in the United States of America

HAESSNER PUBLISHING, INC.,
NEWFOUNDLAND, NEW JERSEY 07435

CONTENTS

Foreword 6

AJS 7

Ariel 12

BMW 17

BSA 22

Bultaco 26

Ducati 31

Greeves 36

Honda 41

Husqvarna 46

Jawa 56

Lambretta 62

Matchless 67

Montesa 72

Moto Gilera 81

Moto Guzzi 85

Norton 91

NSU 96

Ossa 102

Puch 107

Royal Enfield 112

Triumph 117

Velocette 122

FOREWORD

The past decade has witnessed a tremendous increase in the popularity of the motorcycle in the United States. Along with this new found popularity has come many new riders, most of whom have little knowledge of the great history of our sport.

Most of these new motorcyclists, along with the more seasoned riders, are interested in the history and evolution of the motorcycle. It is for these curious afficianados that I have written this book, and I only hope in these pages you can capture the spirit of invention that has made the motorcycle such a fascinating form of transportation and sport.

I have attempted in this book to cover the sporting history of each marque featured, since motorcycle racing and competition experience has had such a great deal to do with design improvement down through the years. There is something about the motorcycle, compared to the automobile, that is more sporting in nature, and it is this feature that has made the history of the motorcycle so varied and appealing.

In preparing this book we have had a great deal of assistance, without which it would have been impossible to prepare and illustrate the manuscript. We would, therefore, like to acknowledge the following: Bavarian Motor Works, Birmingham Small Arms Company, Bultaco, Ducati Meccanica, Greeves, Honda Motor Company, Husqvarna, Jawa, Lambretta, Matchless, Montesa, Moto Gilera, Moto Guzzi, Norton-Villiers, NSU, Ossa, Puch, Royal Enfield, Triumph and Velocette. In addition we are indebted to the Ariel Owners Motorcycle Club, The Motor Cycle, Temple Press Ltd., Motor Cycle News, Bagnall Publishing Company, B. R. Nicholls, and Joseph C. Parkhurst for supplying photographs and making it possible to publish this book.

In this book I have tried to produce a concise and readable history of 22 of the most important makes of machines in the history of the sport. I sincerely hope it will be considered a valued addition to the knowledge of the motorcycle, and I am pleased to dedicate this work to all of those who believe that motorcycling is the most fascinating sport on earth.

The history of motorcycling is captivating and the legacy is great. I hope in the pages of this book you can feel the nostalgia that I do so that we may share it together.

Richard C. Renstrom
January 20, 1977

AJS

In the colorful annals of motorcycling, there are a few manufacturers which have been pioneers of design progress as well as creators of legend in competition. One such company is AJS-a British marque that possesses a great legacy of success in trials, motocross and road racing, and which has exerted a driving force for better motorcycle design during the first half of the 20th Century.

The story of this progressive concern began in 1897 when an engineering blacksmith named Joseph Stevens gathered his five sons about him to design and produce an internal combustion engine. The new gasoline burning device was soon put into production, and within a short time it was powering such early day motorbikes as the Werner and the Wolf.

This engine proved to be a reliable little chugger, and the reputation of the Stevens family was established. Thus encouraged, the business expanded and production of motorcycle frames and other proprietary parts was initiated. By 1900, the 2.25- and 3.25-bhp single-cylinder engines were available in both air and water cooled versions, and the little company was on a firm financial base.

By 1909, the Stevens family was eager to try its own hand at producing a complete motorcycle, so the plans were drawn up and production was started. Named the AJS after the A.J. Stevens name, the new motorbike featured a 2.75-bhp single-cylinder engine mounted in a bicycle frame; belt drive was used. The model proved to be as reliable as any during those early days.

By 1911, the infant company was producing a genuine motorcycle with a heavier frame, a 298-cc (70 by 77.5mm) side-valve engine, belt drive, and a three-speed gearbox. This use of a separate gearbox was a most unusual feature, as the majority of manufacturers still were using either a single-speed belt drive, a two-speed rear hub gear, or an expanding-pulley belt

drive arrangement. Two of these AJS machines were entered in the 1911 Isle of Man TT, but 15th and 16th places were the best obtained.

In 1913, the factory made a really noteworthy design advance when it produced the 350-cc model with bore and stroke measurements of 74 by 81 mm. The engine was a side-valve unit that produced 2.75 snarling bph, and this power was transmitted by

Canadian rider Mike Duff at speed on an AJS twin in 1968.

The 1937 AJS Single was available in 350- and 500-cc sizes. Peppy ohv engine, four-speed footshift and rigid frame were standard.

The 1932 AJS model T-2 was a smooth-running side-valve V-Twin in 800- or 1000-cc sizes. A handshift three-speed gearbox was used.

an all-chain drive. The earlier three-speed gearbox was dropped in favor of a two-speed unit. Another progressive idea was the use of an internal expanding brake on the rear wheel. A caliper type brake was still used on the front wheel. One of these thumpers was entered by the factory in the famous Isle of Man TT, and it garnered a creditable 9th place.

The following year, the 350 was improved by the fitting of a double chain and sprocket arrangement from the engine to the clutch, with a lever and cable sliding one or the other set into engagement. The two chains ran on engine sprockets with an off number of teeth, and this provided four speeds when used with the hand-shifted two-speed gearbox.

The side-valve engine was also developing greater power, with the remarkable engine speed of 5000 rpm possible on the road. The engine, incidentally, had a cast iron cylinder and a steel piston with a slim clearance of only 0.001 in. between them. The lubrication system was still rather archaic. A hand pump and the total loss method were used.

The 1914 Junior TT saw five new AJS machines entered, and they all finished—1st, 2nd, 4th, 6th, and 29th. Eric Williams was the victor, and he won at the record speed of 45.72mph with a record lap at 47.57mph. This magnificent showing greatly enhanced the company's reputation and boosted sales. A move soon was made to larger quarters at Wolverhampton. Then came the Kaiser's war, and the AJS folk were plunged into war contract work.

The war itself taught the Stevens brothers a great deal about metalurgy in general, and the value of aluminum and other light alloys in particular. When peace returned, much of this knowledge was put into practice in motorcycle production. This provided a great leap forward in design progress.

The first post-war TT race, in 1920, provided the marque with another victory in the Junior class. AJS was rather lucky, however, because six of the eight works entries broke down, and winner Cyril Williams pushed his bike in from Keppel Gate after it had ceased to run. Eric Williams did increase the lap record to 51.36 mph, though, which well demonstrated the speed of his Single.

The new AJS actually was a very advanced design for its day, and it can be said to have been the true father of the high performance single-cylinder design. The 350-cc engine had a bore and stroke of 74 by 81 mm, and it featured an overhead valve design. The valves were set at a 90-degree angle to each other, thus providing the now common hemispherical combustion chamber design. The advantages of the hemispherical combustion chamber were better fuel flow characteristics and greater head space for larger valves. Today this is a standard practice for most high performance ohv engines. The head and cylinder were cast iron; a steel piston was used.

The belt drive, by then, was just about dead, and AJS was progressive with its all-chain drive. An interesting feature was the six-speed gear setup (and present-day riders think six-speeds are something new!) which had a three-speed gearbox with the two-speed engine-clutch arrangement. An internal expanding brake was used on the rear, but a caliper brake

was still featured at the front.

During 1921, the factory worked the bugs out of their new ohv design, and reliability took a big jump. The number of gear ratios was reduced to only three by doing away with the dual engine-clutch chain setup, and the gear ratios were 4.9:1, 6.0:1, and 9.3:1. A new frame was used in conjunction with 2.25x26 tires. Dry weight was only 190 lb. Maximum speed was 70-75 mph, which was terifficly fast for those days.

In the Junior TT, the marque scored a smashing 1st, 2nd, 3rd, 4th, and 5th, with Eric Williams the winner at 52.11 mph. Howard Davies upped the record lap to 55.15 mph, then went on to win the Senior TT at the record speed of 54.49 mph-the only time a 350 ever has won the 500 event!

By then, the reputation and sales of the AJS were at a very high level. Profits from production were turned back into research and additional race results. The 1922 models were again improved, with the famous 350-cc Big Port Single heading the range of machines. This thumper ran on a compression ratio of 5.75:1 and had a huge 2.625-in. diameter exhaust pipe. Internal expanding brakes were used front and rear. The model again took 1st and 2nd in the Junior TT with Tom Sheard winning at 54.75 mph.

The following year, the racers were modified by use of aluminum alloy pistons. In 1924, a large inlet valve was fitted to better charge the cylinder. The racing fortunes of the marque declined after 1922, as a result of some peculiarly rotten luck, rather than through deficiencies in design and engineering. A few places were gained in the TT races, plus a win or two in Continental grands prix, but for the time the coveted No. 1 was to elude AJS.

In the meantime, the production range was going strong with sales climbing to previously unheard of heights. By 1925, the range of machines offered was comprehensive and included models for just about every type of riding. For the budget minded there were 250-, 350- and 500-cc side-valve Singles that offered reliable day-to-day transportation at rock bottom prices. For the more sporting minded there were 350- and 500-cc ohv models that provided a spirited performance. For the connoisseur of motorcycles there were the powerful, smooth-running 800- and 1000-cc side-valve V-twin models.

Another 1925 success was the 500-cc Single, built for a bash at the Senior TT. Ridden by Frank Longman into 2nd place, the ohv engine had a bore and stroke of 84 by 90 mm, and weighed only 270 lb. After winning the French Grand Prix, the factory decided to put the model into production for the 1926 season. By then, AJS had won renown throughout Europe for their well designed Singles.

Motorcycle racing in Europe became extremely competitive during the late 1920's. Greater horsepower was required to stay in contention. In response to this, the Wolverhampton firm developed new ohc works racers for the 1927 season. The Single camshaft was driven by chain, and the primitive foot-operated oil pump (total loss) was at last replaced with a double-gear pump and a dry sump system. A new four-speed gearbox also was used, with gear ratios of 4.6:1, 5.58:1, 7.5:1, and 10.29:1

on the 350-cc model, and 4.12:1, 4.99:1, 6.7:1, and 9.19:1 on the 500-cc model. An unusual feature was the foot operation of both brakes. The idea was to leave the right hand free to operate the throttle and gearshift lever.

The new camshaft engines proved reliable, but slow. In the TT, the best the AJS machines could do was a 3rd in the Junior. Jim Guthrie, however, went on to win the 350-cc class in the grands prix of Belgium, Switzerland, Austria, and Germany. Nevertheless, the company decided that the cammer needed more development, so AJS reverted to its pushrod design for the 1928 season-with a fair turn of success in Continental events.

In 1929, the factory reintroduced the ohc engine with small internal improvements, plus a stronger girder fork at the front. Large brakes also were used, with an 8-in. unit on the front and a 9-in. size on the rear. The 350 proved much faster that year with a 2nd place in the Junior TT, plus victories in the Ulster, Austrian, German, and European grands prix.

The 500-cc model generally proved unreliable, but it did set up a new one-hour record at 104.51 mph, plus a 500-cc one-kilometer record of 118.98 mph. The 350-cc model also set a kilometer record at 107.37 mph. Altogether, this marque set over 100 speed/endurance records that year.

During 1930, the standard production range was enhanced by the introduction of a new side-valve V-twin that was aimed at the rider who wished something smooth, powerful, and a bit different. The unusual thing about this new Twin was that the engine was mounted transversly in the frame. The model stayed in production only a few years and was then discarded as being too expensive to produce.

Another model that was introduced in 1930 was the R7 racer. This 350-cc model featured a chain-driven ohc 350-cc engine patterned after the works racer, and it had a rigid frame and girder front fork. The R7 proved to be popular with the private owners, but it never did achieve speeds to match the KTT Velocette or Manx Norton.

The AJS factory also had a bash at the world speed record with a 1000-cc V-twin in 1930, but 130 mph was the best obtained. The engine was a 50-degree V-twin with bore and stroke of 79 by 101 mm. It had chaindriven overhead camshafts. There were two carburetors, with both inlet ports facing rearward and exhaust ports facing forward. Cylinders were of steel and heads of light alloy. The V-twin appeared again in 1933, fitted with a supercharger, but 136 mph was the best speed achieved. The last attempt was made at Tat, Hungary, with 145 mph recorded, but this was 6 mph below the world record.

During the early 1930's, the marque scored a few grand prix wins, plus Jim Guthrie's 1930 Lightweight TT victory. As time passed, AJS faded away from serious contention. The main cause was financial, because the economic depression severly damaged the financial standing of the company. By 1931, the concern was on the rocks, and the doors were closed, but, happily, the name and tradition were kept alive when the Matchless Co. purchased AJS and moved it to Woolwich, London.

This move to London, plus the depression, naturally caused a curtailment of AJS racing efforts, and increased emphasis was put on the standard production models. The side-valve and ohv Singles continued to be the most popular models in the range, and their reliability and performance endeared them to owners throughout Europe. The big side-valve V-twin also was continued, and this long wheelbase model offered about as much rider comfort as could be expected in those days of rigid frames and girder front forks.

There was an AJS reentry into international racing in 1934. From then, until 1939, the 350-cc machines followed the general trend of design. The engines remained basically the same chain-driven ohc units, but they gradually included more light alloy in their construction. Aluminum bronze heads were used in 1934, a bi-metal head with a bronze skull in 1935, and aluminum alloy with screwed-in valve seats in 1937.

Aluminum alloys also were used extensively for the cycle parts. Maganesium alloys were employed for gearbox and engine castings. This all helped keep the weight down to a light 270 lb. on the 1935 model, but the weight climbed to over 300 lb. in 1938 when rear suspension was added. The suspension was by an unusual pivoted-fork that attached to plunger spring boxes at the rear of the frame. Another improvement was the huge alloy front hub-brake unit, and nearly all of these modifications (except the spring frame) were adopted on the 7R model which was produced in limited numbers for the private owner.

By the middle 1930's, the world was on its way to economic recovery, and the AJS higher echelon decided that the expanding sales justified a more intensive racing campaign. Those also were the days when everyone else had the same idea, and international road racing became terribly competitive. Matt Wright, who was AJS' chief design engeneer, thought really big. When his pet project was laid out on the drawing boards it caused even the strongest to gasp.

The basic plot was a 50-degree V-4 with bore and stroke of 50 by 63 mm. The light alloy cylinders and heads were very similar to the 7R design. Overhead cams were driven by a chain in the center of the engine. The valves were controlled by exposed hairpin valve springs, and two carburetors fed the cylinders. Eccentrically mounted rocker arms were used to set valve clearances. The compression ratio was 8:1. The hollow, two-throw crankshaft was supported by five roller and ball bearings. A vertical shaft and bevel gear setup drove the oil pumps and two magnetos.

Two of these Fours were ridden in the 1936 Senior TT by Harold Daniell and George Rowley, but they both retired halfway through the race. The machines were not terribly speedy, and they obviously needed a great deal of development work to make them raceworthy. This Four was put on display at the 1935 Olympia Show. It was to be sold either with or without supercharger; the price was very high, of course. History

Notable for its four sweeping exhaust pipes, this early AJS V-four was of overhead-camshaft layout.

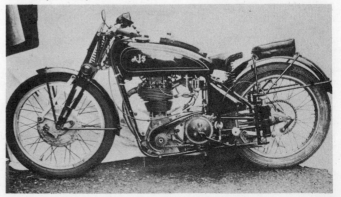

The 1938 model 7R featured a chain-driven ohc alloy engine and unusual pivoted-fork rear suspension with plunger spring boxes.

books make little mention of how many of these supersport road models were sold.

During 1937, the Four was under development and was not raced. In 1938, it reappeared with a new supercharger mounted in front of the crankcase. The new spring frame was also used, as was a hugh 8-in. by 1.75-in. front brake that was housed in a magnesium alloy hub with deep fins. The blown Four proved to be very fast, but overheating and poor steering plagued the model. Little success was obtained.

Meanwhile, the production models were faring exceptionally well. The trend away from side-valve engines to ohv models had been wholeheartedly accepted by the factory, and the 350- and 500-cc Singles were very popular. With Burman four-speed footshift gearboxes the performance was good, even if the rigid frames and girder front forks provided a far from smooth ride. These fine handling Singles were particularly successful in trials competition, and their fame continued to spread the world over.

The final year of international motorsport before the war was 1939; AJS contributed greatly to that classical year of speed. The V-4 model had been converted to water cooling during the winter, and it was ready to do battle with the best. In the Senior TT, the 405-lb. Four was handicapped by the twisty nature of the circuit, plus a need to take on more water, and 11th and 13th places were the best obtained.

Late in the season, in the fast Ulster GP, the great Walter Rusk finally was able to show the speed of the Four, as the 7-mile Clady Straight allowed him lots of room to unleash the blown engine's fury. Walter and Dario Serefini, on a blown Gilera Four, were locked in a terrific battle, and on Lap 3 Rusk pulled clear by 19 sec. and recorded the first ever 100 mph lap. Then came disaster when a front fork link broke, thus ending a colorful era for the AJS V-4.

After the war, supercharging was abolished by the FIM for international racing, and, at any rate, the factories could not have afforded such an expensive luxury. In war-torn England, the most pressing need was to rebuild factories and start production again. To this goal AJS dedicated itself, and a whole new range of machines was introduced.

The basis of the new range was 350- and 500-cc ohv Singles with bore and stroke measurements of 69 by 93 mm, and 82.5 by 93 mm. Both models featured the new Teledraulic front fork, which provided a much smoother ride. Frames still were rigid. These Singles were of an exceptionally sound and rugged design, and riders the world over came to know and love them for their ease of operation and dependability.

These Singles were used by the factory in both trials and the newly founded motocross sport, in which they achieved tremendous success. Hugh Viney, for example, won the coveted trophy in the Scottish Six Days Trial, and other riders kept the marque well to the fore in all types of dirt competition.

The factory also made a return to road racing with a new 500-cc Twin. The Twin was rather unusual, with its engine mounted horizontally in the frame, and spike fins on the head that led to the nickname of "Porcupine." The bore and stroke were 68 by 68.25 mm. The one-piece crankshaft featured two roller bearings, plus a third plain bearing in the middle. Rods of RR-56 alloy were used with plain big-end bearings, and the engine ran "backward."

The drive to the double overhead camshafts was by spur gears. The exhaust valves were sodium filled to facilitate cooling. Oil was circulated at the amazing rate of 45 gph at 7000 rpm. The engine was mounted in a wide duplex cradle frame that featured air-oil shock absorbers on a swinging arm suspension. Front suspension was by the Teledraulic fork with 3 in. of travel. Huge brakes with air scoops were used.

In the 1947 Senior TT, the Porcupine showed a fair turn of speed in the hands of Jock West and Les Graham, but minor teething troubles kept them well down on the finishing list. A few other places were obtained in grand prix events, but additional development obviously was needed to make the Twin a winner.

The following year, the marque intensified its racing campaign with the introduction of the 350-cc 7R model. Produced both as a works and production racer, the 74 by 81-mm Single had the traditional chain drive to a single overhead cam. The "Boy Racer," as it was affectionately called, had a duplex cradle frame, Teledraulic front fork, and huge conical hubs cast from magnesium alloy.

The alloy engine was fitted with a 1.156-in. TT carburetor. A Lucas magneto provided spark. An 8.45:1 compression ratio was used. The engine produced about 30 bhp at 7000 rpm. The four-speed Burman gearbox had ratios of 5.24:1, 5.95:1, 7.07:1, and 10.14:1, which produced a speed of 110 mph in top cog. Other specifications of this sleek new racer were a 56-in. wheelbase, 298-lb. dry weight, 4.75-gal. fuel tank, large megaphone exhaust, a 3.00x21 front tire, and a 3.25x20 rear tire.

In classical racing that year, the team fared well with both the 350- and 500-cc models, but they still lacked the speed of the all-conquering 350 Velocette and 500cc Norton. Many good places were obtained, and private owners did exceptionally well on the 7R model. In dirt competition, the AJS figured

The last of the Porcupines – the 1954 model – this Twin produced 54 bhp, good enough for 145 mph. The engine was mounted at 45 degrees.

prominently. The great Hugh Viney again won the Scottish Six Days Trial

The year 1949 generally is regarded as the greatest in the AJS history. The production range was expanded to include a new 500-cc (66 by 72.8 mm) Twin. All the models could be had with the swinging-arm frame that made the AJS one of the most comfortable bikes in the world. The marque also built special 350- and 500-cc models in trials and motocross trim, and these alloy-engined bikes achieved tremendous eminence in their fields. These were then put into production for 1950.

In grand prix racing, the works team experienced a fabulous year, although Les Graham did lose the Senior TT when his magneto drive shaft broke, just a few miles from victory while he led by a wide margin. The Porcupine was a very speedy model that year, and on the Continent AJS engaged in some epic struggles with the equally speedy Gilera Fours. Les won the Ulster and Swiss Grands Prix, plus taking a 2nd in the Dutch event, and this gave him enough points to win the coveted 500-cc World Championship. Teammate Bill Doran won the Belgian GP and took a 4th in the Ulster and a 3rd in the Monza classic. This enabled the marque to also win the 500-cc manufacturers' championship. In the Junior class the 350 failed to score any wins, but it did provide honest opposition to the terrifically fast dohc Velocette.

In trials competition, Hugh Viney etched his name indelibly in the history books with his third straight victory in the Scottish Six Day Trial. This "hat trick" victory string in the famous trial is, perhaps, one of the all-time greats in motorcycle competition. In motocross, the AJS recorded another great year, and in America the Singles won many of the most important dirt competitions that were held.

In 1950, the AJS did not fare so well in the Senior class, as the new Norton Featherbed was a little too fast. The team placed well in many races, and Les Graham did win the Swiss GP. In the Junior class the Velo was again too fast for the 7R, but Les did score a popular win in the Swiss meeting on wet roads.

During 1951 and 1952, grand prix racing became more competitive, and AJS responded with many technical improvements to its race ware. The works 7R model had the valve angle reduced from 79 to 70 degrees, and the intake port was steepened 12 degrees. The engine also was mounted farther forward in the frame, the wheelbase was shortened to 55 in., a narrower crankcase fitted, and clip-on handlebars were used. Then the height was lowered by using 3.00x19 front and 3.25x19 rear tires, and the front fork was shortened 1 in. These fork and wheel modifications also were made on the Porcupine. Then in 1952, the engine was raised to 45 degrees, orthodox engine fining was used, and the weight was lowered by mounting the oil sump beneath the engine.

For 1952, the factory also designed a unique new works 350 model with three cams and three valves. Two exhaust valves were used in conjunction with two ports and two exhaust pipes. The bore and stroke also were changed to 75.5 by 78 mm, and these measurements were later used on the production 7R in the late 1950s. The three-cam model fared well on the racetracks, and it also set a one-hour record of 115,66 mph for the 350-cc class late in the year at Montlehery, France.

During the next few years, the line of models continued the same with road, trials, scrambles, and the racing 7R models being offered. Improvements were mainly of a small technical nature to the existing sound design, and the sales and reputation of the AJS continued to expand around the world. By 1954, the 7R model was producing 37 bph at 7200 rpm, and it was by then the most popular mount in the world for 350-cc class road racing.

The year of 1954 also was a memorable one for the marque, as AJS won the Junior TT with a three-cam Single in the hands of Rod Coleman of New Zealand. Both the 350- and 500-cc racers were weird in appearance with their huge low-slung 6.5-gal. alloy fuel tanks that required a fuel pump to get the fuel up to the carburetor. The idea was a bit of streamlining, with a non-stop ride for fuel and a lower center of gravity. The 500 Twin by then weighed 335 lb., was breathing through a pair of 1.125-in GP carburetors, and developed 54 bph at 7500 rpm-good enough for 145 mph.

After 1954, the marque lost interest in grand prix racing, and AJS discontinued active participation to spend time on production model development. In 1956, a new 600-cc Twin was produced, along with the traditional 350- and 500-cc Singles in road, trials, and motocross trim. In 1958, a clean looking 250-cc ohv model was added to the range, and, in 1959, the 600 Twin became a powerful 650-cc model.

Meanwhile, the 7R model had been under constant development, and by 1961 it was developing 41.5 bhp at 7800 rpm. With a wide torque range that produced 33 bhp as low as 6000 rpm, the 285-lb. Single delivered terrific acceleration. The compression ratio, by then, had been upped to 12:1, and the Amal GP carburetor had a bore of 1.375-in. The four-speed gearbox had ratios of 4.87:1, 5.36:1, 6.48:1, and 8.67:1, which provided a top speed of 120 mph.

During the early 1960s, the company underwent a great change. The dynamic leadership that had characterized AJS history was lacking. Design progress and sales began to sag. The company continued to make a modest effort in trials and scrambles competition, and Gordon Jackson's magnificent one-point victory in the 1961 Scottish Trial (his only point was for the one dab of his foot) helped to keep the name alive.

Things were not well, though, and, in 1963, the last of the illustrious 7R models rolled off the production lines. Next came the amalgamation with Norton, and the AJS Twin became a Norton with AJS on the fuel tank. This lack of design improvement hurt their image and competitiveness. Just at the darkest hour, when it appeared as though the doors were going to close again, a company, Manganese Bronze Holdings, came forward, and out of this came a new company called Norton-Villiers that held promise of great things to come. Already, the name AJS has been restored to racing by a 250-cc two-stroke of Villiers ancestry, and the company has given a hint that more racing activity is to follow.

During the late 1960s new two-stroke trials and scrambles bikes were produced-both production and works versions, which show great promise for the future. This new effort in the two-stroke field seems rather uncomfortable for the tradition of AJS, and only time will tell if it will be a successful transition.

So this is the story of the AJS-a tale of a make that has a great legacy in both motorcycle sport and production. From the early trend-setting with gearboxes and overhead valve engines to the wonderful trials, motocross, and road racing models, it is a legend that is rich in tradition and engineering achievement.

Mick Andrews was a works rider on the AJS trials team in the middle 1960s. He rode this 245 pound 350cc single to many wins.

ARIEL

One of the most classical stories in all of motorcycledom is the legend of Ariel. Even though Ariels have not been produced since 1965, the marque is still well known throughout the world for its magnificent Square Four-a model that connoisseurs of fine motorcycles consider to be a classic of incomparable stature. The company also has an enviable record in the competition sphere; the illustrious Ariel Singles scored many trials wins in the pre- and post-World War II days.

The story of this colorful British marque began in 1898 when a 2.25-hp tricycle was produced. The head of the infant company was a Scott named Charles Sangster, who had been producing bicycles for quite some time. This single-cylinder trike soon gave way to a 2.5-hp motorcycle in 1903, which had such primitive features as an automatic intake valve (it was sucked open by the downstroke of the piston), a chassis with no suspension, and a single-speed belt drive.

During these years Sangster worked hard to make his motorbike reliable. By 1905 he felt confident enough to enter his first race, the elimination race in the Isle of Man, which determined the British Machines for the Gordon Bennett Race in France. The winner of this elimination event happened to be a 6-hp twin-cylinder Ariel, which averaged 42 mph. The Twin weighed only 110 lb., but it was trounced quite badly in the big Continental event.

In 1906 the company produced a new Single that had mechanically operated side valves, a battery ignition and a sprung front fork. The following year a magneto was used for ignition. These models continued until 1910.

In 1910 a new Single was produced that had side valves and a belt drive with a variable gear ratio. In 1912 the 3.5-hp thumper featured a chain drive and two-speed gearbox in the rear hub. In 1913 this was changed to a three-speed countershaft gearbox with a belt drive. This model proved to be an exceptionally

sound design, and Ariel proceeded to win the team prize in both the English and Scottish Six Day Trials. The Single was followed in 1915 by a two-stroke, but at this time the factory was converted to wartime production.

After the war the range consisted of a 3.5-hp Single and a 6-hp Twin, with belt drive still being retained. The company also experimented with a spring frame, which had a triangulated fork that worked on coil springs mounted just below the seat. Nothing much became of the springer, and it was soon dropped as an expensive and impractical proposition.

By 1922 Ariel was firmly established as one of England's leading names, and a comprehensive brochure listed no less than eight models. The first was a 500-cc Sports Single with measurements of 86.4 by 85mm. A three-speed gearbox with ratios of 14.3:1, 7.75:1 and 4.6:1 was used in conjunction with a belt drive, but a surprising innovation was a hand clutch lever. Cog swapping was done by hand, and the oil pump was also hand operated. This 3.5-hp thumper had a magneto ignition and girder front fork, with the tire size being 2.40x26. The fuel tank held 2-1/8 gal. and the oil tank held 2.5 pt. The wheelbase was a long 56 in., and the weight was only 235 lb.

The next model had the same engine but with a foot clutch, and the gear ratios were 16.5:1, 8.75:1 and 5.3:1. This Touring model weighed 275 lb. and had 4.25 in. of ground clearance.

The third and fourth models listed were 6- to 7-hp 796-cc V-Twins, one with a sidecar and one solo. The Twin weighed 300 lb., and had gear ratios of 14.3:1, 7.75:1, and 4.6:1. One other Twin was listed in the brochure which had a 994-cc MAG (Motosacoche of Geneva) engine with a bore and stroke of 82 by 94mm. This engine was of the inlet-over-exhaust valve design. The model weighed 334 lb.

Ariel also produced a huge 665-cc Single then that had a bore and stroke of 92 by 100mm. This 4.5-hp beast was produced in both solo and sidecar trim, and it featured a chain drive. Two other sidecar models were produced at that time. It is interesting to note that several of these 1922 Ariels had internal expanding brakes in place of the common caliper brakes on the wheel rims.

During the middle 1920s the British industry was gradually changing from side-valve engines to the overhead valve design. Ariel introduced their first overhead valve Singles in 1926, and these models proved to be so sound that they soon became one of the largest manufacturers in the world. The 500-cc ohv models had a mechanical oil pump (double plunger). In 1927 the bike became more modern looking when the "saddle" fuel tank was adopted that went over, instead of between, the top frame tubes.

By 1928 Ariel was recognized as a leader of the industry. Their range of models included both side-valve and ohv machines. The side-valvers were 557-cc Singles with a bore and stroke of 86.4 by 95mm and had an alloy piston and Lucas magneto ignition. Output was 5.5 hp, and a three-speed Sturmey-Archer gearbox had ratios of 14.0:1, 7.6:1 and 4.75:1. The frame was a strong single-loop cradle type, and braking was accomplished by a 7-in. internal expanding unit. Gear shifting was still done by hand, while the weight had risen to 280 lb. The tire size was 3.00 x 26 on this model, and a 2-gal. fuel tank was fitted. A deluxe version was also offered that had wider fenders and a Burman three-speed gearbox.

The 500-cc ohv Single had measurements of 81.8 by 95mm and weighed 290 lb. The pushrod model had most cycle parts in common with the side-valve model, but it produced 5.0 hp and had gear ratios of 13.0:1, 7.6:1 and 4.75:l. A super sports version was also available with a two port head and polished ports. An optional close-ratio gearbox was produced, making the sports model a popular mount with the more sporting minded riders. Wheelbase on all of these Ariels was 55 in. The appearance was beginning to take on a more modern look.

The actual power output of these early Ariels is not known since the company rated one horsepower for each 100cc in their brochure. The SV models would do 75 to 80 mph and ohv models about 80 to 85 mph-respectable speeds for those days. These Ariel Singles were also used in the big trials events of the day, their reliability and performance enabling them to win a goodly share of the awards. It might be mentioned that the trials of that era were more of an endurance type than the observed type, with stamina being more important than performance.

During the late 1920s England assumed undisputed world-wide leadership in motorcycle design and sales, and a great rivalry existed between the companies to produce a superior machine. Motorcycling had become very popular, with the increasing sophistication of the machines that were available, and a great demand was created for a refined machine of superior performance.

Ariel was one who had its eyes on this new market. Plans were laid to produce the most luxurious motorcycle ever offered to the public. Because it took several years to design and test the brainchild, it was not until 1931 that the model was listed in the brochure. This new Ariel was called the Square Four, and it created a sensation that has endured to this day.

The new Four had a unique design, which used two crankshafts at a right angle to the frame. These two shafts were geared together in their center so that they counter-rotated toward each other. The advantage of this design was its superb engine balance and compactness; the smooth flow of power was a revelation to a world that knew only the throb of a Single.

The con-rods all used roller bearing big-ends, but the timing side mains were all plain. Large roller bearings were used on the drive side shafts, and the alloy crankcase was naturally quite large. The cylinder and head were both of cast iron, with one exhaust port being used on each side of the head. The valves were mounted in a parallel position in the head, since a hemispherical combustion chamber would have required a complicated valve train and large head. The valves were actuated by a single overhead camshaft, which was chain driven from the right side of the engine. A single carburetor was used, and ignition was by a magneto.

The massive engine was mounted in a wide duplex cradle frame, and a four-speed handshifted gearbox was mounted in plates behind the engine. Burman made an optional footshift conversion kit, since those were the days when England was changing over to the footshift gearbox. The frame was still rigid, of course, and a girder front fork was used.

This first Square Four was a superbly finished mount for the aristocratic rider, with the 500-cc engine providing a smooth but rapid performance. In 1932, Ariel decided to increase the bore and stroke to 56 by 61mm, thus providing 600cc. In 1933 the oil tank was dropped in favor of a wet sump system. This made the Ariel run much cleaner, since the oil lines were done away with, and the Ariel Four became known as the "Rolls Royce of motorcycles."

The Square Four continued in production through 1936 in this trim, and soon it had a reputation all over Europe as the prestige machine "par excellence". Top speed was listed as 90 mph, and acceleration was second to none. The Four never did sell in really large numbers, due to its high cost in the post-depression days of the middle 1930s, so the man who rode one was considered a man of substantial means.

Meanwhile, the company was aggressively improving its line of Singles in an attempt to compete with the many fine Singles produced at that time. In 1931 the company produced

The 1950-53 VCH below weighed 290 lb. and was a popular trials machine. The engine developed 25 hp. MK III model, right, was to be most luxurious roadster ever, but Four was dropped from production.

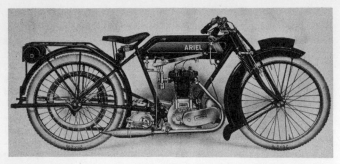

The 1922 500-cc Ariel Single featured side valves, a belt drive, hand-shifted three-speed gearbox and caliper brakes.

their famous 30 degree "sloper" in both side-valve and overhead valve designs. The side-valve model was 555cc, while the ohv model was available in both 250- and 500-cc sizes. Ariel even produced a special four-valve model that was tuned for high-speed performance and won many grass track and scramble races.

The next big change came in 1933 when the slopers were phased out and a new line of vertical Singles introduced. In this era of great classical motorcycles in England, Ariel was right at the forefront with a superb range of machines. The following year Ariel expanded their range even further, listing ten magnificent models in the 1935 brochure.

One of these bikes was the old 550-cc side-valve Single that was still popular as an inexpensive and reliable sidecar model. The compression ratio was a mild 5.0:1, and either a 3- or 4-speed handshift gearbox was available. Then came the 250-cc overhead valve model with measurements of 61 by 85mm. This utility Single ran on a 6.0:1 compression ratio. The 72 by 85mm 350-cc Single and 81.8 by 95mm 500-cc thumper came next, and these sloggers all had hand gearshifts and 19 in. wheels.

The models that appealed to the sports minded riders were the 250-, 350-, and 500-cc Red Hunters, special bench tested Singles that had many exciting specifications. The idea was to produce a fast sports Single that would streak down a country lane. A wide range of options allowed an owner to purchase a Red Hunter in trials or scrambles trim.

The 250-cc model ran on a 7.0:1 compression ratio and had 3.00x20 tires, a 2.5-gal. fuel tank and sports cams. The performance was listed as 70 mph, which was remarkable for those days. The 250, like all the Red Hunters, had a black frame and a red fuel tank with gold striping plus a footshift gearbox.

The 350-cc Red Hunter was tuned to run 80 mph on a 1.0-in. carburetor. This model also had a 2.5-gal. fuel tank and a 0.5-gal. oil tank. The big 500-cc model was available for use with 50/50 petrol/benzol fuel. The carb size was 1 1/8 in., and the fuel tank size was 3.25 gal. The oil tank held 0.75 gal. The 500 was available with either a one- or two-port exhaust system, and top speed was listed as 100 mph. The rear tire was a 3.25x19 block tread, front was a 3.00x20 rib tire.

All of the Red Hunters had racing cams, ground and polished ports, a polished con-rod, and a bench tested engine. The brakes were up to the performance, too, since the 7-in. binders had wide 1.25-in. shoes, and ribs were cast on the brake drums to help dissipate heat. A sports type of quickly detachable headlight was fitted, and a buyer could order his Single in competition trim with an upswept exhaust, crankcase shield, small fuel tank, magneto, knobby tires, sports fenders, and special bars.

These Red Hunters performed magnificently in trials events, as was attested by the 1935 brochure which proudly listed wins in the Scott, Colmore, Kickham, Victory, Bemrose, Cotswold, Mitchell, Wye Valley, and Gloucester Grand National events. Ariels also won the 250- and 500-cc classes of the famous Scottish Six Days Trial, and Gold medals were won on both the "A" and "B" teams in the ISDT.

The most prestigious model in the range was, naturally enough, the luxurious Square Four. The Four had 3.25x19 tires

and 3.25-gal. fuel tank. It had a classically elegant appearance with gold striping on a black finish.

The next improvements came in 1936 when the side-valve Single was increased to 600cc (86 by 104mm), and all the models had a foot gearshift. The marque also offered the 500-cc Red Hunter in genuine competition trim. These models were soon tuned by men such as L.W.E. Hartley to clock 109 mph on alcohol fuel. Perhaps the most remarkable record was set in Australia, when Art Senior clocked a fantastic 127 mph on his Single. The Australian record was set in 1938, and it stood for many years until after the War, when a 1000-cc Vincent finally exceeded this speed. The works trials and scrambles team included such greats as Jack White, Len Heath and Jimmy Edward, all of whom continued the Selly Oak tradition by winning many events.

The next change came in 1937 when the overhead cam Four was dropped in favor of a new pushrod engine. The new Four had a redesigned lower end in which the coupling gears were located on the left crankshaft ends, and plain rod bearings were used in an effort to lower production costs and make the engine quieter. A centrally located camshaft operated the pushrods and made the external appearance much cleaner.

Perhaps the most notable item about this new Four was that a massive 1000-cc version joined the earlier 600-cc size in the stable. The brutish 1000 had measurements of 65 by 75mm, and it produced 38hp at 5500 rpm. This much pressure made the Four a genuine 100-mph model, and its acceleration was by far the fastest of any production roadster available then. The new Four also had a Burman four-speed footshift gearbox, a single-loop cradle frame and a dry sump lubrication system.

In 1939 the marque made another great step forward when they produced an optional spring frame on all but the 250-cc models. The design was rather unique in that it had swivel links connected to the plunger boxes containing coil springs. The idea was to provide axle movement in an arc, which helped maintain constant chain tension. The suspension gave about three inches of travel, making the Ariel an exceptionally comfortable bike for those days. A modification was also made to the girder fork when a pair of small auxiliary dampening springs were added to control the rebound.

The range for 1939 was much the same as before, except that a Deluxe Four was produced for the connoissuer which had deeply valanced fenders, a pair of fishtail mufflers, lots of chrome and an impeccable finish. There were also many small technical improvements to the Singles.

The final few years of pre-war sport had Ariels winning a goodly share of the awards. In 1938 G.F. Povey won the Scottish classic on his 350-cc model, and Ariels won four gold medals in the 1938 ISDT. Other pre-war Ariel achievements include a 96-mph clocking by L.W.E. Hartley with a 557-cc SV model and Ben Bickell's 111.42-mph lap at Brooklands with his 500-cc Four that had a Powerplus supercharger fitted.

During the war Ariel met military needs, but in September of 1945 the company was able to resume production of roadsters again. In 1947 Mr. Sangster sold out to Birmingham Small Arms, but Ariels continued as before with 350- and 500-cc Singles, the 1000-cc Four, and 600-cc SV models being produced. For 1947 Ariel improved their range by adopting the telescopic front fork with hydraulic dampening.

The marque participated in most of the early post-war sporting events. In trials and scrambles events Ariels were always well placed; the Singles even got involved in road racing when the Isle of Man held their now defunct Clubman races for standard machines. In 1947 Senior Clubman TT G.F. Parsons captured 3rd, and other riders placed well until 1950 when the other companies' pseudo-racers made their debut. Perhaps the most surprising Ariel showing was in the 1947 Dutch Grand Prix, where a fellow by the name of J. Schot piloted his Red Hunter into 6th place-the first and only time that the marque had gained a world championship point!

The following year Ariel created a sensation with their 1949 brochure, which listed a wide range of models that included the Singles, a new 500-cc Twin, and a redesigned Four. The 63 by 80mm Twin was available with either a rigid or spring frame, and it was produced in two versions: a 25-hp (at 5500 rpm) model that ran on a 6.8:1 compression ratio and a 27-hp (at 6000 rpm) model that used a 7.5:1 ratio. These Twins had a very cleanly designed engine, but they never experienced the popularity of the Red Hunters or the Four.

The new Square Four, called the MK I, was a vastly improved motorcycle with its all-aloy engine that reduced the weight from 420lb. to 385 lb. (the springer weighed 25 lb. more). The alloy engine ran much cooler, and the appearance was sheer artistry in metal. Operating on a 6.0:1 or 6.8:1 compression ratio, the Four developed 34.5 hp at 5400 rpm and ran 95 to 100 mph. The acceleration was fantastic, with standing quarter-mile times of around 13.5 sec. being reported. The MK I model was the most luxurious roadster produced anywhere in the world; even today these beautiful Fours are highly prized by collectors.

In 1950 the company turned its thoughts to producing a genuine competition model named the VHC or Comp Red Hunter. The idea was to produce a 500-cc Single that was suitable for both trials and scrambles, and the empahsis was on light weight and fine handling. The 81.8 by 95mm alloy engine ran on a 6.8:1 compression ratio and churned out 25 hp at 6000 rpm, with great torque being produced at low engine speeds. Two gearboxes were available, a close ratio box for motocross racing and a wide ratio box for trials events. The ratios on the two boxes were 15.3:1, 9.7:1, 7.2:1, 5.75:1 and 19.1:1, 12.6:1, 9.16:1, and 6.05:1 for the wide ratio box.

The VHC model was quite light at 290 lb. Its stamina soon made it popular with trial riders, many of whom won several of the top events then. Bob Ray of the works team was one of the most successful riders. Ariels were always a force to be reckoned with in trials events. Harold Lines proved to be the marque's best motocrosser, but he seemed to lack a wee bit in the horsepower department compared to the BSA Gold Stars, Matchless Singles, and FN thumpers.

The next big year for Ariel was 1954 when they introduced a new swinging arm frame on all but the Four, which retained the old plunger suspension. The new frame kept the Ariels totally modern, as everyone was making the change at that time, and the riding comfort reached a new high. The company also produced a new 650-cc Twin called the Huntmaster that produced 40 hp at 6200 rpm, and a 200-cc Colt was added to the range as an inexpensive utility model.

The 500-cc Singles were also improved by using alloy for the cylinders and heads, while the Red Hunters had the pushrod tunnel cast into the cylinder in an effort to provide a cleaner running engine.

The model that really made the news than was the fabulous Square Four that was truly the Rolls Royce of motorcycles. The MK II had a completely new engine with a massive alloy cylinder and head plus an improved lower end. The head featured a set of bolt-on exhaust manifolds that had two ports each, so the MK II soon became known as the Four Port model. This engine produced 42 stampeding horses at 5800 rpm, and the top speed was increased from 105 to 110 mph. The acceleration was shattering, and several road tests obtained standing quarters of 12.9 to 13.2 sec.

The appearance of the MK II was impressive. A huge 6-gal. fuel tank was used that had a concave chrome panel near the top on each side. A buyer could have his choice of either a solo or dual type seat. The weight of the MK II was 450lb., the wheelbase was 56 in., and the tire sizes were 4.00x18 rear and 3.23 x 19 front. A new Burman gearbox was also used with ratios of 11.07:1, 7.1:1, 5.46:1 and 4.18:1, which gave the MK II a high cruising speed combined with shattering acceleration.

Meanwhile, Ariel had not forgotten about the competition scene and designed a pair of new models for trials and motocross racing. These two sports had developed to the point where one design was not suitable for both events, so a more specialized mount was designed for each.

The trials model was named the HT. This bike was destined to achieve fame and glory a few years later when Sammy Miller became a works rider. The HT featured an alloy engine with a 25 hp output that ran on a 5.6:1 compression ratio. The bore and stroke was the classic 81.8 by 95mm, and slow cams and heavy flywheels were used to obtain low speed pulling power.

The frame, a light swinging arm type, was very special since 1955 was the year when most factories dropped the old rigid frame in favor of a springer. The wheelbase was only 53 in., and the fork angle was very steep for precise steering at slow speeds. The dry weight was only 290 lb., due to the use of alloy for the fenders and the 2.0 gal. fuel tank. The wide ratio gearbox had ratios of 19.3:1, 14.7:1, 9.46:1 and 6.02:1. Ground clearance was 7 in.

The HS model had a bench tested engine that developed 34 hp at 6000 rpm, and this was slotted into a rugged frame with a close ratio gearbox that had ratios of 16.1:1, 10.2:1, 7.9:1 and 6.02:1. The compression ratio was 9.0:1 and the dry weight was 318 lb. The tire sizes were 4.00x19 rear and 3.00x21 front; the same as the HT model. This scrambler was a good bike, though it never achieved the success that its less powerful brother did in trials events.

During the next few years the Ariels underwent only minor changes, but in 1957 the Square Four was given a facelifting with a larger oil tank, a headlight nacelle, and a large full-width front hub that was cast in alloy. These changes made the luxurious Four even more appealing, and it continued to be the most prestigious (and expensive) motorcycle in the world.

However, change was In the air. Sales were falling off in Europe due to the rise in the standard of living that allowed the populace to afford automobiles. Ariel responded by producing the 250-cc Leader, a two-stroke Twin with sheet metal paneling that provided excellent weather protection. The Leader was followed by the Arrow and Arrow Sports, which were unstreamlined standard models. A tiny 50-cc ohv Pixie came next, an attempt to build a "schoolboy" model at a very low price.

These new Ariels proved to be so popular with the everyday rider that a decision was made early in 1959 to halt production of all the big four-strokes in order to meet the demand for the new two-strokes. This was a tragedy. The company had already designed and tested the MK III Square Four, the most luxurious motorcycle the world had ever seen. The MKIII had an Earles leading-link front fork similar to those on the BMW, and it was claimed to provide the most comfortable and stable ride ever produced on a motorcycle.

As it transpired, the MK III never saw the light of day. This model would have been the most regal of a long line of magnificent Fours. Even today there are few machines which could approach its luxurious specifications.

Meanwhile, during the middle 1960's, the Japanese manufacturers were making serious inroads into the world market with their lower priced lightweights. Ariel sales began to fall, and soon the company was failing to show a profit. If Ariel had had a line of big bikes to fall back on, they might have survived. But the desire of the Burman company to sever their contract (due to the smaller numbers that were involved) was the final blow that felled the marque. In the autumn of 1965 the last Ariels left the factory.

The 1957 500-cc Twin had a compact engine with an alloy head and the swinging arm frame. Twin was stylish, but never sold well.

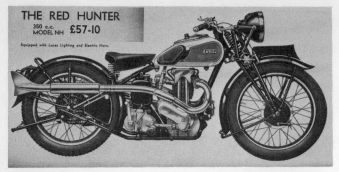

Red Hunters of 1935 were good looking mounts with tuned engines. Upswept exhaust was optional. 500-cc model would run 100 mph.

There was one final chapter to the Ariel story, and this one proved to be the greatest. For this story we must go back to 1956 when Sammy Miller of Ireland was hired onto the works trials team. Sam spent the first few years in learning how to set up his big Single and master the toughest courses. By 1958 he showed enough class to finish 2nd to Gordon Jackson (AJS 350) in the famed Scottish Six Days Trial.

During the next few years Miller dedicated himself to modifying his Ariel. First came a smaller front brake and an upswept exhaust. Then came some mods to the steering geometry. An alloy oil tank and slimmer fuel tank came next, followed by a new Reynolds 531 tubing frame, designed to contain the oil tank. Miller also used a Norton front fork and fiberglass for the fenders, primary cover, magneto shield, seat pan, chain guard and number plates. The dry weight finally ended up at an unbelievable 242 lb. Wheelbase measured 52.5 in., and the ground clearance was 9.0 in.

This thumper proved to be a magnificent trials machine, enabling Sammy to win the coveted British Championship in 1959 by defeating his arch-rival Gordon Jackson. Sammy then proceeded to dominate the British Championship, taking the title the next five years in succession (1960-'64). The "maestro" also won the coveted premiere award in the Scottish classic in both 1962 and 1964. Then financial problems caused the factory to terminate its contract with Miller. This proved to be a significant turning point in trials history; Miller went to Bultaco and thus started the trend to 250-cc class trials machines. It can truly be said that when Ariel passed from the trials scene,

the lusty big single passed too.

The Ariel, however, refuses to pass from the scene. The Ariel Motorcycle Owners Club and thousands of afficionados are keeping the name alive through their dedicated restoration of all the great classics. To some, the majestic Square Four is the most regal. Others appreciate the pre-war Red Hunter classics, which are the prototypes of the era of great Singles. Then there are those who love the HT trials model, the last big Single to win the Scottish. All of these magnificent models well represent that proud era when Britannia reigned supreme; perhaps the greatest era that motorcycling has ever known.

The 1955-59 HT trials model was made famous by Sammy Miller. The 500cc single weighed only 290 pounds.

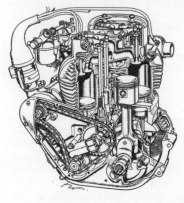

This drawing reveals the many interesting details of the 1949 Mk I Square Four engine. Courtesy of Motor Cycle.

The 1935 Square Four had 600-cc ohc engine and handshifted gearbox. Burman unit was available to convert to footshift. Top was 90 mph.

BMW

Something there is about a BMW that sets it apart from the others-it doesn't handle the best, nor is it the fastest, but in its quiet, imperturbable way it exudes the aura that here is the very best. Like a Rolls Royce it is smooth, seems to run forever, and it has a finely finished look that lasts and lasts and lasts.

Today, without a doubt, the BMW is **the** machine that has the reputation all over the world for finest quality of design, materials and workmanship. It has been a uniquely distinctive machine with its opposed twin engine, shaft drive, and unusual swinging-arm suspensions both front and rear.

And yet, if this is such a great motorcycle, why are there not more BMWs seen on the road? The price may have something to do with it, for quality seldom comes cheap. But that is not entirely it, as many, many experienced motorcyclists have no desire whatsoever to own a BMW. Maybe it is that gentlemen-gentlemen who also happen to like bikes-make the best BMW owners. For a BMW, like a gentleman, has fine manners.

The BMW owner is usually a proud man-proud that he owns **the** prestigeous machine of motorcycling. He also appreciates good engineering; not the kind of engineering that has double overhead cams, 10,000 revs and road racing brakes, but rather the good engineering that makes a bike as quiet as an owl in flight, as clean and vibration-free as an electric motor, as comfortable as a living room chair, and that will run for 100,000 miles and still be alive to serve more.

The story of the Bavarian Motor Works goes back many years to 1883 when a boy was born in Wurttemberg, Germany to the family of Fritz. Young Fritz later became Dr. Ing. Max Fritz, a mechanical genius who helped start the BFW airplane engine manufacturing concern in 1916. In 1912 Dr. Fritz had designed the first successful small aircraft engine used in Germany, and in 1916 his company was called upon to serve the Kaiser's army by designing and producing airplane engines for the war effort.

After the war the company began producing a motorcycle engine that was used in the Victoria machine during 1921-22. The engine was a side-valve 500cc job that produced 6.3 hp at 3000 rpm.

It was in 1923 that the actual BMW company came into existence with Dr. Fritz as its chief designer, manager, and president. Dr. Fritz worked in this capacity until the end of World War II, then continued on as a technical advisor. One of the first projects was the designing and building of a complete motorcycle, and to this end the infant company dedicated itself with Teutonic skill.

When the first model was displayed at the Paris Motor Salon Show in 1923, the mold was cast in the direction the company would pursue for the next 50 years. The engine was an

First BMW was 1923 side-valve 500-cc model R-32. Front brake was an internal expanding unit; rear employed a friction dummy rim.

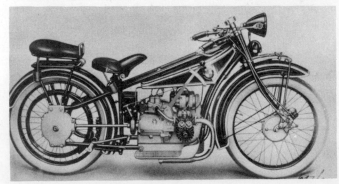

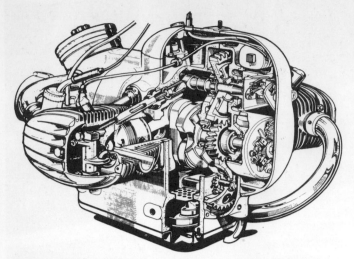

Engine of 1923 R-32 had a power output of 8.5 hp at 3300 rpm. Opposed twin layout and shaft drive were featured from the start.

250cc model that developed 6.5 hp at 4000 rpm. Here was the second BMW axiom-anything under 500cc would be a vertical single, and anything else would be an opposed twin. It was in that same year that the first 500cc OHV engine was used which was good for 16 hp at 4000 rpm. All those early BMWs had an enternal expanding front brake, a dummy-rim rear brake, a castiron pipe frame, hand gearshift, and a leaf-spring front fork.

In 1916 the internal expanding brake was adopted on the rear wheel, and in 1928 a new 750cc side-valve engine was available which produced 18 hp at 3400 rpm. Later in the year a 750cc OHV model was introduced which had 24 hp at 4000 rpm. In 1929 the company began using an unusual pressed steel frame which they called the "star" frame, and it was a wide affair that passed outside the gas tank. A hand gearshift was still used for the three-speed gearbox.

During the middle 1930's BMW became a leading machine, and the company took an aggressive but methodical approach to improving their product. Always a pioneer in building a comfortable mount, BMW began experiments with an improved front fork in 1935. The new fork was a pressed steel type with coil springs. This innovation was probably the forebearer of the modern telescopic fork.

opposed twin with shaft drive with the engine and gearbox in one unit, and there lies the story of the BMW. While the modern BMW is certainly a vastly improved machine compared to that 1923 model, the original basic design has never been altered.

In 1925 the company produced their first single, an OHV

For 1936 the company truly took the lead when the sleek R-5 model was introduced. The new 500cc OHV engine produced 24 hp at 5400 rpm, which gave it a brisk performance for those days. The talk of the motorcycling world was the new frame and fork, though. The old star frame had been dropped

R-11 model of 1929-30 sported a husky 750-cc side-valve engine that produced 20 hp at 4000 rpm. The R-11 was popular for sidecar work.

Tubular telescopic front fork made its debut on the 1936 BMW. This R-5 model had 500-cc ohv engine that developed 24 hp at 5400 rpm.

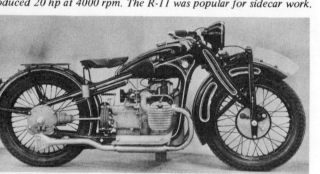

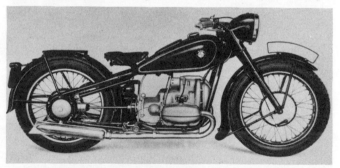

A much revered BMW was 1938 model R-61. The 600-cc side-valve model was ultimate in riding comfort with telescopic front fork.

George Meier is seen at speed at Quarter Bridge on his way to victory in the 1939 Senior Tourist Trophy race.

and a new steel tubing frame was used with a modern telescopic front fork, thus setting a new trend in riding comfort. The R-5 had a particularly "clean" look about it, and even today it would be considered a nice appearing bike.

Not content to rest upon their laurels, the Munich factory produced the very ultimate in 1938. Called the R-51 and R-66 models, the new 500cc and 600cc OHV engines were mounted in a new frame that featured a plunger rear suspension. Here was the very best in comfort and handling then, and with 30 hp at 5400 rpm the R-66 was a speedy roadster, too. The 750 side-valve model was still produced, as well as a 200cc single which kicked out an economical 8 hp at 5400 rpm.

Then came World War II and the factory was taken over by the Nazi government for war production purposes. At the war's end Germany was occupied by her conquerors, and the bulk of the company's tools and equipment were distributed to sixteen nations as spoils of war. More tragic was the loss of the company records, technical specifications and historical data; and much of this has never been recovered. It might be fitting to mention here that the factory made great efforts to provide material for this book, but many technical questions went unanswered as the material is lost-forever.

In 1946 the factory began producing farm tools, household goods, and motorcycle replacement parts. In 1947 the production of motorcycles resumed. In 1948 a new 12 hp 250 single was added to the 500cc twin production, and the factory was once again on its way. In 1952 the 600cc model R-68 was introduced which had a 35 hp rating at 7000 rpm. By 1953, no less than 100,000 BMWs had rolled off the production line since 1947.

In 1955 the BMW acquired its classical appearance when it

Terrors of the Grand Prix classics during the late thirties were supercharged 500-cc models of BMW works team. Power was 68 hp at 8000 rpm — good enough for 140 mph on 50-50 petrol-benzol. The 1953 BMW works racer, below, featured a swinging-arm frame.

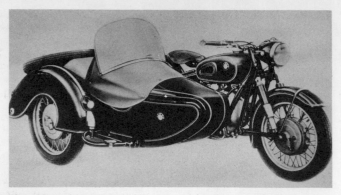

The 600-cc ohv model R-60 is a natural for three-wheeled use; in Europe this combination is considered most prestigious by owners.

came out with a swinging-arm suspension both front and rear. The range then consisted of a 250cc single, a 500cc twin, and two 600cc twins. The star of the range then was the R-69S model, which would comfortably exceed the 100 mph mark. The output was 42 HP at 7000 rpm.

In the history of international competition the BMW factory has had some very great moments. The first racing efforts were made during the early 'twenties, but it was not until sales reached goodly proportions during the early 'thirties that the company could afford a serious racing program. Always faithful to their opposed twin, shaft drive layout, the BMW successes are a tribute to years of patient development that were not always strewn with roses.

It was during the early 1930's that intensive work began on a 500cc Grand Prix machine, and as the rules then allowed it, a supercharger was used. In 1936 the world first received notice of what was to follow, when works riders Otto Ley and Karl Gall carried off the last race of the season in Sweden by trouncing World Champion Jim Guthrie (Norton) rather badly.

Ley's BMW averaged 91.8 mph on the fast Swedish course, and there lies the crux of BMW's problem to ascend to the Senior Class racing throne. Fast as they were, the bikes just were not the best handling or most roadable on the circuits, and on the curves and corners they were getting carved up badly by the Nortons and Velocettes. It was only on a fast course with few sharp corners that their fierce performance advantage could offset the superior roadholding of their unsupercharged British competitors.

Methodically, the GP machine was developed. The rigid frame gave way in 1937 to a plunger rear suspension. The BMW had been plagued during the '36 season with torque reaction from the driveshaft layout. Previously, twisting up the wick on the blown twin had created some disastrous effects when heeled over in cornering. The factory started the year by sending Jock West to the Isle of Man for the Senior TT, and fifth place was the best he could win. More work was needed.

The next race was the Dutch TT, and the trophy went to Munich after Jim Guthrie's Norton retired from the race with mechanical troubles. Then, in the Swiss and Belgian events, Guthrie showed the world that he still was champion by soundly trouncing the field. The next race was the home country Grand Prix on the Hohenstein-Ernstthal circuit, and Karl Gall and Otto Ley captured the prize for the fatherland. It was rather a hollow victory, as Jim Guthrie was leading the race only one mile from the finish when he crashed and died later from his injuries.

The balance of the season was a mixed picture. BMW with Jock West took the Ulster Grand Prix; BMW also took the Swedish again; Velocette won the French, and Gilera the Italian. So 1937 ended with the Munich concern winning four out of nine classic races, Norton still champion, and the BMW was still at a disadvantage on all but the fastest courses. During the long winter many problems would have to be sorted out in Munich.

In the spring of 1938 the new contender came out of the race shop, and here was truly a magnificent racing machine. Rear

plunger suspension was retained. Braking power was greatly increased with two full-width hubs, cast in alloy, which provided stopping power to match the speed. The vane-type Zoller compressor was still used, and the engines were producing no less than 68 hp at 8000 rpm on petrol-benzol fuel. The engine, incidentally, had a bevel gear and tower shaft drive to the overhead camshafts, and ignition was by magneto. The gearbox had four speeds.

The season started off poorly in the Isle of Man. Gall crashed in practice, the brilliant newcomer Georg Meier had a spark plug stripped out just before the start of the race, and Jock West came home fifth, over three miles per hour behind the Norton of Harold Daniell. The next race was on the fast Belgian course, and Meier and West took first and third. Things were looking up.

The Swiss classic was held on the slow tortuous Geneva circuit that year, and once again it was Norton first and second. On to the Dutch TT and these tables were reversed-BMW first and second with Meier picking up another eight points toward the title. Back to Germany for the Grand Prix d' Europe, and Meier once again pushed the Nortons of Harold Daniell and Fred Frith in 2nd and 3rd.

For the Ulster GP the factory sent over only Jock West, but that was all it took to win the event at the record speed of 93.98 mph-the highest speed ever recorded in a Grand Rrix race. The last race of the season was at Monza, Italy, and BMWs scored a convincing one-two again with Meier taking the trophy. The season's total was five out of seven races, with Georg Meier the World Champion. Only one race remained to be won-the TT!

In June of 1939 the factory sent their works team to the Isle of Man full of confidence. Their splendid twins had been clocked at 140 during the 1938 season, and Georg Meier had developed into a truly great rider. During the very first practice lap Karl Gall crashed and was killed, but Meier and West came through to lead the practice times by wide margins.

In the TT itself Meier rode a magnificent race with steady consistant cornering, and then scorching down the straight stretches nearly 20 mph faster than the Nortons and Velocettes. The result was a record speed, and to this date that 1939 event is the only Senior TT that BMW has ever won. Just for the record let's list the leader board:

1. George Meier (BMW) 89.38
2. J.M. West (BMW) 88.22
3. Fred Frith (Norton) 87.96
4. Stanley Woods (Velocette) 87.91
5. J.H. White (Norton) 85.92
6. Les Archer (Velocette) 84.31

The balance of the 1939 season was less rewarding, as the Italian Gilera-Rondine supercharged four was faster than the Munich twins. Then Meier crashed in the Swedish event and was unable to ride the balance of the season, and so the championship was lost.

After the war, Germany was on "probation" and could not compete in international racing until 1952. The racing spirit was kept alive on homeland courses though, such as the 1950 Rheyit Circuit race where Meier used the pre-war compressor model to average a fantastic 129.87 mph, with a record lap of 134.21.

In 1953 a new BMW, the 500cc Rennsport, made its debut as both a works and production racer. With the post-war ban on supercharging, the new racer had normally aspirated twin carburetors. A new frame was also adopted, which had swinging-arm suspension both front and rear.

While the post-war BMW success in Senior Class racing has not been nearly as good as during the pre-war days, Walter Zeller did garner a great number of second through sixth places in World Championship racing from 1953 through 1957. An experimental fuel injection system was used on Zeller's machine, but the speed just wasn't sufficient to stay with the Italian fours. In recent years the factory has not supported a works team.

If the post war solo successes have not been too great, then the sidecar championships must certainly make up for it. With the exception of 1968 and 1971 when Helmut Fath stove everybody in his home-built "four," BMW has won the title every year until 1975. The flat twin with its low center of gravity is a natural for the sidecar class, and the record now stands at 19 out of 23 titles since 1954 plus that fantastic fifteen straight championships in a row.

There is another facet of competition where the Bavarian concern has prominently figured, and this is the world of absolute speed. They first hit the news in 1929 when Ernst Henne took the World's Fastest title at 134.75 mph for the kilometer. His bike featured a 750cc pushrod OHV engine with a Zoller compressor.

Henne lost his title, and then gained it back at 137.86 in 1930. Again his crown was taken, and again he took it back at 151.76 in 1932. He then pushed it up to 159.0 in 1935, still using the 750cc engine.

Henne startled the world in 1936 with his 168.9 mph clocking, and that record was set with only a 500cc OHC road racing engine. The bike had a complete shell for the record attempt, which was probably the first successful use of full streamlining. During 1937 the title was again lost, and so, late in the year, Henne rolled out on the Frankfurt Autobahn and recorded 173.88 mph. That record stood for fourteen years.

Today the BMW still holds the official World Sidecar speed mark at 174.0 mph, plus a great number of long distance sidecar speed records. Willi Noll is the man who wears the crown, and his mark was set in 1955 with a 500cc engine.

So this is the story of the Bayerische Moteren Werke-never any panic or quick decisions. Like making a fine German cheese, it takes time, and the end product will always be good. It can be said that BMW has never produced a poor motorcycle, and few there are that can make that claim.

Today the work goes on to improve the breed. Way back in 1965 the factory was experimenting with a works special in the International Six Days Trial. The bike had a telescopic front fork, a new frame, and it weighed 80 pounds less than the production models. In 1970 the experiment finally went into production, along with a fast 750cc model, proving that it takes time to fully test at BMW.

Time is something they seem to have a lot of at Munich.

The 1975 range of BMWs includes 600, 750 and 900cc twins — expensive but universally acknowledged for their quality.

BSA

Fourteen men, gunsmiths by trade, sat around a long boardroom table in Birmingham, England, and watched as Mr. E. Otto prepared to demonstrate his invention-a bicycle. In 1861-the gunsmiths had formed the Birmingham Small Arms Company, and as the musket business had been poor in 1880-they were looking about for a new item to produce.

Mr. Otto proceeded to demonstrate his bicycle by lifting it onto the table, riding it the length of the table, down the stairs, and then out the door and down the street. So impressed were the gunsmiths that production was started, and in the next few years over 1,000 BSA bicycles were manufactured and sold.

In 1888, the company forsook the bicycle trade and returned to gun manufacturing. The armament demand soon slacked off again, and so, in 1893, the gunsmiths returned to the transportation field and began making parts for bicycles. The concern produced their own complete bicycle in 1906, and from then on BSA was to stay in the two-wheeled field.

It is not intended to say that BSA is concerned only with two-wheeled transportation, for the BSA group was later made up of 35 separate corporations which produced everything from motorcycles to rare metals, machine tools, guns, plastics, car bodies, and coal mining equipment. From the humble beginning of five gunsmiths banded together in 1692 to produce muskets for King William III's army, the BSA group grew until it became an industrial giant of England.

It is in the motorcycle field that BSA is best known, though, and in 1905 the company experimented with their first motorcycle. It was not until 1910 that the first BSA models were manufactured, and these were 3½ and 4½ hp models with belt drive. The two 500cc singles had a bore and stroke of 85mm x 88mm, measurements that were to become legendary in the BSA line.

BSA motorcycle development followed standard practice in those early days with single cylinder side-valve engines, belt drive, and dummy-rim brakes being accepted practice. To test the soundness of their design, the company had a bash at the Isle of Man TT race in 1913 with a team of six 500cc singles. Only one finished in seventh place. An experimental two-speed hub was tried which proved to be successful.

After World War I the motorcycle boom was on, and the Birmingham group fielded an extensive line to garner their share of the rapidly expanding sales. To augment the 500 and 556cc single cylinder models, a 770cc side valve V-twin was added to the range in 1919. The new twin featured a three-speed transmission and dummy-rim brakes on both wheels. That same year the company produced a "light" car powered with the 90 degree V-twin engine, and BSA was to dabble in this field until World War II.

In 1921 the factory again had a try at the TT races, but they met with such failure that they eschewed racing for many years after. Six 500cc models were built with single cylinder engines canted forward to give a "sloper" appearance. Dummy-rim brakes were still used, but the three speed gearbox and chain drive had replaced the belt drive. All six machlines failed to finish the race.

Returning to the drawing boards, the BSA engineers made up for their racing failure by producing some outstanding road models. In 1922 the company produced their first 350, a side-valve single which was followed the next year by an OHV version. That same year the 250cc SV "round tank" model was introduced, and this thumper quickly extablished an envitable reputation for its reliability, ease of handling, and low maintenance expense. The 250 featured a two-speed gearbox. In an attempt to satisfy the demand for a more powerful machine, in 1922 BSA made a 985cc V-twin to further enhance their growing line.

The year 1927 was a momentous one, as this was the year the company began producing good OHV singles that were destined to become the hallmark of BSA. The famous 500cc "H" or "sloper" model was introduced which featured an 85mm x 88mm single cylinder engine mounted in a duplex cradle frame. The three-speed gearbox was standardized on all BSA's, and the new single had internal expanding brakes. Due to the oil sump being low in the crankcase, the sloper had a low center of gravity and therefore handled very well, and it proved to be quite fast and very popular. The price was a modest 65 pounds.

By 1930 the BSA range had been expanded to no less than 17 models. BSA had well and truly assumed world leadership in motorcycle production, and they were destined to wear this title until the mid-fifties when the scooter and mo-ped craze took over. During that year, one out of four motorcycles sold were from BSA.

The smallest in the range was the 174cc two-stroke. Next came the 250cc SV single, the 350cc single in either SV, OHV or sloper OHV form, the 500cc single the same as the 350 range, the 557cc sloper, and the 770cc and 986cc SV V-twins. In addition, the popular 500cc OHV sloper could be had in "tuned" trim with a red star on the engine's timing cover. The Red Star model had a higher compression ratio and special valves, springs, and cams. It produced 24 hp at 5,250 rpm (compared to the 18 hp of the standard model), and had a top speed in the mid-eighties. The tuned version cost 6 pounds extra.

During the early thirties the sloper design was dropped and emphasis was placed on the vertical singles, forerunners of the B-31 and B-33 models so popular after the war. As with the Red Star models, special tuned versions of the vertical singles were offered in both 350cc and 500cc sizes. These were called the Blue Stars, and they were capable of 75 mph and 85 mph respectively.

In 1935 an improved series of singles was introduced, and once again there were the "Star" models for the motorsportsman. Called the Empire Star, the model was available in either 250cc, 350cc, or 500cc sizes. The Empire Stars featured engines that were almost identical to the post-war B-31 and B-33. A fast road machine, the Empire Star was attractively finished with a black frame and a dark green gas tank with the now famous Star Emblem.

In 1937, after a 16-year absence from the racing game, BSA decided to compete at the famed Brooklands track with a specially prepared 500cc Empire Star. The famous racing man, Walter Handley, was engaged, and the goal was to capture a coveted "Gold Star" award given to those lapping the track at over 100 mph.

On June 30, 1937, the alcohol-burning single was successful; Walter won a race at 102.27 mph and lapped at 107.57, thus

BSA's first complete cycle, a 3½-hp single, belt-drive "mo-ped." Below, a 1915 model with chain-cum-belt drive.

350-cc BSA of 1925, owned by J. Smazek, shown here with his wife, has been in regular use without major repairs since purchased.

An outstanding performance demonstrations in the twenties was the climbing of Snowdon by four BSAs. Here one of them nears summit.

BSA's first Gold Star in 1938 sold for about $385. Right, last of Gold Stars was 1963 model, discontinued in favor of unit twins.

bringing home a Gold Star award.

BSA continued to lead the sales field and offered the greatest range of motorcylces of any manufacturer in the world. Take the 1938 range, for instance. No less than 17 models were available: 250cc SV and OHV models, a 350cc SV and two OHV models, a 500 SV and 500cc OHV model, a 600cc SV model, a 750 OHV V-twin, and the 1000cc SV V-twin. In addition, there were 250cc, 350cc and 500cc Empire Star models for the rider desiring a fast road machine, and a special 350cc trials model with upswept exhaust, small gas tank, narrow chrome fenders and knobby tires.

The above machines total only 14, though, and the last 3 models were the ones that gladdened the hearts of British motorsportsmen. Patterned after Walter Handley's Empire Star, the new model was appropiately named the Gold Star. Available in either road, track, or trials trim, the 500cc Gold Star was the most specialized mount that BSA had ever produced. Money was not the most plentiful item in those post-depression days, and many European motorsport enthusiasts could not afford both a "pukka" OHC racing model and a street machine. Here was BSA's answer then-a high performance OHV machine that could serve as both a competition model and a street bike.

The technical specifications of the M 24 Gold Star were interesting. The bore and stroke were 82mm x 94mm, and peak horsepower was 30 at 5,800 rpm with 6,500 rpm listed as peak permissable revs. The compression ratio was 7.5 to 1 for gasoline or petro-benzol and up to 10 to 1 for alcohol fuel.

The cylinder and head were cast in aluminum alloy, with inserted valve seats and a cylinder liner. Double-coil valve springs were used, and the carburetor was an Amal TT type with a 1-5/32" bore.

Possessing a rather "cobby" appearance, the Gold Star had a large 3½-gallon fuel tank for road or track use, and a girder fork was standard at the front. Tire sizes were 3.00 x 20 in. front and 3.50 x 19 in. rear. The brakes were a husky 7 in. x 1-3/8 in. and provided exceptional stopping power. The Gold Star weighed in at 325 to 350 lbs., depending on whether the machine was stripped for competition or fitted with full road equipment. Standard top gear ratio was 4.8 to 1 on the road model and up to 4.2 on the racing machine. This provided speeds of 95 and close to 110 mph for the two models. A trials model was also available for any dirt type of event.

For 1939 the range of models offered was the same as in 1938 except that the faster Silver Star replaced the Empire Star in the 350 and 500cc sizes. The 250cc Empire Star was dropped and replaced by the C10 and C11 models. The Gold Star model was also available with a special close ratio gearbox. In late 1939 BSA also built a few hairpin valve spring Silver Stars, but then World War II halted production of all sporting machines.

In the pre-war era, BSA machines won a fair share of trials and other types of competitions, but it was not until after the war that the Gold Stars would really come into their own. Probably the most noteworthy pre-war racing result was in 1938, when E.R. Evans rode his Gold Star into 5th place in the Ulster

Grand Prix at 79.04 mph. Ahead of Evans were only the winning supercharged BMW at 93.98 mph, two works Velocettes and a privately entered Manx Norton.

After the war there was little need for sporting motorcycles for a few years, and BSA concentrated on getting back on wheels. The 350cc B-31 and 500cc B-33 models were the mainstay of the range with the new telescopic front fork and a rigid frame. In 1947 the competition variants made their debut, and there iron-engined models were basically trials machines. The 125cc Bantam two-stroke also proved popular in the post-war era, and in 1947 the 500cc Star twin made its debut.

In 1949 the Gold Star model was re-introduced in 350cc form, and this was followed in 1950 by the 500cc model. The new Gold Stars were redesigned. The stroke on the 500cc model was shortened to 88mm with an 85mm bore, and the 350 had measurements of 71mm x 88mm.

The two engines had alloy heads and cylinders, and produced 33 hp and 25 hp respectively. A new plunger rear suspension was adopted, and an 8 in. front brake provided exceptional stopping power.

The Gold Star was progressively developed, and in 1954 an improved engine was produced. Possessing massive square fins, the 500cc and 350cc engines were producing 37 and 30 hp in road racing trim. The connecting rod was shortened, the rockers were eccentrically mounted to do away with the "nut and bolt" tappets and thus lighten the valve gear, and a Nimoc 80 exhaust valve was used. Reliability at racing speeds was further enhanced by the use of a "timed" mechanical crankcase breather and an EN.36 crankpin. The frame had previously been changed in 1953 to a duplex front-down-tube cradle frame with swinging-arm rear suspension. The Gold Stars were available in clubman, trials, moto-cross, or road racing trim.

In the early fifties, American motorcyclists were asking for more powerful British motorcycles, and BSA responded with the Golden Flash, a fast 650cc vertical twin. The big twin was subsequently developed and could be had in sports road trim or as a scrambler. The 1960-1972 , twins sported alloy heads and "tuned" engines which offered the discriminating buyer a very fast sports machine.

In 1965 the BSA range had something for everyone. There was a 75cc OHV lightweight, several 175cc two-strokes, 250cc road, trials, and scrambles models, 350cc road and enduro models, and 500cc and 650cc vertical twins in several degrees of tune and specifications. Lamentably, the illustrious Gold Star was dropped from production at the end of the 1963 season.

Probably the most exciting model in the range then was the new 441cc Victor, which was developed from the works motocross models. This single was available in road, enduro, or motocross trim, and it had a bore and stroke of 79 x 90mm. The big feature of the Victor was its light weight-288 pounds in Enduro trim and only 255 pounds in scrambles trim. The scrambler had an "oil tank" frame, but it was dropped after two years when the big 360cc two-strokes took over.

In 1969 BSA startled the world with their new 750cc-a "three" that churned out 60 hp at 72 rpm. This beast had a top speed of over 120 mph, and its acceleration was shattering.

In 1971 BSA made news again with the re-introduction of a new Gold Star along with a Victor Trail and a Victor Moto-Cross. These 84 x 90mm alloy singles were also developed from the works moto-cross bikes, and they featured a Ceriani type front fork and conical alloy hubs. The Gold Star produced 34 HP at 6200 revs and weighed only 310 pounds, while the scrambler had a 38 HP engine (at 6200 rpm) and weighed a very light 240 pounds. The MX model had the oil reservoir in the frame plus extensive use of alloy. The marque also designed a new DOHC 350cc twin with a five-speed gearbox, but this model was never put into production.

The BSA competition policy was much the same during the post-war era as in the pre-war days. Rather than build special "works" type racing models, the philosophy was to sponsor a factory team in sporting events, particularly trials and scrambles, and to use the standard Gold Star model. Nevertheless, their competition record is impressive indeed.

Bill Nicholson added many lustrous chapters to the BSA story by dominating the 1952 and 1953 European trials events, and Jeff Smith obtained a third place in World Moto-Cross standings. In 1955 the Scottish Trials again fell prey to BSA with Smith the victor, and John Draper garnered the World Moto-Cross championship with other Gold Star riders in second, fourth, and sixth positions. BSA fortunes then dropped a bit, as Draper could do no better than third in the 1958 Moto-Cross season; and Broer Dirks, fourth place in 1959.

In 1960 the new 250cc Star scrambler was used in the "Coup d'Europe" Moto-Cross Championship, and Jeff Smith rewarded the factory with the second place in championship standings. The little 250 was also used by the factory team in the 1963 and 1966 Scottish Trials, and Arthur and Sid Lampkin promptly plonked home the winners.

The BSA "Stars" returned again, and after a mediocre sixth place in 1962 moto-cross standings, the Birmingham group came back strongly with a new lightweight mount based not on the old Gold Star, but on an enlarged 350cc B-40 model. Jeff Smith upset the invincible Swedish aces.

In 1964 with his 420cc model, and in 1965 he trounced the field on a 441cc version. In 1966 Jeff slipped to third behind Paul Friedrichs and Rolf Tibblin on the new CZ 360, but he came back to finish second in 1967.

Jeff then retired from the scene and John Banks took over

with a full 500cc single. John finished close seconds in 1968 and 1969 after leading during the season, but in 1970 an injury stopped his efforts. In 1971 the company dropped the works moto-cross bikes because of financial crises; this robbed the sport of its last four-stroke single.

During the early 1970s all was not well with the company, however, since a series of poor decisions had virtually bankrupted the once proud name. In 1973 it appeared as though the BSA and Triumph would soon be a thing of the past, but at the last minute Norton-Villiers came forward with an offer to merge and thus save the names. Triumph was the only name to be saved, however, so that the BSA also became a marque to be remembered in the history books.

The 1966 441cc Victor Enduro was a popular model in the United States with its light 288 pound weight and generous ground clearance.

The 1965 650cc twin was a sleek roadster that would clock 100 mph with a single carburetor. Faster versions were also produced.

The 750-cc BSA Rocket 3, when introduced, was the first British multi intended for the mass market since the demise of the Ariel Square 4.

BULTACO

Many of the world's motorcycle manufacturers began production under peculiar circumstances, but none can equal the bizarre tale of the Spanish Bultaco. Born quite literally in a barn, the Bultaco has nevertheless, become one of the most famous names in the world among the more sporting-minded motorcycle enthusiasts. The company still operates from a farmyard. The narrow, rutted lane that leads to the sprawling set of buildings is a rough dirt affair that handily serves as a testing ground for new suspension systems.

The story of this young Spanish concern began in May 1958, at a board of directors meeting of the famous Montesa Company. Francisco Xavier Bulto was in attendance that day; he was one of the directors of the company, as well as being one of the original founders in 1946. The topic of discussion was whether Montesa should continue to participate in international grand prix road racing; the majority vote was negative.

This decision greatly saddened Francisco Bulto, because he had been the driving force, as well as the brains, behind the little 125-cc Montesa road racer which had performed so well during the middle 1950's. Sick at heart, Bulto resigned his position at Montesa to devote his time to other business interests–a textile plant and a piston manufacturing concern.

Senor Bulto soon learned, however, that he was not the only one who had resigned from Montesa, for within a few days he was invited to a dinner by former technical staff, mechanics, and riders of the company. At this dinner, the former employees asked the wealthy Fransisco to start a motorcycle manufacturing company–one that would have a deep love for sport.

Greatly inspired by these men, Bulto quickly agreed to set about the task of creating a new name in the motorbike field. On June 3, 1958, a group of 12 technicians met at Francisco's country home to design a 125-cc single-cylinder roadster that would sell in transportation-poor Spain. The long-range goal

was more sporting, of course, but a sound production program was essential before emphasizing the racing game.

Later that month, the embryo company moved to a farm at San Adrian de Besos on the northern edge of Barcelona, where the offices were established in old outbuildings. To give some idea of the primitive conditions under which Bulto began his company, the lathe was set up in the barnyard with only a tin roof to cover it. Within four months, the design team had finished its work, and the lathes, boring bars, and milling machines soon turned the mechanical drawings into a real motorcycle. Senor Bulto rode the little Single 40 miles to his home that night. Then the work began to iron out the many little "bugs" that are inherent in any prototype design.

By February of 1959, the time had arrived to hold a press day for the new motorcycle, but no one had thought of a suitable name for the company. John Grace finally came up with the now famous "Bultaco" handle, which was a contraction of Bulto and Paco–the latter name being a nickname for Francisco in Spain. John Grace is an Englishman, but he was, and still is, an influential member of the Bultaco concern. John also was a road racer in those days, and he was one of the energies behind Bultaco's sporting image. The "thumbs up" trademark of Bultaco was conceived by Francisco himself, who had witnessed British road racers give the thumbs up sign to signify all was going well when they flashed by their pits.

This first Bultaco, named the Tralla 101, proved to be a good bike. It helped to establish the company at this critical point in its existence. The powerplant was a two-stroke Single with a bore and stroke of 51.5 by 60mm, which gave 125cc. The engine was tuned to pump out a very healthy 12 bhp, which put it in the "sports" class. Top speed was 71 mph, which was really moving for a 125-cc model in those days.

This new Bultaco was quite advanced for 1959, with a

four-speed gearbox in unit construction behind the engine. The frame featured a swinging-arm suspension, and the front fork was especially flexible. A comfortable dual seat, large fuel tank, low handlebars, and good sized brakes set in alloy hubs combined to make the Tralla 101 a good looking model that appealed to the Spanish riders. No less than 1136 models were sold during the first year.

Just two months later, in May of 1959, Bulto entered his first team in competition. The event was the "Clubman" or roadster class of the Spanish Grand Prix, and Bultacos finished 2nd, 3rd, 4th, 5th, 7th, 8th, and 9th positions. John Grace was the marque's fastest rider, and he finished only six inches behind the winning Montesa.

Bulto then decided to modify a Tralla 101 by replacing the 22-mm carburetor with a larger 29-mm unit, plus removing the muffler. This bike was entered in the Madrid International race in October. Other than a polishing of internal engine parts and stripping of excess weight, the "works" racer was nearly identical to the stock roadster version. Nevertheless, Marcello Cama rode the little Single into 6th place behind the established racing stars of the day.

The next week, at Zaragoza, the team again entered the production class. They had realized that they had little chance of defeating the great Carlo Ubailli on his double-knocker MV Agusta or Bruno Spaggiari on his desmodromic Ducati. The officials, however, decided that the Bultacos were much to noisy to compete in the production model class, so the team was forced to compete in the pukka racing class. The mechanics toiled all night in an effort to convert the road bikes to "racers," and the next day the team apprehensively went to the starting line.

Then came the rain, and on the slippery track the fine handling little Bultacos sailed around the more powerful, but heavier, four-stroke MVs and Ducatis in every corner-only to lose advantage on every straight. Spaggiari then unloaded, leaving only world champion Ubbaili to hold off the pack of

"Buls." Two laps from the end, Carlo also unloaded, but this time he fetched off Johnny Grace who was right behind him. Marcello Cama, close behind also, went on to score a suprising and popular win for the barnyard concern from Spain.

This win was a tremendous encouragement for Francisco to proceed with the development of a real racer. It also gave the company added prestige, which helped boost sales of the Tralla 101. The winning 125 Single pumped out 13 bhp at 8800 rpm, and would turn 9000 revs in the lower gears.

In 1960, Bulto expanded his range of machines by offering two new models-one for touring and one for off-the-road play. The new touring bike was called the 155 model; it was more refined than the Tralla 101. Top speed was 62 mph, and this "Taco" became known as a comfortable, good looking, reliable, and fine handling touring bike. The rough-stuff model, the Sherpa N, had a larger 155-cc engine, wide ratio gears, upswept exhaust, and knobby tires. Produced as an enduro model, the Sherpa N helped boost sales to 4171 during 1960.

During 1961, Bultaco continued to make small changes in its basic design-they were making a good bike even better. The company also continued to compete extensively in Spanish production model road races, and it gradually began to dominate these events. This competition activity stimulated sales further, and total sales jumped to 7039 in 1961.

Bultaco still was known only in Spain, however. Factory leaders realized the company's growth would continue only if a substantial export business were established. The question was how to gain the world's attention. The unanimous decision was that competition was the best route. With the export goal in mind, Bultaco accelerated its research program in the race shop during 1960.

The first significant result of this research came in October 1960, when a specially prepared model was taken to Montlhery, France, for the purpose of breaking long-distance speed records. The Bultaco was a 175-cc two-stroke with standard piston-port induction (Bulto still scorns rotary valves as

In 1960 streamlined 175-cc Bultaco went 24 hours at 81.82 average.

1964 Sherpa S scrambler had 29 bhp, put Bultaco on the map in U.S.

First TSS road racer in 1961 had 125-cc single with 20 bhp.

The great Sammy Miller in action on the original Sherpa T in 1965 Scottish Six Days Trial, first victory for a non-British bike.

too expensive, tempermental, and unreliable). A sleek, streamlined shell completely covered the bike, but not the rider.

The powerplant was a 60.9-by60-mm Single, and it ran on a 9.0:1 compression ratio. Peak power was pumped out at 8000 rpm, with 18 bhp the output. Top speed was 107 mph, and lap speeds of 105 mph could be attained around the high banked bowl at Montlhery.

The riders were John Grace, Francisco Gonzales, Marcello Cama, Ricardo Quintanilla, and Frenchman Georges Monneret. The bike ran perfectly for 10 hours at well over 90 mph, only to develop a frame tube break. After a brief examination, John Grace restarted to complete the 12-hour record at 89.27 mph. Then the bike was pulled in to spend one and a half hours in replacing the frame. The streamliner then went out and nailed down the 24-hour record at 81.82 mph, which was a record speed for even the 250- and 350-cc classes! Finally, just to show the world how good his engines really were, Senor Bulto had John and Pierre Monneret go out and complete six laps at over 100 mph. This 24-hour record still stands in the FIM record book. It certainly increased Bultaco's recognition throughout Europe.

In 1961, Bultaco decided to take advantage of its racing knowledge by introducing the TSS road racing model. This four-speed 125-cc Single was a beautiful bike, and it proved to be just about the best production 125-cc racer available then. The lusty mill churned out no less than 20 bhp. This model, known for its fine handling and powerful brakes, soon was in demand by enthusiastic private owners. The letters TSS, Bulto's designation, signify nothing. However, Francisco was a great fan of the overhead cam KSS (sports roadster) and KTT (racing) Velocettes, and it is rumored that he wanted his racers to bear letter designations similar to the classical old Velos. (Francisco was a 1936 Spanish racing champion on a camshaft Velo, and, in 1949, on a Montesa.)

The TSS models made a good start in 1961, with R.B. Rensen piloting his racer into 6th position in the Isle of Man ultra-lightweight TT. Rensen, the first private owner to finish, averaged a respectable 83.26 mph. The one point earned was Bultaco's first point ever in world championship racing. John Grace followed this up with a 5th place in the Spanish GP, with Ricardo Quintanilla in 6th. TSS models also won national championships in Spain, Argentina, and Uruguay.

For 1962, the firm concentrated on improving its roadsters and introduced a new 200-ccMetralla model. It had a bore and stroke of 64.5 by 60 mm, and it pumped out 22 bph at 7000 rpm. Top speed was listed as 84 mph, and the model was known for its good looks, fine handling, and powerful brakes. In this, its initial export year, the firm sent 470 machines abroad, while total sales jumped to 8796. The U.S. received just 82 bikes (good things often start on a modest scale.)

The TSS model continued to do well in international road racing. By this time, any enthusiast worth his salt was well aware of the excellence of the Bultacos-racer and roadster alike. Dan Shorey, on an experimental 200-cc model, pegged down a 6th in the Isle of Man TT. John Grace pulled a 5th in the German GP 125-cc class, with another privateer getting 6th in the French event. TSS models also won national championships in Peru, Argentina, France, Sweden, and England; and Shorey won the British 250-cc crown on the works 200-cc model. Other notable achievements were the first 125-cc placing in the rugged 24 Hour Grand Prix d'Endurance at Barcelona and a pair of gold medals in the International Six Days Trial at Garmisch, Germany.

In 1963, the marque maintained the pace of design improvement with the new Tralla 102-a 125-cc mount with more power, better acceleration, improved road holding, and more powerful brakes. A new TSS road racing model also was added to the stable. Its 200-cc engine pumped out 30 bhp at 9500 rpm. Sales rose to 11,836 units-885 of which were exported. The U.S. consumption was 606 that year, so the Bultaco still was a fairly rare bike in this country.

The greatly expanded sales rate had provided funds for Francisco to pour all of his passion into the racing game, and the race shop became a place of frenzied activity. Water cooling and six-speed gearboxes were incorporated into the works bikes, and the latest bomb was given it's baptism in the 1963 Monza Grand Prix. In the 125-cc race, John Grace came home in 5th position at 92.2 mph-only two miles down on the winning Honda. This was a fantastic performance for such a simple engine design, and technicians the world over marveled at Bultaco's two-stroke knowhow. Other Bultaco placings were 5th and 6th in the Argentine GP. A modified Metralla model also won the European Grand Prix d'Endurance trophy for long-distance production machine racing.

For 1964, the marque branched out even further by introducing new motocross models in 125, 175, and 200 sizes. Called the Sherpa S, these new bikes featured a Ceriani front fork that set a new standard in riding comfort. Performance was simply devastating. These three engines had the same bore-stroke measurements as previous models, but compression ratios were 13.0:1, 12.0:1 respectively. Larger carburetors provided power outputs of 22, 26, and 29 bhp. All three models had a four speed gearbox, a 54-in. wheelbase, and 19-in. front and 18-in. rear tires. The dry weights of 182, 187, and 189 lb., respectively, made handling excellent. Because of these new scrambles bikes, exports to the U.S. shot up to 2161 of total export of 2429 bikes. Total production was 13,449.

The TSS road racers continued to be highly successful in the hands of private owners. Bultaco riders generally were the first 125-cc private owners to finish. The 200-cc models also did well, and Oriol Puig Bulto, son of Francisco, won the Spanish 250-cc Motocross title. "Buls" were beginning to be used for scrambling all over the world.

For 1965, Bulto really warmed up the dirt end of the sport, with the introduction of the 152-cc Campera, the 250-cc Sherpa T, and the 250-cc Pursang-Metisse. The Campera was a combination street and boondocking cycle, no doubt designed for the American market. In 1966, the Campera was enlarged to 175 cc, with a power output of 16.5 bhp. The super-fine suspension offered a generous 6 in. of front fork travel, and wide ratio gears were used. The Campera helped boost Bultaco sales to 17,392 in 1965 and 20,042 in 1966, with U.S. exports of 4906 in 1965 and 7199 in 1966.

The Sherpa T model, a pukka trials mount, was designed by the factory with the help of the great Irish trials rider, Sammy Miller. The Sherpa T had a wide ratio four-speed gearbox, a 4.00x18 rear tire, 2.75x21 front tire, a 53-in wheelbase, and a dry weight of 202 lb. Power output from the 72- by 60-mm engine was 18 bhp at 8000 rpm. A tiny 24-mm carburetor was used, and the compression ratio was 8.0:1.

The Pursang-'Metisse was a fire-breathing 250-cc motocross model that blended the famous Rickman-Metisse frame to a 36-bhp engine. A 32-mm carburetor was used, and the compression ratio was 12.0:1. This scrambles model became very popular with American riders for the fast TT-type scrambles races because of their terrific power. The Pursang helped establish Bultaco as a leader in the American rough-stuff competition scene.

Improvements to the TSS road racer for 1965 included water cooling and the increasing of the 200-cc model up to a full 250 cc. These were magnificent road racing models for the private owner, and their performance was good enough to win many national championships in the 125 and 250 classes. The addition of six-speed gearboxes also helped, and a constant improvement in the frame design, suspension, and braking strengthened overall performance.

Significant successes during 1965 included 3rd places in the 125 and 250 classes of the German GP, and 2nd in the Spanish 250 class, a 3-4-5 in the 250 French, 6th in the Ulster 125 and 250 races, 6th in the Finnish 250, and a 4th in the Monza 250 with a 6th in the 125 race. Then Sammy Miller won the famous Scottish Six Days Trial-the first time a non-British bike, or a two-stroke, had ever won this prestigious event. Sammy also won the British Trials Championship-something he did every year since until 1970.

In 1966, the marque did even better in classical road racing, with a 6th in IOM 250, 4th and 6th in the Spanish 250, as well as a 6th in the 125 race, a 6th in the Dutch 250, a 5th in the Czech 250, a 4th in the Finnish 250, and a 4th in the Italian 250 race. Then, in the fast Ulster GP, Ginger Molloy headed a Bultaco 1-2-3 win when the exotic Japanese 250-cc works multis tore their innards to shreds down the long straights. This was and still is the only outright win by Bultaco in world championship racing. It was earned by privateers who certainly had their day of glory.

The Bultaco line continued to expand for 1967. Models such as the four-speed Matador and the five-speed Pursang were two big reasons for the marque's popularity in the U.S. The Matador was a combination street and boondocking model that was pushed out to five speeds (wide ratio) for 1968, while the Pursang is a brutal 34-bhp scrambler, always hard to beat in the 250 class.

The Sherpa T, after winning the 1967 Scottish Six Days Trial, was made a five-speeder for 1968, and Miller won again that year! The gear ratios on the T model are so wide with this box that first gear is low enough for the worst obstacles, yet fifth is fast enough to really motor between observed sections. This gearbox, plus the 203-lb. weight and superb suspension, are probably the big reasons why Bultacos now dominate the European trials scene.

By 1968, the Bultaco range had been expanded to 21 models, a far cry from the one model that rolled out of the barnyard only nine years earlier. Included in the range were 100, 125, 175, 200, 250, 350, and 360 models in roadster, scrambles, enduro, trials, and road racing trim. The really big news in this lineup was the red hot 360-cc El Bandido motocross model that punched out a ghastly 43.5 bhp at 7500 rpm from its 85- by 64-mm engine. The new 360 used a four-speed gearbox, and the weight was only 251 lb. The El Bandido featured the use of fiberglass in a rather striking manner for the fuel tank, fenders, and seat. Wheelbase was a longish 55.9 in.

Another popular model with American riders was, and still is, the Matador-a five-speed 250 combination street and woods bike complete with lights. With 22 bhp at 5500 rpm and a 247-lb. weigh, the Matador is a fine dual purpose machine that performs exceptionally well in the rough. Its superb suspension offers the ultimate in rider comfort.

Probably the most popular model with the European crowd is the Metralla MK II-a fast 250-cc roadster with a strong psuedo-racer accent. The Metralla mill shoves out a healthy 27.6 bhp at 8700 rpm, which provides a maximum speed close to the 100-mph mark. The sleek Single has a five-speed gearbox with ratios of 5.87, 6.44, 7.71, 10.0 and 17.24:1. Wheelbase is 51.0 in. The Metralla is known for its big, powerful brakes (which are housed in truly beautiful alloy hubs); the front binder has twin leading shoes and a massive air scoop. The Single, also known for its superb handling, will scratch around tight corners in true road racing fashion.

Another bonus with the Metralla is the "bolt-on" racing kit, which can be used to convert the roadster into a competitive racing bike. The kit includes a small head fairing, larger fuel tank, clip-on bars, seat, a rearset brake-gearshift-footpeg setup, a special cylinder with wilder porting, a special squish head, larger carburetor, a piston, and an expansion box exhaust system. By fitting these parts, plus a set of road racing tires, an owner can go road racing in respectable manner-especially in "production" model races.

The race-kitted Metrallas have done well in international production model road races, such as the 1967 IOM 250-cc race where they took 1st, 2nd, and 6th. The winning model averaged

The Metralia can be modified for racing with special kit. Performance is nearly unbeatable in production racing with 110-mph speed.

Despite simplicity, water-cooled 125 and 250 Bultaco TSS singles develop 29 bhp at 11,500 rpm and 38.8 bhp at 9500 rpm respectively.

Metralia MK II, introduced in 1967, featured five-speed gearbox, powerful brakes and 100-mph speed. U.S. version has higher bars.

Bultaco's early lightweight roadsters, like this single, had conventional piston port design, full fenders, rounded fuel tank.

TSS was a two-stroke single for road racing, with 125- and 250-cc displacements. It was water-cooled, preventing wide use in U.S.

88.63 mph, a good speed for this type of bike.

For the read grand prix enthusiast, the 1968-69 TSS models were the bikes that made fhe pulse pount. They were held in high esteem by private owners. The water-cooled 125 and 250 models, which have been under constant improvement, pump out 29 bhp at 11,500 rpm and 38.8 bhp at 9500 rpm, respectively. The performance through a six-speed gearbox is fantastic for a single-cylinder piston-port engine. Top speed with a fairing are claimed to be 118 and 130 mph. The gear ratios of the 125-cc racer are 7.3, 7.8, 8.5, 9.6, 11.5, and 15.5:1, while the 250's are 5.2, 5.5, 6.2, 6.8, 8.2, and 11.1:1. The wheelbase is a short 51.0 in. on both models. Dry weights are 205 and 212 lb., respectively.

The TSS range was expanded late in 1968 with the addition of the new 350-cc model, a Single with bore and stroke of 83.2 by 64 mm. The new 350 is air cooled and runs a compression

ratio of 11.0:1 (compared to 13.5:1 on the smaller racers), and the mill pumps out 50 bhp at 8500 rpm. Bulto claims a speed of 137 mph for the 350 which combined with the 242-lb. weight and a five-speed gearbox, made life interesting for other 350s. Carburetion on the 350 is by a 32-mm Amal GP unit, compared to a 30-mm size on its smaller brother.

These TSS models have continued to display an impressive performance in international grand prix racing, as well as winning many national championships. By 1968, the 125 and 250 TSS "Buls" generally were regarded as the finest production racers available to European private owners. In 1968, the marque was especially successful; Giner Molloy placed 3rd in the 125-cc World Championship behind the exotic Yamaha V-4s, and S. Cannelas tied for 5th place. Molloy also finished 4th in the 250 class, as well as tying for 4th in the 350. All this on a simple piston-port two-stroke Single against the most exotic disc-valve two-stroke multis going today. In addition, are the magnificent victories of Sammy Miller in the 1967 and 1968 Scottish Trial, plus his 1968 and 1970 European Trials Championships.

Since 1969, Bultaco has not been so interested in road racing and has concentrated more on "dirt" bikes. The latest Yamaha 250 and 350cc water-cooled twins have proven too fast for the Bultacos, so the TSS models were dropped from production in 1972. Bultaco did prepare a prototype 360cc single that won the prestigious Barcelona 24 Hour Race in 1972 plus take a second in 1973, just to prove how fast their singles were over a twisty course.

The new 175, 250, and 325cc Alpina models have more than made up for the loss of the TSS racers, as have the 250 and 350cc Sherpa trials bikes. The Alpina is a delightful dual-purpose trail and trials bike that weighs just 215 pounds, and it is famous for its fine handling and plonking power. In competition, Martin Lampkin won both the British and European Trials Championships in 1973, while Malcom Rathmell took the 1973 Scottish and the 1974 European title. In moto-cross, American Jimmy Pomeroy won the Spanish 250cc Grand Prix for Bultaco's first win in this rugged game.

So ends this story of Francisco Xavier Bulto-a modern day genious of the international motorcycle scene. True, Bultaco never may be the world's largest selling motorcycle, but somehow this doesn't seem very important to Senor Bulto. The man appears to be a sportsman first and a manufacturer second, and upon such giants as this does the sport of motorcycling rest its case. Born in a barnyard and still a farm-based operation, the Bultaco was already a legend at the ripe old age of 13 years.

The 1975 Sherpa T is generally recognized as the finest trials bike in the world. It is produced in both 250 and 325cc sizes.

DUCATI

In discussing many of the world's motorcycles we speak of their great days in the past when the marque produced scintillating mounts for the more sporting minded rider, or when they added illustrious chapters to the colorful saga of motor racing. When we speak of Ducati, we speak of the present, because the Ducati is truly one of the most modern of all the motorcycles being produced today.

The story of this Italian masterpiece began only a few years ago in 1950 when the Bologna factory was rebuilt after the devastation of the war. Previously, the company had never produced motorcycles, but it was decided they would enter the motorbike field because post-war Italy needed personal transportation at a price that the rather poor populace could afford.

With the capital stock partly owned by the Italian government and the Vatican, the company had the financial resources to launch a line of 48cc and 65cc motorbikes and a 175cc scooter. These models proved to be well-designed, peppy little mounts, and the company was on its way to success.

As post-war Italy flexed its economical muscles, the standard of living slowly increased, and, quite naturally, the Ducati concern grew right along with it. In 1954, the factory hired Ing. Fabio Taglioni to head up the design work, and this proved to be an excellent one as Taglioni's genius was soon manifest.

By 1955 the Ducati was rapidly becoming a best seller in Italy, and the inexpensive little 65TS model was probably the star of the range. This 65cc four-stroke model produced 2.5 hp at 5,600 rpm for a maximum speed of about 44 mph. The suspension system was very advanced for those days, with a swinging-arm on the rear and an orthodox telescopic fork on the front. A comfortable dual seat was fitted, and, to satisfy the Italian desire to be a "racer," a small racing type windscreen was mounted over the handlebar. This windscreen bit

seems very strange on a 44 mph motorbike to anyone except an Italian, but it made the 65TS a "sports" mount and this must have been important to the Latins, because the motorcycle sold in great numbers.

In 1956, the more affluent natives had their eyes on the 98S model, which offered more spirited performance than the 65cc Ducati. The new 98cc ohv motorbike had a more potent powerplant, producing something like 6.5 hp at 7,000 rpm for a maximum speed of 56 mph. The 98S model looked considerably more rugged than the smaller edition, and it had a heavier "open" type frame along with larger brakes to match the performance. The front tire was a 2.50 x 17 inch and the rear was a 2.75 x 17.

Still catering to the Latin desire for a "racer", the 98S had a small handlebar fairing complete with a tiny racing

The 98-cc ohv Ducati of 1956 was popular motorbike in Italy. 56-mph roadster had a racing type fairing to please sporting Italians.

The first of the ohc Ducatis was the 1957 175-cc model. This one is shown in export trim for the American market.

This racy looking 100-cc Ducati was produced in 1958 – a popular mount for racing-conscious Italians. Ohc engine gave 65 mph.

windscreen. With low handlebars the mount was supposed to look very fast, at least to the Italians, and this rather humorous accessory on a 56-mph motorbike helped sell the 98S model in goodly numbers.

Ing. Taglioni had not been hired just to design roadsters. His great passion in life was in fire-breathing racing engines. Hard at work on his brainchild, Taglioni was destined to produce a truly great racing engine-and on a meager budget at that.

It was not until the 1956 Swedish Grand Prix that the new racer appeared, but the impact of the design was tremendous, as it set the whole motorcycle racing world to talking. The engine displaced 125cc and featured a desmodromic cylinder head that allowed fantastically high revs with no fear of valve float. Desmodromics, for those of you who are unfamiliar with the term, means positive valve control, and in the Ducati this meant simply that there were a pair of cams to push open the valves and another pair of cams to pull them shut. Valve springs, therefore, were dispensed with, and this positive mechanical process meant that valve float was eliminated right along with the dangers of "holing" a piston or failing the valve gear through overstressing the components. At any rate, Degli Antoni astounded the racing world by riding the "desmo" machine to victory over its more established rivals in its first race. Then, just to seal the company's reputation, the Ducati team of Fargas-Ralachs rode a 125cc model into first place in its class in the Barcelona 24-hour Grand Prix d'Endurance-a true test of stamina and reliability at speed.

The early success of the marque declined a bit during 1957, when the company concentrated its resources on the introduction of the new 175cc ohc "T" and "S" (touring and sport) models, and these were followed in 1958 by the 100 and 125cc "Sport" models. By then, Ducati's goal was obvious;

they were out to expand their sales to all corners of the world. To do this meant two things: they would have to produce a line of really good motorcycles, and then they would have to get the message across to riders all over the world. The new ohc Ducatis certainly fulfilled the first requirement, and for the second it was decided, and wisely so, to conduct an aggressive campaign on the world's grand prix tracks. This racing effort would have to be conducted on a slim budget, though, because the company was still rather small and the funds were not too plentiful.

As far as the world-wide sales were concerned, Ducati had a really fine machine in the new 175cc ohc model. The 175cc alloy engine, with a 62mm bore and a 58.8mm stroke, produced 11 hp at 7,500 rpm for a maximum speed of 68 mph. Carburetion was handled by a 22mm Dellorto, and the valves were inclined at 80 degrees to each other. The compression ratio was a modest 7:1.

The engine's lower end featured a rugged ball and roller bearing assembly, and the crank and transmission cases were cast in one clean-looking unit. The gearbox had four speeds. This engine-gearbox case was mounted in an exceptionally well designed frame which used a swinging-arm rear suspension and a telescopic front fork of outstanding quality. The brakes were very large and were housed in beautifully finished alloy hubs. The whole bike had an exceptional finish, and the engine had Allen-type screws instead of slotted screws on the covers.

These 175cc models were followed by the 100 and 125cc sports models in 1958, which were produced more for domestic consumption. The little 100 Sport model proved very popular with the Italians because it provided a speedy little tourer to very sporty specifications at a cost factor that they could afford. Similar to the 175cc models except in size, the engine had a 49mm bore and a 52mm stroke. A compression ratio of 9 to 1 was used along with an 18mm carburetor, and the little lunger pumped out 8 hp at 8,500 rpm. Top speed was listed as 65 mph.

During 1957 the factory spent their time in developing the 125cc desmodromic engine and improving their standard production range. Their racing successes, quite naturally, declined a bit. Just to keep their name alive and to prove that 1956 was no fluke, the factory sent Bruno Spaggiari and Albert Gandossi to Spain for the 24-hour Barcelona event. Once again the 125cc ohc proved to be reliable as a team garnered first place at record speed in the 125cc class.

In the winter of 1957-58 the factory shops were very busy. The Ducati management had aggressively set up an extensive dealer network all over the world, and retailers in the European countries, North and South America, the Orient, and Australia, all had this new line of ohc singles to sell. The management promised these new dealers all over the world that, by the end of the year, Ducati would be renowned as a great motorcycle.

To get the Ducati recognized meant just one thing-successful participation in world championship racing. To this end the factory dedicated itself in the spring of 1958. It would take some determined work to show the world the brilliance of Ing. Taglioni's designs. Still a relatively small company, Ducati did not have the finances to hire the very top riders or conduct a massive racing campaign. Still, they had the desmodromic engine, and, by choosing their battlegrounds, they just might steal the whole show.

The very summit of international racing is the Isle of Man TT, and the marque decided to start the season there. Handicapped by not having riders with a great deal of experience on the island course, the Ducati team didn't really expect to defeat Carlo Ubbiali and his MV Agusta. The team did put up a courageous battle, however, and Romolo Ferri, Dave Chadwick, and Sammy Miller took second, third, and fourth places.

The next battleground was the Dutch Grand Prix at Assen, and, when the little 125s were pushed off the grid, it was Alberto Gandossi and Luigi Taveri who led the first lap. After a fantastic battle it was Ubbiali again, though, with Taveri,

Gandossi, and Chadwick taking second, fourth, and fifth places. Taveri was beaten by just a few yards, though, and he did have the honor of making a record lap.

Then followed the Belgian GP at Spa, and this was where the tide turned. The previous races had been on the slower, more twisty courses where Ubbiali's brilliant riding gave him an advantage, but now the season was to enter the faster courses where horsepower would show. The result was a smashing victory for Ducati, with Gandossi, Ferri, Chadwick, and Taveri taking first, second, fourth, and sixth places.

The next race was the German event at the Nurburgring and once again the Ducatis streaked into the lead. Displaying superior speed over the world champions, the Ducati riders steadily pulled away. Then, disaster struck. Ferri crashed, Taveri's engine went off song, and Gandossi's model broke down.

Then followed the Swedish Grand Prix at Hedamora, and Gandossi and Taveri once again were the victors with Ubbiali taking a bad drubbing into third place. Next was the fast Ulster event, only that year the race was run in a driving rain. Gandossi rode like a tiger that day and, with two laps to go, he held Ubbiali at bay-clocking 107.9 mph on the Leamthemstown Straight. Then, on the hairpin, Gandossi lost the model on the slippery road. He was able to remount and finish fourth, with Taveri and Chadwick in second and third; but with his crash went his last chance for the world championship.

The final event of the 1958 season was at home on the fast Monza circuit. With great prestige at stake here, the two antagnists made great preparation for the race. This final chapter in a season of torrid racing was destined to be Ducati's, though, as the marque quite literally slaughtered the mighty MV's by taking the first five places. The final order was Bruno Spaggiari, Gandossi, Francesco Villa, Chadwick, and Taveri. All Ducatis were desmo singles except Villa's mount, which had a new twin cylinder engine.

So the curtain fell on a courageous effort by a small factory-and it very nearly proved successful, too, as only Gandossi's spill in the waning laps of the Ulster Grand Prix stood between him and the championship. This racing campaign was eminently successful for what it was intended to do, however, and that goal was to put Ducati "on the map" all over the world. Almost overnight the marque became famous and sales sharply increased. The year of 1958, then, must be regarded as the turning point for Ducati. And just to add some frosting to the cake, the team of Mandolini-Maranghi once again took the 125cc class at the 24-hour Barcelona event to cap a really great year.

For 1959 Ducati planned a racing campaign that would keep them in the news, but it was neither as extensive nor expensive as the all-out effort of the previous year. Some remarkably good results were obtained, however, with outright victories by Ken Kavenagh In the 125cc Finnish Grand Prix and by Mike Hailwood in the Ulster event. Hailwood also garnered a

third at the Isle of Man, and other Ducati riders took fourth, fifth, and sixth in the Ulster, as well as a third in the Monza classic. Then, once again, the Ducati team of Flores-Carrero won the 125cc class at the 24-hour Barcelona grind on a standard production 125cc Sport model.

In 1959 the standard production range was increased with the 85cc Bronco, which was derived from the older 98cc model, and this was later enlarged to a 125cc powerplant. During 1960 the ohc 175cc models were enlarged to 200cc, and, in 1961 and 1962, the Piuma Sport and Falcon 48cc two-strokes were added to the range of motorcycles.

During 1960, Ducati racing successes took a sharp turn downward as the factory changed its competition policy. Racing in world championship classics had achieved what the company wanted in the way of publicity and sales, and so the factory turned its efforts toward improving production models and building racing bikes for the private owner. These production racers have achieved a great number of victories and placings in Europe, Argentina, Canada, the United States, Africa, Venezuela, Brazil, Uruguay, Ecuador, Chile, Australia, and the Orient, and in all these places the Ducati name had become synonymous with performance.

This knowledge gained in racing has been incorporated into the stahdard production models, and the 200cc ohc engine was enlarged to 250cc in 1962 and produced as a super sports model (Diana), a tourer (Monza), and a scrambler. In 1963 the factory began production of the 100cc Cadet and Mountaineer models, and then the 48cc and 100cc scooters. Lastly, in 1965, the 250 acquired a five-speed gearbox and new 160cc and 350cc ohc models made their debut.

The Diana MK III was the star of the 1966 range, and this 250cc sportster is for the enthusiast who liked to play road racer on weekends. American road tests have obtained speeds of around 104 mph on this bike, which is a truly remarkable performance. The fine handling and powerful brakes are also exceptionally good, and the Diana is probably about as close as a fellow can come to running a pukka road racer on the street. The fittings on the Diana were all rather sporting with low bars, an extra megaphone exhaust, tachometer, and rear-mounted footpegs and brake-gearshift levers as standard equipment for the machine.

For more sedate touring the Monza model was the answer, with a lower performance engine and more comfortable accessories. For motocross fans there was the 250cc scrambles model. The 350cc Sebring and 160cc Monza Junior models completed the range.

In Europe the Ducati line was slightly different than in the U.S., with the Mach I replacing the Diana model. This Mach I is claimed by Ducati to be the fastest standard production 250cc motorbike in the world, and few there are that argue with this claim. Several British road tests have attained 106 mph with the muffler intact-which is about two mph faster than stateside tests of the Diana with a megaphone. Chief differences

The fabulous 150-cc twin-cylinder desmodromic racer which Mike Hailwood used for many victories. Only the one model was built.

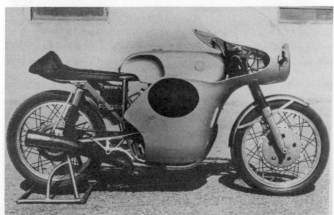

Available only in Europe, the 250- and 350-cc Ducati road racers had special frame; outputs were 34 and 39.5 bhp respectively.

between the Mach I and Diana are battery ignition, low bars, fuel tank, seat, tachometer drive, larger valves, and a different camshaft.

For Pukka racing there were 250cc and 350cc racers available which offered excellent performance on the track. The Ducati racer featured a massive double, twin-leading-shoe front brake and a full duplex cradle frame. The lower half of the engine was similar to the works racers, but the top half had the conventional single overhead camshaft. Power output was rated as 34 hp at 8,500 rpm on the 250cc engine and 39.5 hp at 8,000 rpm on the 350cc version. Both engined had twin spark ignition and five-speed gearboxes.

Ductai's aim in producing these racers for European sportsmen is to supply a racing bike that handles well, performs reasonably well, is reliable, and yet sells at a cost low enough so that almost anyone can afford it. A more powerful engine could, no doubt, be supplied, but the cost would soar and reliability would decline as a result.

Since the change in racing policy from exotic works desmodromic engines to production racers and clubman-type racing, Ducati has continued to establish an enviable reputation. In the classic 24-hour Barcelona race for production or prototype models, the team of Villa and Balboni took a 175cc model into a remarkable first place ahead of the works 600cc BMW in 1960. The next success was in 1962 when the Fargas-Rippa team took another first, this time in the 250cc class.

Then, in 1964, came perhaps the marque's greatest hour when the team of Bruno Spaggiari and Guiseppe Mandolini took a 285cc single ohc model into an outright win going the record distance of 2415 kilometers-the first time that 100 kph had been achieved for the 24 grueling hours. All this was done, mind you, against the finest big-engine teams that Europe could produce. Still displaying their stamina, stemming from good engineering, the Ducati team of Cere-Giovanardi again took a first place overall in the 1966 Imola Six-Hour Race, one of the big races counting for the Coup d'Endurance award. Behind the winning Ducati 250 were many big motors up to 750cc.

In 1968 Ducati became interested in the road racing game again with some proto-type models that included the predecessor of the production desmo models. They achieved some

notable placings in the 250, 350, and 500cc classes, but it was not truly serious attempt at any championship.

In 1968 they also won the 250cc class in the Barcelona 24 Hour Race-finishing third in the 750cc class. These efforts seemed to be more of a try out for their new designs, but it did give them a fair amount of publicity around the world. Their present policy seems to be much the same, with only an occasional outing to reveal any flaws in a new design.

In 1968 Ducati introduced a potent 350cc scrambler that became popular in the U.S., and in 1969 their new Desmodromic 250 and 350cc models caused a great sensation for their technical excellence. The big advantage of the desmo setup is lack of valve float, which makes for reliability at high engine speeds. A 450cc model was also produced.

Late in 1970 Ducati announced their entry into the super bike field with a potent 750cc V-twin that had OHC heads and a five speed gearbox. The dry weight is only 374 pounds, which should combine with the 70 HP at 8,000 rpm for a terrific performance.

This new 750cc twin had proven to be a superb sporting motorcycle, with works "desmo" versions taking first and second in the 1972 Imola Formula 750 Race plus a second in 1973. The twin also won the prestigious Barcelona 24 Hour classic at record speed in 1973.

And so ends the story of the growth of Ducati. But, before we leave this speedy little Italian, let's go back to that fabulous tiny desmodromic engine and take a peek under the gas tank. A truly great classic in the annals of European motorsport, the 125cc Ducati is the only successful desmodromic motorcycle engine to have ever been raced. Produced by a brilliant engineer, the project was handicapped by a slim racing budget and a shortage of really top-flight riders. Nevertheless, it achieved some dramatic victories and added a chapter to motorsport history.

Taglioni first sketched out his desmodronic layout in 1948, but it was not until 1954, when he was hired by Ducati, that he could get down to the actual design work. In 1955 the first engine was assembled, and in 1956 it was entered in its first race in Sweden.

The little 125cc desmo engine had a bore and stroke of 55.25 x 52mm, and was the same as the marque's single and double overhead cam engines from the cylinder top downward. The two cams that opened the valves were located on spur gears in much the same manner as a double overhead camshaft engine. On the middle shaft was located the closing cams which had, of course, an inverted profile, and these closed the valves via short rocker arms. These rocker arms were attached to the valve stems through flanged collars located by split wire rings sprung into grooves in the stem. The valves were closed to within 0.012 inch of their seats, and the internal compression pressure then closed them onto the seats.

The valves themselves were inclined at an 80-degree angle, and the inlet and exhaust lifts were 8.1mm and 7.4mm, compared to 7.5mm and 7mm on the standard twin-cam Grand Prix model. The throat diameter of the valves were 31mm on the inlet and 27mm for the exhaust. Carburetor bore size was 22 or 23mm for use on tight, twisty courses which put a premuim on acceleration, 27mm for typical grand prix courses, and 29mm for very fast circuits such as Monza or Spa-Francorchamps. The compression ratio was 10 to 1.

Power output was 19 hp at 12,500 rpm, compared to 16 hp at 12,000 rpm on the twin-cam Grand Prix model. The little desmo twin that Francisco Villa used in the 1958 Monza classic had a bore and stroke of 42.5 x 45mm and pumped out 22.5 hp at 14,000 rpm; but at the time the single was more raceworthy because of its wider torque range. The maximum speeds with dolphin fairings were 112 mph for the single and 118 mph for the twin.

The frames that these splendid little engines were mounted in were quite orthodox for their day and the handling was never reputed to anything exceptional. Five- or six-speed gearboxes were used, depending upon the circuit, and twin-coil ignition was employed. The oil sump was contained in the crankcase and the oil lubricated both the engine and transmission. A castor-base oil of SAE 20 weight was used, and fuel consumption averaged about 45 mpg.

Another interesting Ducati produced in 1959 was a 250cc desmodromic twin that turned to 11,800 rpm. The factory produced just this one model, built especially for Mike Hailwood. and then lost interest in racing. On this fabulous twin Hailwood set his homeland short circuit races alight, as the screaming Ducati smashed many a race and lap record.

Today, the racing efforts of the marque are concentrated toward the European production machine racing where they do so well and the improvement of their rather secretive experimental models. The regulations for the Coup d'Endurance racing trophy allow some modifications from standard production practice for experimentation, and Ducati has taken advantage of this. The result has often been some surprising victories against much larger engines, and the company has benefitted immensely from the publicity.

All this participation in racing their production models has had its benefits to Ducati, and the knowledge gained is usually incorporated into the standard production range. With a constant technical improvement to their basic ohc design, the present-day Ducati range must be considered one of the most modern in the world.

From scooters and inexpensive lightweights on up to the fabulous 750cc V-twin, here is a motorbike that appeals to the knowledgeable enthusiast. Quality of workmanship and race-bred design go hand in hand at Bologna.

This exploded drawing reveals the details of the famous 1959 Desmodromic 125cc engine. Courtesy of Motor Cycle.

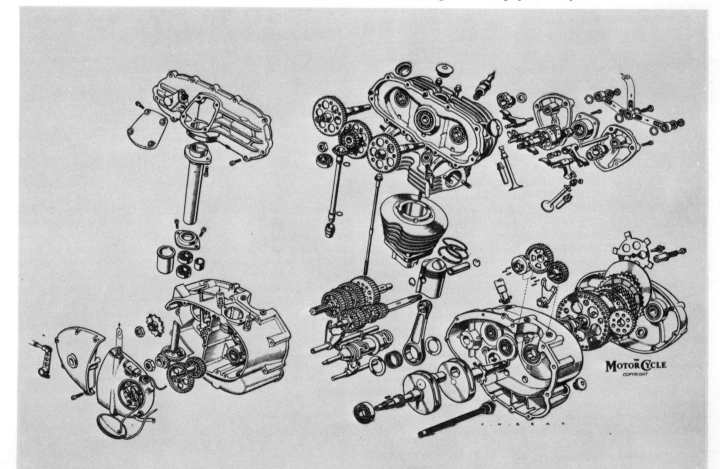

GREEVES

The history of a motorcycle manufacturing company has often begun in some unusual ways, but the establishment of Greeves is unique. The manufacturing of a gasoline engine powered wheelchair for severely disabled people may not seem to be the way to start a motorbike business, but, nevertheless, that is exactly how one Britisher made his mark in the world of two-wheeled sport.

What is truly unique about this venture is that today, despite its ancestry of a motorized wheelchair, the Greeves concern produces nothing but fire-breathing competition machines that are definitely not for the faint of heart. From wheelchairs to motocross championships is their motto, and what fabulous results have been obtained for such a tiny manufacturer!

The story of this venture began in 1945 when Derry Preston Cobb, who now is sales manager of the Greeves concern, complained to his cousin, Bert Greeves, that his battery powered invalid car was hopelessly inadequate for getting about the countryside. To Bert Greeves this was a challenge, particularly after Derry put a 30-cent wager on the deal, so he went to work designing and building the rig. The result was suprisingly good, so the pair of them decided to go into business producing the machine.

The little business prospered and the tale might have ended there had it not been for the creative genius of Greeves. Now Bert was, and still is, a dyed-in-the-wool motorcyclist, having been a rider since 1919 when, as a 14-year-old, he began his studies on a 225-cc James. Today there are 15 bikes in his garage, ranging from a 1912 Triumph to a 1951 Vincent "Black Shadow" that still is known to occasionally travel down the Southern Arterial at well over the 100-mph mark.

So Bert Greeves is, above all, a dedicated motorcyclist, and it was only natural that someday he would get the desire to build his own motorbikes. In the early 1950s, he got down to the designing and testing of his theories, and in the 1953 Earls Court Show the first models were put on display. Delivery was promised in early 1954, and the two models certainly whetted the appetites of the sporting minded riders.

These first Greeves motorbikes used the popular 200-cc Villiers engine, a common practice in those days among a host of British manufacturers. The two models were for competition-one was a trials mount, the other a scrambler. Powerplants had bore and stroke of 59 by 72mm, and they were the tried and proven two-stroke design. Both models featured four-speed gearboxes, with the scrambler having a close ratio box and the trials model having wide ratio gears.

It was in the chassis and suspension that Bert manifested his theories, and even today some of the basic ideas are retained. The model 20-S motocross machine was particularly cobby looking with its leading-link front fork, unusual swing-

Very first Greeves was 1954 trials model, powered by a 200-cc Villiers two-stroke. I-beam frame member is still Greeves feature.

Dave Bickers flies at Glastonbury, England. This works Greeves sports a Ceriani fork, since adopted for production machinery.

ing-arm rear suspension, and I-beam front downtube frame member.

The front fork featured an unusual rubber suspension with friction dampers, and the suspension characteristics were quickly adjustable at trackside to suit local conditions. The rear suspension system was a very early attempt at the swinging-arm principle, and it used spring loaded units with friction pads for damping. The massive I-beam frame member was cast of magnesium alloy, for light weight with great strength.

The rest of the specifications were functional. A short open exhaust pipe was used, and the alloy fenders were mounted well above the tires for plenty of clearance on suspension and for mud clinging to the tires. A small fuel tank was used, and the seat was the now common dual type.

The trials model was similar to the scrambler, except it had an upswept exhaust pipe with muffler, a speedometer, and trials tires instead of the gripster tread. The trials model was very light, and its handling in rugged going was considered to be exceptional.

After introduction of his bikes, Bert Greeves set about improving the breed. During those years, the world's manufacturers all were experimenting with some sort of rear suspension, and Greeves was one of them. That was the era when many were changing from the rigid frame, or plunger suspension, to the now common swinging-arm type, and Greeves decided to join the throng.

The new frame used Girling telescopic shock absorber units, and it followed accepted practice in its basic design. The unusual leading-link front fork was retained, however, but it was modified for better suspension characteristics. All in all, the Greeves was a good little bike, but it was still barely known outside England.

About that time, Bert decided that, if his name were to grow, he would have to gain some publicity. If sales could be increased, there would be more profits for research and development, and this would provide a better bike that would sell in greater numbers. There were several avenues open for promotion of the Greeves but the sporting nature of the designer made the competition route the only logical answer.

To proceed in this direction required a top flight rider, as those were the days when motocross racing was becoming immensely popular in Europe. Bert obtained the great rider he needed. To the late Brian Stonebridge goes a great deal of credit for putting the marque in the news. Brian was a truly fine motocross rider, with a wealth of both British and continental experience to bring to the tiny factory.

So, in January of 1957, a great partnership was formed, and the pair forged ahead in racing and improving the scrambler breed. During 1957, Stonebridge concentrated on British events, winning his share and establishing a fine reputation for the eager young company. All this activity and success naturally helped the sales of the company's product, and the future looked bright.

In 1958, the **Federation internationale motorcycliste** (FIM) decided to establish a **Coupe d'Europe** trophy for 250-cc class motocross machines, and a series of races were scheduled in various countries throughout Europe. Stonebridge was anxious to enter this series, as he had a great wealth of continental experience upon which to base his campaign. Bert was also agreeable to the idea, because no British lightweights at that time were capable of upholding British prestige.

So the still tiny company embarked enthusiastically on its giant-killing mission, and what a battle it was. All season long the lanky Stonebridge battled it out with the best that the world had to offer, and in the end he came 2nd to Jaromir Cizek on his flying Jawa. The season's tally also gave a big boost in Greeves motorcycle sales. The company was on its way!

The following year proved to be another battle all season

long for Stonebridge, and again he garnered a 2nd place in the championship standing. That year, the Britisher had the statisfaction of trouncing his Czecholosvakian rival, only to lose out to Rolf Tibblin (Husqvarna). The success and publicity that Stonebridge gained continued to help expand Greeves sales, and for the first time the export business became important to the company.

Meanwhile, the founder had been busy at his drawing boards. One of the most important advances was the new 66-mm bore cylinder to boost the Villiers engine from 197cc to a full 246-cc powerplant. This was followed by a new head, and these two components gave the engine a square appearance. A systematic development of port shape and exhaust tuning also yielded an increase in horsepower, which was essential to keep up with the fast charging continentals.

The following year saw a new name on the works machines, as Brian Stonebridge had tragically lost his life in an automobile accident. The new ace was Dave Bickers. His forceful riding was destined to be the second great chapter in the story of the Greeves.

During 1960 and 1961 Bickers rode a greatly improved machine with such gusto that he was crowned European champion both years. These magnificent results really put the seal on the reputation of the marque, and sales rapidly expanded. Exports also increased until 20 percent of the total production was leaving the mother country to do battle all over the world.

With such fabulous international competition success it was only natural that the factory would expand its production into the roadster field. The 1962 catalog, for example, listed a total of 11 models-four roadsters and seven competition machines. The roadsters included 200- and 250-cc Singles, and a 325-cc Twin-all with standard Villiers engines. All the road models featured the proven I-beam front frame member and the leading-link front fork.

The seven competition models were all 200- and 250-cc single-cylinder trials and motocross mounts. Both were available with either the stock Villiers engine or with the more potent Greeves alloy cylinder and head components. These competition machines established a great reputation all over the world in the hands of private owners, and the sales of the company continued to expand.

All this activity in the engineering department curtailed the international competition program, and Bickers was able to compete in only the British round of the 250-cc series. Dave did win that event, though, just to show that the marque had lost none of its touch.

For 1963, the range of machines offered was expanded into a new area, but the number of models offered was reduced to nine. The roadsters were all 200- and 250-cc Singles, and they were little changed from the previous year. The two 250-cc trials models were identical except for engines-one with a standard Villiers engine, the other with a Greeves alloy cylinder and head. The trials models featured wide ratio gearboxes with ratios of 7.75:1, 10.5:1, 18.6:1 and 27.9:1.

Two scramblers were offered that year, and both were similar except for engines. The Hawkstone model used a Villiers Mark 36-A engine that developed 19 bhp at 5500 rpm. Dry weight was 223 lb. The Moto-Cross model used the Greeves square alloy head and cylinder on the Villiers crankcase, and it produced 23 bhp at 6000 rpm. The compression ratio was 12.7:1 as compared to 10.0:1 on the stock engine, and both had gear ratios of 10.0:1, 12.7:1, 17.8:1, and 25.0:1.

Probably the most talked about Greeves that year was the new Silverstone road racing model. The inexpensive racer was produced for the private owner who had to watch his expenses very carefully, and yet the bike was capable of an outstanding performance.

The frame of the Silverstone was based on the successful motocross model, but with small modifications to make it suitable for road racing. The wheels had alloy rims laced on full width cast alloy hubs, and the tire sizes were 2.75x19 front and 3.25x18 rear. A sleek 2.75-gal. fiberglass fuel tank was fitted, and an orthodox road racing seat was used.

The engine was a modified Villiers 250-cc unit with the Greeves alloy head and cylinder. Modifications to the port sizes and location combined with an expansion box exhaust system provided a power output of 26-27 bhp at 7500 rpm. The power spread was quite wide, with good punch coming in at 3000 rpm.

During 1963, the company was engaged in a great deal of development work, and the success in international motocross was not quite so great as in previous years. The continental machines were getting faster and the competition had become intense. The continued development work on the Villiers engine was paying off in horsepower, but the added stress on the lower end and gearbox was causing a notable increase in mechanical failures. By then it was obvious to Greeves that piecemeal modifications were no longer good enough-a whole new engine was needed.

During late 1963 and early 1964, the creative genius of Bert Greeves was hard at work. By March of 1964, the world got a taste of things to come when the new "Challenger" scrambler model was introduced, and this was followed in late summer by the Silverstone Mark II road racing model. Both of these bikes featured the "all Greeves" Challenger engine. In time, the complete range of models offered was to use this engine.

The lower end of the Challenger engine was a compact built-up unit made by the famous Alpha Co. The crankpin was pressed into the flywheels and an orthodox roller bearing rod was used. The alloy cylinder and head were made by Greeves, and these new components had a 50 percent greater cooling area than did the earlier Villiers-Greeves engine.

A great deal of experiment went into the port shape and location on the scrambles and road racing engines, and in the end both units produced power characteristics well suited to the tasks at hand. The motocross model breathed into the crankcase through a 1.187-in. Monobloc carburetor while the Silverstone used a huge 1.375-in. Amal GP type. Both engines had

The 1962 Mark II roadster, powered by a 250-cc Villiers twin. Greeves discontinued model to concentrate on competition machinery.

First Silverstine had Villiers engine with Greeves squared cylinder barrel and head. Powerplant gave 27 bhp at 7500 rpm.

the intake port inclined-the road racer 22 degrees and the scrambler only 8. Both intake systems are inclined another 9 degrees by the forward tilting of the engine in the frame.

For a gearbox, Greeves went to the famous Albion concern, which designed a rugged four-speed transmission for the scrambler and a new close ratio five-speed unit for the Silverstone model. The frames remained much the same as in previous years.

These new Challenger engines were considerably more powerful then the previous Villiers-Greeves units, and the reliability was also notably improved. The scrambles model produced 25 bhp at 6000 rpm, combined with good torque at anything above 3000 revolutions. The Silverstone engine produced 30 bhp at 7500 rpm after a full 5 min. at full throttle on the test bench. The engine would pull 33 bhp for a brief flash reading, but the inevitable 10 percent loss after the engine was hot was a truer indicator of actual track performance.

So, out into the world went the new Challengers. They became a smashing success! There were naturally a few minor problems to sort out, but the basic design seemed to perform well in addition to being reliable. Dave Bickers continued to mop up in the home country motocross events, and his sashays on the continent were treated with profound respect by his rivals.

Meanwhile, the Silverstone model also was distinguishing itself. Earlier in the year, Joe Dunphy had garnered the first points ever won by a Greeves machine in world championship road racing when he took a 5th in the 1964 Daytona classic. This was followed in September by the smashing victory of Gordon Keith in the 250-cc Manx Grand Prix. Gordon's average speed in this race for "amateurs" on standard production racing machines over the famous Isle of Man course was a speedy 86.19 mph.

With all this fabulous success in both motocross and road racing events, it was only natural that Greeves sales continued to expand. Exports in particular grew in importance, as the fame of the British two-stroke spread all over the world. And, with Don Smith's winning of the European Trials Championship, the marque was acquiring an outstanding reputation as a trials machine.

For 1965, the range of Greeves machines was narrowed to seven models-four competition mounts, and three roadsters all with standard Villiers engine. The low priced 250cc trials model also used a Villiers engine and this dirt plugger was popular in the hands of private owners for club trials and competitions.

For the real enthusiast, the three "pur sang" competition mounts were the only thing. First was the "Scottish" trials model with a Villiers-Greeves engine, and this model was establishing an outstanding reputation in international trials. Then there were the powerful Challenger scrambles model for motocross racing, and the Silverstone road racing machine.

The record chalked up in 1965 by the small British marque again was impressive. After a rather frustrating time in getting

Don Smith, twice unofficial European Trials Champion, progresses up a rocky ledge in 1954 Scottish. Note typical Greeves fork.

the bugs worked out of his motocross bike, Dave Bickers had a serious bash at the 1965 world motocross title. The season proved long and torrid, with Dave coming home 3rd in the championship standings behind Victor Arbekov and Joel Robert on their potent CZs. Dave did have the satisfaction of winning the British 250-cc title for the fifth time, though, and all this helped give the name even greater renown.

In road racing, the Silverstone acquitted itself most admirably, with Greeves taking 1st and 3rd in the 1965 Manx Grand Prix classic. The winner was Dennis Craine at the record average of 88.37 mph, and a new lap record was chalked up to the tune of 89.84 mph. This win, combined with the many victories on local race courses all over the world, certainly accomplished what Bert Greeves had set out to do-build a good and inexpensive racer for the private owner.

During 1966, the factory reduced its range to only five models, but those that remained were all notably improved. These five were a 250-cc trials model, a 200-cc single-cylinder road model, the 250-cc Challenger scrambler, and the Silverstone road racer. The rubber suspension front fork, so long a Greeves trademark, finally gave way to a leading link

The 1967 Silverstone model featured all-Greeves engine, rated at 30 bhp at 8000 rpm. Top speed with fairing approached 120 mph.

front fork with Girling hydraulically damped spring suspension units. There were other less noticeable changes made to the five models, and a new 360-cc motocross machine also was in the experimental stage.

During 1966, the company lost the services of Dave Bickers who had joined the CZ camp, but newcomer Freddie Mayes pipped Dave by one point to give Greeves its sixth British 250-cc scrambles championship. On the continent, the marque faired less well, as Greeves had no riders with the necessary experience to challenge the top European aces. In the trials sphere, the marque was kept well to the fore by Don Smith, who again won the European Trials Championship.

Meanwhile, the design improvement work went on, but for 1967 the range of models offered was reduced to only four. All of these were competition machines-the company had decided to specialize on the sporting end of the game. The first model was the 250-cc Anglian trials mount, which could be had with either a Greeves or Ceriani front fork. This machine was a replica of the works bike used by Don Smith and it offered the mud-pluggers a truly competitive mount.

Next in line was the 250-cc Challenger scrambler, which had a new frame and redesigned four-speed gearbox. The weight was a light 217 lb. and the wheelbase was 51.5 in. A new 1.75-gal. fiberglass fuel tank was used, and the Greeves-made front fork used Girling shock absorber units.

The 360-cc Challenger is the model that excited the motocross riders, and this mount also could be obtained with either a Greeves or Ceriani front fork. The powerplant featured a bore and stroke of 80 by 72mm. Compression ratio was 10.0:1. The weight of the 360-cc model was very light at 226 lb. and the wheelbase was 54.5 in.

The Silverstone model also was continued with minor modifications, with its power output fractionally increased. Maximum speed with a fairing was not far shy of the 120 mph mark, which was really tramping for a production 250. Peak power was reached at 8000 rpm, and the acceleration through the five speed gearbox was competitive on the short British racing circuits.

Then, after gradually reducing the number of models offered, Greeves came back with something of a bombshell for 1968, announcing an eight-model range which included an all-new 350cc road racer. Named the Oulton in honor of a British race circuit, the 350 was developed from the 360-cc scrambler. Its piston displacement of 344.3 cc is achieved by retaining the motocross engine's 80-mm bore, while a special crankshaft provides a stroke of 68.5 mm. Traditional Greeves design appears in the leading link front fork, and alloy beam front down tube on the frame.

Other new models include two machines intended mainly for export to the U.S. One is the 250-cc Ranger trail bike, the other is a special TT racer based on the Challenger. Also new is a Wessex trials bike, equipped with a all-Villiers 250-cc power unit. The idea behind this machine is to offer a low priced machine for novice and less serious riders. The 250-cc Challenger motocross model featured a modified short stroke engine. Anglian, Silverstone, and Challenger 360 models continued almost unchanged.

On motocross circuits, the company did not maintain its devastating success of previous years. Leading factory riders were two dashing young men, red-haired Arthur Browning, and crewcut Bryan Wade. Both were competitive on English circuits, but the company only rarely ventured to the continent. However, developments at the factory were a 390-cc version of the 360 engine, in an attemp to keep pace with the ever growing displacements of Continental two-stroke Singles, and an experimental all-tubular frame.

In 1969 the marque had its finest hour in classical trials competition, when Bill Wilkenson scored a stunning upset victory on his trusty old 250 in the rugged Scottish Six Days Trial. This was a fitting tribute to the marque, since they had faithfully supported the trials game for many years.

The tubular frame was finally proven, and in 1969 Bert Greeves announced his new Griffon models-thus ending the unique I-beam frame that had so long been a feature of the marque. A sad note was the dropping of the Silverstone from production-a silent admission that the "Boys Racer" single just wasn't fast enough to keep up with the Yamaha twins.

So, this is the story of the Greeves a modern day legend of a man very dedicated to the motorcycling sport. In this age of mass production it is refreshing to find such interesting personalities and down to earth machines, and one cannot help but admire the men who have achieved so much with so little behind them. Today the Greeves still is comparatively small in the production of motorbikes, but to many motorsportsmen the world over, the name means a great deal. From wheelchairs to motocross-it is a saga rich in honor.

The only British built two-stroke 360-cc motocross machine available in 1968: the Greeves Challenger, with Ceriani fork.

HONDA

In all the annals of motorcycledom, a unique story standing apart from all the others is that of Soichiro Honda, the world's largest producer of motorcycles. It is a rags to riches legend that is second to none.

Born in 1906 in Hamamatsu, Japan, Soichiro grew up in a small village atmosphere where his father was a blacksmith. With a confessed interest in engines at the early age of five years, Soichiro recalls that when he was in the second grade of schooling, the first automobile came to their town. It leaked some oil on the ground when it stopped, and Honda remembers that he literally put his nose to the ground and deeply breathed in the aroma. From that day, Soichiro Honda has been breathing engine oil.

With notable lack of interest in his studies (reading and writing in particular), young Honda left school at 16 to become an auto mechanic apprentice with the Art Trading Company. This business was one of the few repair shops in Tokyo, as cars were still very scarce in Japan. After a period of time in which he did domestic work for his employer rather than learning the mechanic trade, Soichiro Honda finally began his serious studies of the automobile.

Then, only 18 months after he went to work, the city was leveled by the terrible earthquake of 1923, and in the resulting fire, both the city and his master's business were burned to the ground. Following the holocaust, Honda's employer retained his services to repair the many burned automobiles. It was then that Soichiro first came in contact with a motorcycle.

By age 22 he had become a mechanic of some renown, and so he returned to his home town to set up his own repair shop. Business was slow at first, because there were already two repair shops in Hamamatsu. But Soichiro's ability to get the tough jobs running soon manifested itself and his clientele expanded.

It was also in those early days that young Honda got his first taste of racing when he built up a racing car for his old employer. Soichiro first tried a Daimler-Benz six cylinder engine, but later switched on to a 90 hp Curtis airplane engine. Mounted in an old car frame, the primitive racing car proved fast, clocking 100 kph (62 mph) at a Toyko airfield.

Soichiro then decided to build some racing cars at Hamamatsu, and he later raced them with a fair amount of success. At age 31, however, his automobile racing days came to a screeching halt when his supercharged Ford four-cylinder job somersaulted three times, end over end. The event was the All-Japan Automobile Speed Championships and, even though he was given a trophy for the new speed record, his injuries halted any future speed studies.

After leaving the hospital, an indomitable spirit moved Honda to try his hand at manufacturing piston rings. In this venture Soichiro found his product somewhat lacking in quality and, in fact, they were so bad he could not even sell them. With fifty employees on the payroll, he was destitute; he even pawned his wife's wardrobe to get the money to attend a metal casting school.

Just nine months later, the piston rings he produced were among the finest in Japan, and the little company prospered. During World War II the concern produced piston rings for the Japanese military effort, and after the war the business was sold.

Soichiro then spent some time trying to make salt out of sea water, and later manufactured a rotary type weaving machine. These efforts proved fruitless. So in 1948 the Honda Technical Research Institute was founded in Hamamatsu. The original plant was a truly breathtaking industrial spectacle — a 12- by 18-foot wood frame shack, one rickety belt-driven lathe, a dilapidated machine tool, a couple of desks, and 12 hungry men.

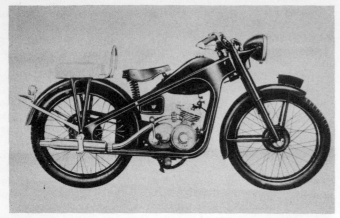

The 1949 D model was 100-cc two-stroke with 2.3 bhp. Looking like mid-thirties German machine, it was Honda's first production bike.

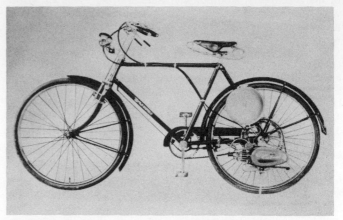

The 50-cc Cub model was introduced in 1952 and public response was so great that production soared to 6500 units per month.

In the completely disrupted society of the immediate post-war years, one of the most pressing Japanese domestic problems was that of transportation. The country was despirately poor, and the masses were forced to crowd into the archiac trains, busses, and taxis to get to their jobs. In this atmosphere, Honda correctly decided that a motorized bicycle was just the ticket for cheap and speedy transportation.

The first product featured a small two-cycle engine that the Imperial army had used to power communications equipment, and these little lungers were mounted on a bicycle. The production was only one unit per day, and the engines ran on a fuel extracted from the roots of pine trees. These primitive motorbikes sold like hotcakes in transportation-starved Japan, and the supply of 500 engines was soon exhausted.

This lack of engines called the hand of the aspiring industrialist, and he responded to the challenge by designing a one-half horsepower 50cc two-stroke engine. When initial tests were completed, the new powerplant was refined and then put into production. The motorized bycycle met with tremendous public acceptance, and production came nowhere near to satisfying demand. With this modest but burgeoning foundation, the Honda Motor Company was incorporated in 1948 with 34 employees and $2,777 capitol.

This event proved to be a great milestone in the industrialization of Japan, as the country has economically lagged well behind Europe and America for the greater part of this century. Just consider, for instance, that in 1940 only 3,000 motorcycles were produced, and in 1945 it had declined to the meager sum of only 446 bikes turned out by Japanese manufacturers, and this production rate increased to only 1,394 by 1950.

When the Honda Motor Company was organized in 1948, there were only eight motorcycle manufacturers in Japan. However, none of these companies made both their own frames and engines, and this complete motorcycle production goal was one of Soichiro's dreams. In August of 1949 his dream came true when the 100cc D model rolled off the assembly lines. The new D model featured a 2.3 hp two-stroke engine which drove through a two-speed gearbox and chain drive. The frame was a pressed steel type and it had no method of rear suspension. The front end has a clean looking telescopic fork.

The new Honda was called the "Dream" by the company since it fulfilled the maker's dream of the first complete Japanese motorcycle. The D model was well ahead of Japanese competition too, but its introduction happened at the wrong time, as the country was hard hit by an economic depression. Sales dropped, collections were slow, and the company was on the verge of bankruptcy.

By now, Soichiro had come to realize that while he was an engineer and technician par excellence, he was not a financier or salesman. He decided then, and wisely so, to hire Takeo Fujisawa as sales and financial director. With this new management team, the company pulled through the crisis and established itself as a small, but sound Japanese industry.

In 1950, the company expanded by opening a new office in Tokyo, and Honda was able to obtain a $5,555 loan from the Japanese government to purchase new machinery. Production and sales increased, and soon 300 Dream models were rolling off the assembly lines each month. This was a truly remarkable feat, as all the other Japanese manufacturers together were producing only about 1,600 machines per year.

During the early 1950s Japan began a rapid industrial growth, and Honda grew right along with it. With the standard of living in a sharp rise, Soichiro decided that the luxury of a four-cycle engine could be afforded by the populace, and so the 150cc E model made its debut. The initial testing of the E model was a tense moment at the factory though; on the day of the test a typhoon raged over Japan. The factory test rider rode the new 150 to the top of Hakone Mountain and back in a driving rain. The rider's evaluation was that Honda had a real winner in the E model, and into production it went.

The E model featured a 5.5 bhp engine mounted in a pressed-steel frame as had its predecessor, the D model. Still rather primitive and looking like a mid-1935 German motorcycle, the E model nevertheless was a sensation in Japan. With a top speed of 50 mph, the new Honda sold to the tune of 32,000 in 1953-an unheard of figure in the Japanese industry. With the mushrooming sales, the company continued to expand, and capitol was listed at $166,000, sixty times what the concern was worth only five years earlier.

In May of 1952, the company again returned to the motorized bicycle field with the introduction of the 50cc Cub. unit. The public response to the little one-half horsepower two-stroke was tremendous, and production was soon up to 6,500 units per month. This Cub model, which was designed by Soichiro, himself, garnered more than seventy per cent of the domestic "clip-on" market, and this feat earned him the coveted Blue Ribbon Medal by the Emperor.

By then a greater percentage of the company's profits were being plowed back into research, while a succession of great models began emerging from the designer's desk. In June of 1953, the 90cc four-stroke Benly came off the line, and this model found an immediate acceptance by the motorcycling public. The new Benly produced a healthy 3.8 hp and it had a three-speed footshift gearbox. The frame was an entirely new pressed sheet-steel type, with a telescopic front fork and a type of torsion-arm rear suspension. The Benly was a much more modern looking Honda than the previous models, and production was soon up to 1,000 per month.

By this time Honda had reached the limit with his archaic machinery, as nearly all of his factory equipment was either pre-war or domestically produced. The engineering ability of his technical department exceeded the production capabilities of his machinery. Additionally, Soichiro had ideas of world-wide marketing of his Hondas, but his plant was incapable of producing a machine that could successfully compete in the world market.

Soichiro announced that $1,111,000 worth of American, German, and Swiss machine tools were being pruchased to make his factory one of the most modern in the world. The timing of this expansion was once again a critical factor in the history of the company, as Japan again experienced an economic recession in 1953 and 1954. After some anxious financial moments, managing director Fujisawa brought the company through to quieter waters and the expensive new machinery began paying its way.

With the company once again doing well and his confidence restored, Soichiro announced in March of 1954 that Honda would soon enter the very pinnacle of motorcycle racing, the famed Isle of Man TT races. Honda's reasoning was most logical; in order to expand sales worldwide, it would be necessary to successfully compete against Europe's best to demonstrate the superiority of the Honda. With this in mind, the company president made a trip to the Isle of Man to gain some experience for their upcoming venture.

So off to the 1954 TT races he went, full of confidence that his machines, which were used in Japanese racing, could be competitive to the best that Europe produced. Two weeks later Soichiro returned home, half in shock and half in despair. He found the European racing bikes developing three times the best power he could raise, and the overall technical superiority of their bikes was devastating to his confidence. All he promised was that he would be back; when, he didn't know, but he would return.

Back in Japan, he turned his efforts toward improving his range of machines, and in 1955 several new models made their appearance. One, the SA model, was a clean looking OHV 250 with a swinging-arm rear suspension. With the standard of living constantly increasing, the home country populace could afford more comfort, more performance, and more luxury.

The program continued to expand in 1958, with another great milestone in the company's history-the 50cc Super Cub. This new Honda was not designed for the motorcyclist, but rather for the "everyman-on-the-street." An enclosed engine and step-through frame made this the most popular of Hondas, with moms, dads, and kids all in on the fun.

This was followed in 1959 by the expansion of Honda throughout the world, including the United States, and the subsequent introduction of the overhead camshaft twins. Since then, Honda sales charts go in a nearly vertical direction, and today they are undisputed sales leaders in the world.

In the whole story of Honda, the really great rise of the company occurred when their racing bikes began winning on the classical grand prix road racing courses of the world. After Soichiro visited the Isle of Man in 1954, the company contented itself with winning their homeland races until 1959, when they returned to the TT races with a team of 125cc twins. The little DOHC Hondas produced a claimed 18.5 hp at 14,000 rpm, and the camshaft drive was by bevel gear and vertical shaft. The front fork was a cumbersome looking leading link affair, and the total weight was 176 pounds.

The race results netted the little twins sixth, seventh, eighth, and eleventh places, which was good enough to win the team prize, as no other team finished intact. Their speed seemed to suggest that the horsepower claim was a bit exaggerated, and

The 150-cc E model, Honda's first production four-stroke. It had unusual "three valve" layout with two inlet valves, one exhaust.

1955 SA model was first Honda with swinging-arm rear suspension. Ohv 250 looks modern compared to Hondas of just a few years before.

A truly great classic, 250-cc Honda four-cylinder Grand Prix machine is sleek 150-mph racer. Four was developed to give 48 bhp.

The 1966 Super 90 had 8-bhp ohc 90-cc engine with speeds to 65 mph. This Honda, weighing only 176 pounds, is a "sports" model.

The 1966 305-cc Honda scrambler was suitable for road or dirt use. It weighed 337 pounds and developed 27 bhp at 9000.

The 1966 Honda Sport 65, an inexpensive ohc 65-cc model with a healthy 6.2 bhp at 10,000 rpm; it is popular for beginning riders.

the handling was described as being "plain terrible." Obviously, Honda had a lot to learn.

Back to Japan they went, and the 125cc twin was joined by a 250cc four-cylinder model for the national Asama Championship race. Hondas made a clean sweep of the two classes, before being recalled to the design shop for a winter's work.

In 1960, Honda returned to Europe with the new 125cc-twin and 250cc-four cylinder racers. Gone was the old frame and fork; in its place a more orthodox frame with a telescopic fork. The engines were canted forward in the frame to give better cooling, and the camshaft drive was changed to a set of spur gears. Another innovation was the four valves per cylinder arrangement, an idea copied from their earlier experimental 125cc twin.

The handling of the new racers was notably improved, and horsepower was obviously greater. Ridden by both Japanese and experienced European grand prix riders, the team put up a respectable showing. In the TT, a 125 took sixth place, and the 250 class had Hondas in fourth, fifth, and sixth places.

In the Dutch GP, a sixth was obtained in the 125 class. Then followed the fast Belgian event and Honda drew a blank. Next was the German event and the 250-four garnered a third and a sixth place. Honda followed this up with a second and fifth in the Ulster GP. The last event of the season at Monza had 250 models in second, fourth, fifth, and sixth places, as well as fourth and sixth in the 125cc class. Altogether it was a good year, but still down on speed from the European machines.

Another winter's work yielded more horsepower plus a general refinement of the two models. The little twin was by then developing 25 hp at 13,000 rpm for a top speed of about 112 mph. The 250 four was rated at 45 hp at 14,000 rpm for a maximum speed of 137 mph. Both models featured six-speed gearboxes and had the four valves per cylinder arrangement.

Soichiro, always a quick one to recognize talent, had come to the conclusion that his Japanese riders were just not good enough to successfully compete against the more experienced grand prix riders. By hiring such aces as Jim Redman, Southern Rhodesia; Tom Phillis, Australia; Luigi Taveri, Switzerland; and Mike Hailwood, England; to head up the racing effort, Honda had a truly formidable team. In addition, the great Bob McIntyre was engaged just before the Isle of Man classic.

In the opening race of the season, Tom Phillis notched Honda's first grand prix win when he garnered the 125cc event in Spain. Gaining momentum, the team swept on to the TT races, where Hailwood took both the 125 and 250 events, and in the latter race McIntyre put in his incredible 99.58 mph lap from a standing start. By the end of the season it was Hailwood with the 250cc World Championship and Phillis wearing the 125 crown.

During 1962, the Hondas continued their domination of lightweight class racing with a new 50cc-single added to the range for the just recently included 50cc class. Hailwood quit

the team and went over to MV Agusta, and Irishman Tommy Robb joined the team. Hondas swept the board in the 125 and 250 classes, but in the 50cc class, their little single was getting slaughtered by the Kreidlers and Suzukis.

Luigi Taveri, their popular little Swis rider, took the 125cc Championship, and Redman won the 250 crown. A big suprise was Redman also winning the 350cc class on a 250 model bored out to 285cc. Altogether a truly great year.

For 1963, Honda's interest in racing seemed to sag a bit, and Redman proved to be their only rider winning a championship. Jim easily won the 350 crown, but in the 250cc class he had to win the final event in Japan to defeat Tarquinio Provini and his embarrassing fast Morini-single. The season's score was only 15 classic wins, and six of these were in the "competitionless" 350 class.

For 1964, Honda made a determined effort with a new 50cc-twin and a 125-four, both turning to something like 19,000 to 20,000 rpm. Horsepower on the 250-four was up to 48 for a speed of about 150, and the 56 hp 350 was capable of around 156 mph.

The new 50cc twin proved very fast, but Suzuki retained their title by winning the last event of the season in Finland. On the remarkably fast 125, Taveri squashed the two-stroke opposition, and Redman had a walkover in the 350 class. In the prestigious 250 class, the 250-four was beaten back by the speedier Yamaha two-stroke twin. Honda, obviously, could not endure such humiliation, and so late in the season a new 250 six-cylinder made its debut.

Once again making a determined effort in 1965, Honda unveiled the very ultimate in GP equipment. The 50 remained a twin, the 250 a six, and the 350 a four, but the new 125 had a rather unusual number of five cylinders and with revs up to 22,000. The 1965 Hondas all proved to be very fast, and they certainly represent the ultimate in four-stroke engine technology. In the Isle of Man, for instance, riders were timed through a two-mile section that has several curves and swerves. The little 50cc twin rocketed through at 109 mph, Jim Redman's 350 clocked 133 mph, and even the 125s averaged 122 mph.

After several years of trying, a little 50cc twin finally won the championship in the hands of Irishman Ralph Bryans, and Redman once again took the 350 crown after a torid battle with Giacomo Agostini on the MV Agusta "three." In the 250 class the Yamaha still held the edge, as did Suzuki in the 125 class.

Honda had obvious intentions of gaining back their lost prestige, and in the fall of 1965 they announced that Mike Hailwood had joined their team. By adding the world's best rider to their team they were serving notice on the racing world that they would make a determined effort in 1966. They also promised Mike a full 500cc model to challenge the MV Agusta, which was expected to really make the sparks fly.

The 1966 racing season proved to be a long hot one, and in the end Honda riders gained the 125, 250c and 350cc championships. The new 500 proved to be terrifically fast, but a series of mechanical failures plus obviously poor handling killed any chances for the title. Giacomo Agostini and his MV 3 were crowned champions-despite Hailwood's 172 mph clocking on the Masta Straight in the Belgian Grand Prix!

In 1967 Hailwood again won the 250 and 350cc titles, but once again he lost out to the dreaded 500 MV Three after a torrid season of racing. The expense involved in all this racing plus an exotic twelve cylinder grand prix car proved to be too much for even Honda to afford, though, so it was announced during the winter that they would race no more. The world's most highly developed four-strokes thus disappeared from the tracks, and to this day no one else has come forth to take their place. An era was ended.

The real goal of Honda, however, has been to offer a comprehensive range of motorcycles for the everyday rider. In 1966 the 450cc model with a DOHC engine set the world to talking, and in 1968 the company announced a more European looking 350cc twin that proved to be popular. In 1969 the fabulous 750cc OHC "four" made its debut, complete with a five speed gearbox and 125 mph top end.

Since then Honda has greatly expanded their range with 500, 350, and then 550cc fours, plus 250 and 350cc four-valve singles in enduro trim. In 1973 the first "modern" Honda two-strokes appeared--fire-breathing 125 and 250cc moto-cross singles that have won many championship in America. This range of machines is the most comprehensive ever offered by any manufacturer in the world, and it has kept Honda in an unassailable first place in sales.

The highlight of the range is, no doubt the 750cc single overhead camshaft model. Designed to satisfy the most discriminating buyer of a motorcycle, the Four develops 68 hp at 8000 rpm for a top speed of more than 120 mph. With the first overhead cam four-cylinder engine ever featured in a road bike, the Honda set a trend in performance, combined with such luxury touring features as an electric starter.

Today there is a Honda for everyone from 50cc up to the luxurious Four. Surely, Soichiro Honda must go down in history with such names as Daimler-Benz and Henry Ford as being a truly great milestone in the transportation era.

This cobby little 125cc single marked Honda's entrance into the trials bike market in 1974. The weight is 210 pounds.

In 1963 and '64 Honda produced a very few replica road racers for sale. This is a 250cc DOHC twin with a six-speed gearbox called the RC72.

The 750cc four, introduced in 1969, is still one of the finest touring bikes in the world. Silky smooth, it will do 125 mph.

HUSQVARNA

Sweden is a beautiful country with its many blue lakes, deep green forests, and miles of scenic coastline. Located in the northwestern corner of Europe, it is not far from the Artic, and quite naturally, the climate is rather severe. With long, cold winters and large areas of rugged mountains, it would seem logical to assume that these descendents of the Vikings would have achieved little in the way of international motorcycling success.

The record, however, speaks differently, as one rather small Swedish manufacturer of motorbikes has chalked up by far the finest record ever achieved in both the European and World motocross championships. And this isn't all, either, as the efforts of this Norse concern in the terribly competitive grand prix road racing classics during the early and middle 1930s were of great enough note to indelibly etch many a first place into the pages of history.

This story of Swedish excellence in the motorbike field had its beginning was back in the year of 1689, when the Royal Arms Company was founded. The idea was to produce armaments for the Swedish Army, which was constantly engaged at war with somebody, and expanding sales provided the fledging company with a sound financial base. Unfortunately, Carl XII decided to have a go at Russia, and even though production reached new heights while the battle was on, a sharp depression hit the company when Russia won.

For many years after, the concern just managed to keep its financial head above water. In 1867 matters finally turned for the better when Erik Dahlberg reorganized the company under the name that is still used today-Husqvarna Vapenfabriks AB. Then followed more wars and the new company prospered, but then, after the Franco-Prussian war in the early 1870s, the demand for muskets once again dropped off.

This time the company management decided to branch out into other products that would meet more peaceful needs. The move proved to be a wise one as Sweden at last entered a more

peaceful era, and sewing machines were soon rolling off the production line. Production of these domestic items has continued, and today Husqvarna is famous for its household appliances, timber saws, fine guns, sewing machines, lawn mowers and furnaces.

The most important item that Husqvarna has ever produced, at least to the world's motorsportsmen, is none of the above products, though. For to the aficionado of fine motorbikes the mention of Husqvarna means just one thing — fabulous motocross machines that have garnered a total of twelve European and world championships.

The story of this modern day terror of rough-stuff competition began in 1903, when the industrial revolution was making itself felt in Sweden. In that year the factory produced its first motorbike-an orthodox 1-¼-hp single-cylinder, belt-driven mount with caliper type brakes on the wheel rims. The engine was a Belgian-made FN, and bicycle pedaling gear was used for starting and on the hills. The single-speed Husqvarna proved to be a reliable method of transport, and the reputation of the company was established.

During those early years of the motorcycle the Husqvarna tried what most other European factories did-experiment to find a sound design. This experimentation finally led to a Husqvarna bicycle with a Swiss made Moto-Reve engine, and the plot proved to be a great deal faster and more reliable than anything that they had previously produced.

The engine was a 500cc V-twin, and it drove the bicycle through a single-speed belt. There were pedals for starting, and a caliper type brake was used on the rear wheel. The Moto-Reve engine was available in 2-½ and 4 horsepower, so the performance was considerably quicker than the first Husqvarna single.

The next big step forward came in 1916, when Husqvarna designed and produced their own engine. This new "Husky" was rather advanced for its day, and it went a long way in establishing their name all over Scandinavia. The powerplant was a 50-degree V-twin with bore and stroke measurements of 65 x 83mm. The 550cc engine featured side valves, and the cylinders and head were both cast iron. The output of 11 hp was transmitted through a three-speed gearbox, and gear shifting was by a hand shift on the right side of the fuel tank. Both the primary and final drives were by roller chain, and the clutch lever was operated by the left hand.

The frame used was the rigid type, and the only method of suspension was by the coil springs in the girder front fork. A "vintage" era gas tank was mounted between the two top frame tubes, and only one caliper brake was used on the rear wheel. The oil was pumped to the engine by a hand pump that built up pressure in the lubrication system, and a single carburetor fed both cylinders.

This side-valve twin formed the basis of the Husqvarna production during the 1920s, and the model was subsequently improved by adopting such features as internal expanding brakes, improved lubrication, a greater engine output, and a better electrical system.

By 1930 another engine type was setting the world on fire, though, and this was the overhead valve engine with its superior performance. The Husqvarna engineers were quick to accept this modern trend, and the 1930 sales brochure well illustrated this policy with five of the ten models listed having ohv powerplants. Carl Heimdal was the chief designer and engineer at that time, and his machines reflected his brilliance even if the Husqvarna was still little known outside of the Scandinavian countries.

The lowest priced Husqvarna that year was the model No. 25, a side-valve 175cc mount that provided reliable day-to-day transportation. The little engine had a bore and stroke of 60 x 62mm, and it developed 5.5 hp. A three-speed hand shift gearbox with ratios of 8.3, 12.6, and 23.2 to 1 was used, and the drive was by roller chain. As was common in those days, a girder front fork and rigid frame were featured, and the only brake was an internal expanding unit on the rear wheel.

Next in the catalog was model No. 30, a 250cc side-valver that produced 7.5 hp. Engine measurements were 64.5 x 76mm, and gear ratios were 6.9, 10.5, and 19.3 to 1. The 250 was similar to the 175cc model except that it had a front brake and a more refined accessory list.

For the customer who wanted even more performance in the side-valve design there was the No. 50-S model-a 550cc job that developed 14 reliable horsepower. The 50-S had a bore and stroke of 79 x 101mm, and the gearbox had ratios of 5.3, 9.0, and 14.1 to 1.

The final side-valve single listed in the catalog was the No. 61 model. This machine had a 600cc engine that produced 16 hp, and the bore and stroke were 86.8 x 101mm. This model was produced with a touring type sidecar only, and the beefy torque from the powerplant was ideally suited for the task.

In the early 1930s the Swedish riders, like most all European enthusiasts, became more performance conscious, and to meet this demand the factory produced a range of overhead valve singles. The first was the No. 30-A, a 250cc model that developed 11 hp on its 5.6 to 1 compression ratio. The bore and stroke were 65.5 x 80mm, and internal expanding brakes were fitted to both wheels.

Then there was the No. 50 "Turistmodell," a 500cc job that developed 20 hp. The big single had measurements of 85.7 x 85mm, and the gear ratios were the same as the 500cc side-valve model. Both wheels had hefty internal expanding brakes, and a girder front fork was used with a rigid frame.

The two models that really made Swedish pulses pound were the models No. 50-A and 50-B. Called the "Sportmodell" and "Super Sportmodell." These two bikes were for the fellow who wanted the very best in Swedish design and performance. Both machines were similar to the "Turistmodell" except that modifications to the cams, valves and carburetors boosted the power output to 25 at 4,600 rpm and 30 at 5,800 rpm respectively. The wheelbase on these 70- and 85-mph speedsters was 55.6 inches, and the dry weight was 363 pounds. The muffler

fitted was a large "Brooklands" type, and the healthy exhaust note announced that a mighty rapid motorbike was coming down the road.

The last page of the 1930 catalog listed a very specialized machine for its day-the 500cc "Specialracer Motorcykel." This ohv thumper was built for the man who wanted to compete in the long distance cross-country races that were so popular in the Scandinavian countries in those days. A lightweight rigid frame was used along with an open exhaust, and the engine developed the remarkable output of 33 hp. These old Swedish cross-country races were actually a long distance scrambles, and the speedy and rugged 30-inch single chalked up an enviable record in these events.

The Husqvarna range continued to expand during the 1930s as the industrial revolution gradually put people on wheels. In 1931 a new 350cc side-valve model was added to the stable, and this 9 hp model had a bore and stroke of 71 x 88mm. The 4,000 rpm side-valver was followed up in 1932 by an ohv model that developed 14 hp at 4,500 rpm.

During the middle 1930s the affluence of the Swedish people was on the increase, so it was only logical that Husqvarna would add a luxury class machine to their range. called the "Modell 120," the new mount was a 990cc V-twin introduced in 1933. The side-valve powerplant had measurements of 79 x

One of earliest Husqvarnas was this 1913 V-twin. Engine was Swiss 4-hp Moto-Reve. Single-speed belt drive was accepted practice.

The 1917 Husqvarna 550-cc V-twin featured side valves and chain drive. The only brake was a caliper type on the rear wheel.

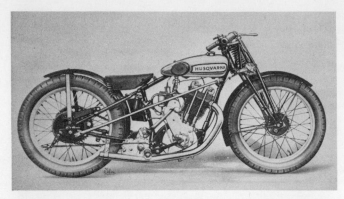

1930 Husqvarna "Specialracer," 500-cc forerunner of the modern scrambler. Old single produced 33 hp; note unusual shift lever.

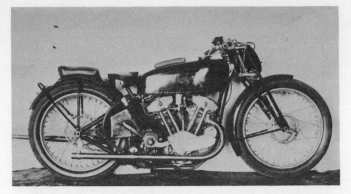

The V-twin that Stanley Woods rode in 1934 Senior TT. The 500-cc mount developed 44 hp at 6800 rpm; maximum was 110 to 115 mph.

101mm, and its 26 hp was produced at 3,500 rpm. The gear ratios were 4.10, 6.35, and 10.1 to 1, and the big twin was noted for its mile-eating lope. The wheelbase was rather long at 58.8 inches and the dry weight was 429 pounds. The "120" model was a very finely finished machine, and it was truly one of the world's most elegant motorcycles in its day.

The following year a new 500cc ohv model replaced the earlier versions. This machine was uniquely destined many years later to make its mark in international competition. Named the "Modell 110 TV," the new powerplant had measurements of 79 x 101mm. Maximum power was 22 at 4,200 rpm, and the pushrod engine had an outward similarity to the old British Ariel. The gearbox was also a new four-speeder, with ratios of 4.8, 6.0, 8.1, and 12.8 to 1.

This new "Husky" was a more attractive bike than the previous ohv models, and such things as totally enclosed valve springs helped make the bike run much cleaner. The whole range of Husqvarnas was improved in detail during the next few years, and they became known as exceptionally well designed motorbikes.

In 1936 the catalog listed a total of five models. First was the 350cc side-valve single that produced 9 hp at 4,000 rpm. Next was its ohv stablemate that developed 14 hp at 4,500 rpm. Then came the 15 hp side-valve 500cc that turned to 4,200 rpm, and the last single was the 500cc ohv that churned out 24 hp at 4,800 rpm. These singles all featured a rigid frame, girder front fork, good brakes, and the traditional white fuel tank with the painted on emblem. The 500cc ohv model was packing a top gear ratio of 4.55 to 1, which provided the respectable speed of 80 mph.

The last model in the lineup that year was the big 990cc side-valve V-twin. The twin could be had with several types of sidecars for both touring and commercial purposes; and it proved popular with the Swedish riders.

After 1936 the policy at the company took a different direction, and the singles and big V-twin were dropped from production. Maybe it was the long cold winters combining with increased income levels that put people into cars or maybe it was the rugged sales competition from England, but at any rate, the factory switched over to producing lightweight models. These new, inexpensive two-strokes were produced up until the war, and they did prove popular with the Swedes.

And so ended the pre-war story of Husqvarna's motorcycle production. But it certainly is not the whole story of the marque during those early years. It could be said, and rightfully so, that Husqvarna's bikes were not quite good enough to compete in the rough and tumble worldwide market place, and they failed to make a really significant impact on the international motorcycle scene. There was however, a chapter in the company's story that did make a notable impression in the history books, and that was their participation in the colorful road racing classics of the day.

The competition record of Husqvarna can be divided into two distinctive efforts-the pre-war grand prix chapter and the post-war motocross chapter. Of these two, the post-war effort has

been by far the most successful. But for pure exotic machinery in a colorful setting, it is hard to beat the days of the grand prix Husky.

The story of their road racing days began in 1930 when Folke Mannerstedt came back from Belgium, where he had been employed by the FN concern. Folke was hired to design a road racing bike, as the factory had decided that the best way to gain international publicity was to win races. The idea was to field a works team on bikes that could win, even if the company's sales figure was not high enough to expend as much on racing as some of the larger European factories.

Mannerstedt went right to work, and by late summer of 1930 he had a team ready for the Swedish Grand Prix. The racers were beautiful bikes, too, but they proved to be too slow and unreliable to hold off the all-conquering Nortons. Tha basic layout of the 500cc Husqvarna was a pushrod operated overhead valve V-twin engine mounted in a rigid frame with a girder front fork. It was obvious that more development work would be needed to make the twin a race winner, and so back to the shop it went.

In the spring of 1931, an improved GP machine made its appearance, and that year saw an amazingly good record chalked up in minor grand prix events all over Sweden, Denmark, and Norway. In the classical Swedish Grand Prix, the team again saw Jimmy Simpson streak away on his Norton single, and once again, Folke was faced with raising more horsepower.

During the long, dark Artic winter the lights glowed very late in the race shop, as more performance was sought from the twin. By summer Eng. Mannerstedt was certain that he had a winner and that his bikes could conquer the "unconquerable" Nortons. The famous British ohc single, however, had won all eight of the 1931 grands prix, plus taking the first three places in the 1932 Senior TT, so it was certainly an impressive champion.

When the flag dropped for the 1932 Swedish GP it was obvious to the croud that Husqvarna had a potential winner in their twin, as Ragnar Sunnqvist and Jimmy Simpson locked themselves in a titanic battle. Lap after lap they fought it out, with Ragnar finally scratching over the line first. Like wildfire the news spread over Europe that this upstart Swedish factory had trounced the mighty Norton. Mannerstedt, meanwhile, quietly went back to his shop to further improve his twin, for he well knew that next year Norton would be out for blood.

The following year the Swedish Grand Prix was given the title of "Grand Prix d'Europe," a recognition that was given in the pre-war days to one of the season's races to signify that it was the premier event of all the classics. Quite naturally, all the great racing names of Europe entered the 1933 race, and the tiny Swedish company obviously had the supreme challenge on their hands.

The race proved to be a real thriller, with the works Norton team of Stanley Woods and Tim Hunt holding off the home-country twins. Towards the end of the race, Hunt crashed and Sunnqvist closed on Woods. Then Stanley's engine blew and Ragnar looked like a sure winner. Fate held the cards differ-

1906 Triumph 500cc Single

1962 BSA 500cc Gold Star

1966 Velocette 500cc Thruxton with fairing

1967 Velocette 200cc LE

1964 Honda 250cc CR72

1952 Moto Guzzi 500cc Falcone

1949 Jawa 250cc Single

1947 Norton 500cc International

1958 Ariel 500cc Red Hunter

1939 Velocette 350cc KSS

1960 AJS 350cc 7R

ently, though, as Ragnar's bike lost its chain only one lap from the finish, and his teammate, Gunnar Kalen, romped home the victor.

After such a splendid showing the factory management decided to make a bid for the European Championship in 1934, and Stanley Woods (Ireland) and Ernie Nott (England) joined with Sunnqvist and Kalen to make a truly formidable team. The team planned on contesting most of the classical races of the day, and Mannerstedt even built a 350cc twin with which to enter the Junior class races.

By then the 500cc twin had become an exceptionally rapid machine, and the British press eagerly "discussed" it when it arrived in the Isle of Man for the TT race. The bore and stroke were 65 x 75mm, and the compression ratio varied from 9.0 to 10.0 to 1, depending on the fuel. The powerplant produced 44 hp at 6,800 rpm, which was as good as anyone was getting in those days. The engine breathed through two 1-inch Amal TT carburetors, and the hairpin valvesprings were left exposed for cooling. The twin was surprisingly light at 297 pounds, and the wheelbase was rather short at 52.0 inches. Aluminum alloy was used for the heads, cylinders, and fuel and oil tanks.

The team fared quite well that year, with Nott starting off with a third place in the Junior TT. Stanley was running a strong second in the Senior TT when he ran out of fuel only a few miles from the finish, but he did turn the fastest lap of the race at 80.49 mph. At home, in the Swedish event, Ragnar Sunnqvist once again trounced the field, and there were a few "places" gained in the other continental events.

In 1935 the marque scored only one victory, when Stanley Woods rode the 500cc twin to a win in the Swedish Grand Prix. About the only Junior Class success was the ninth place of Helge Carlsson in the Grand Prix d'Europe in Ireland, and then the marque lost its interest in road racing. The European grand prix scene became intensely competitive during the late 1930s, and it took either government financial backing or a large sales volume to finance a serious racing campaign. Husqvarna had neither, so they bowed out. While it is true that the marque never established a really great record of wins, they nevertheless did add the nostalgia of exotic machines in exciting races that make for an interesting chapter in our sport.

After the war, the factory produced 98 and 118cc two-strokes for the home market, followed by a 175cc "sport" model in the early 1950s. This later model was immediately modified for scrambles competition by the Swedish riders when motocross racing became popular in Sweden, and this has led to the current situation where all the company produces are 250, 350-360cc, and 400cc motocross and enduro machines. This rough-stuff racing ushered in the second great era of the company, and for this we have to go back to 1958.

In the middle 1950s, motocross racing became tremendously popular in Europe, and many factories began developing some highly sophisticated machines for their works riders to race. The FIM established a series of races to count for the 500cc European Championship in 1952, and in 1957 the sport was elevated to full World Championship status. This was followed by a special Coupe d'Europe award in 1958 for 250cc machines, and then this was elevated to World Championship status in 1962.

The Husqvarna factory first became interested in this rugged sport in 1958 when Rolf Tibblin was entered in several rounds of the 250cc class. Rold's bike was a two-stroke, and it performed well and thus encouraged the company to make a more determined bid in 1959.

The motocross bike underwent a great deal of development work during the winter. Then, by spring, a really fine mount was rolled out of the shop. The 1959 works bike has since been improved and put into production, and it has become one of the most successful scramblers ever developed. The single-port, two-stroke engine was orthodox but very rugged, and the light 200 pound weight set a new fashion in the

Stanley Woods and Ragnar Sunnqvist before start of 1935 Swedish Grand Prix. Woods won race, fourth in a row for Husqvarna.

The great Swedish scrambler Rolf Tibblin on 1963 Husqvarna 500-cc single; he was only rider to win both 250- and 500-cc titles.

motocross sport. On this 250, Tibblin easily won the Coupe d'Europe trophy, and other Husqvarna riders took fifth and sixth in the championship standings. The post-war chapter of Husqvarna was on its way!

During the long winter, factory managers made a momentous decision to compete in the 500cc class and sponsor a team of riders. This move was thought by many to be absurd, because the marque had not produced a 500cc engine since 1936, and motocross racing had become a very competitive sport. So the world sat back to wait and see what the Swedish company would come up with, while the factory engineers got down to the task of designing the bike.

In the spring of 1960 the new Husqvarnas made their debut-and what beautiful machines they were. The frame was a double loop cradle type with an Italian Ceriani front fork. The gearbox and rear wheel were from the British AJS 7R road racer, and Girling shocks were fitted to the rear swinging-arm. The choice of a powerplant was the really suprising item, though, as the factory chose the old 1934 pushrod single! The ancient thumper was updated by fitting a Lucas racing magneto, casting the cylinder and head in alloy, using different cams, valves, and piston, and shortening the stroke to 99mm from the original 101 figure. The engine produced 35 hp, combined with great gobs of torque in the middle rpm range. With this bike the pride of Sweden hoped to capture the world title-even if the engine was 26 years old!

The works team consisted of Bill Nilsson, Sten Lundin, and Rolf Tibblin; and the smiles on the faces of the critics regarding the antiquity of those engines was soon wiped off-fast! By season's end, the team had quite literally clobbered the competition, with Nilsson crowned champion, Lundin in second and Tibblin in fourth. Apart from the superb handling of these big singles, the "experts" attributed their success to the light

312-pound weight-a pleasant contrast to the cumbersome 350-pound weight of the popular BSA Gold Star.

In 1961 the big singles battled all season long with ex-teammate Sten Lundin and his Swedish-built Lito; but in the end, the Lito won, with Nilsson in second and Tibblin in fifth positions. The 250 two-stroke faired even worse, with Torston Hallman gaining a fourth place in the title chase. In 1960 the little Huskys had taken fourth and sixth places, so the emphasis on the larger class had definitely hurt the marque's chances in the Coupe d'Europe.

For 1962 the factory made a determined effort in both classes. Their main riders that year were the experienced Rolf Tibblin in the Senior class and the young but promising Torsten Hallman in the 250 class. During the summer season these two Vikings literally flew through the air, and in the end, both were crowned Champion of the World. Then, just to prove that 1962 was the real thing, these same two riders once again won the two world motocross titles. This record is truly remarkable, for it was the only time that a make had won both classes in one year-let alone two years in a row!

After those two magnificent years, the factory lost interest in the 500cc class and concentrated on only the lightweight events. However, during 1964 and 1965 the Czechoslovakian-built CZ had a fabulous string of successes, and Husqvarna was generally pushed into lesser postitions.

During 1966 the marque made a fabulous comeback, with Torsten dominating the 250cc motocross classic all season long. In capturing the 1966 title, Torsten had achieved what no other rider had ever accomplished-win three World motocross championships. But, then, this sort of record is nothing new at Husqvarna, for Rolf Tibblin is the only man to ever win both the 250 and 500cc titles.

In 1967 Hallman once again trounced the CZs, but in 1968

Torsten slipped to second behind Joel Robert. Other Husqvarna riders took fifth and sixth places in the championship, plus a goodly share of the lesser places. The company also made a bid for 500cc class honors that year with a new 360cc single, but Ake Jonsson could do no better that third with Bengt Aberg in fourth.

In 1969 Aberg came on strong to win the 500cc title, and Arne King came in fourth with other Husky riders well placed. Torsten Hallman's back injury finally got the best of him, and Husqvarna did not place so well in the 250cc class that year. In 1970 a fourth and sixth place in the 250 class was compensated by Aberg winning the 500cc class again, but this time Arne Kring and Chris Hammergren took second and fifth places.

Husqvarna's star seemed to fade away then and they were not in contention for the championships. Success finally came their way again in 1974 when Heikki Mikkola of Finland rode his fast 360cc model to a resounding world championship win.

And so ends this story of the Husqvarna; a truly remarkable motorbike from the land of the Vikings. While it is true that their products have never been really prominent in the world market, they nevertheless have added two of the most colorful chapters to the history of motorcycle sport. From the intriguing V-twin grand prix bikes of the 1930s to the post-war motocross singles-this is a story that is rich in color and tradition.

This 1953 175cc model developed 9HP at 6000 rpm and had a three-speed gearbox. In 1959 Rolf Tibblin won the Coup d'Europe motocross title on an enlarged 250cc model.

Most popular Husqvarna in 1968 was the Motocross model, available in two sizes, 250-cc "Husky" and 360-cc "Viking". This 250-cc model put out 29 bhp at 6800 rpm. Bore and stroke were 69.5 x 64.5, compression 11.4:1, weight 202 lb.

Husqvarna's 500-class 4-stroke motocross had conventional push-rod design.

JAWA

In any field of manufacturing enterprise the economic factors involved are always a major force which a company must recognize. If a company ignores or miscalculates the economics of their market, they soon may go broke. Conversely, a proper appraisal of the market can get a ready acceptance of a company's product, and the future of the business is established.

Consider, then, the Czechoslovakian motorcycle industry in the early years of this century. About the only manufacturer of any consequence was the Laurin & Klement concern, and from 1899 to 1908 the Czech factory was influential in the development of the early motorcycle. The secret of their success was the production of well-engineered motorcycles that the average citizen could afford. Then the company quit producing bikes and entered the car manufacturing field, and Czechoslovakia was without a large or significant motorcycle manufacturer.

From 1908 until 1928 the country's motorcycle manufacturing industry continued to decline until nearly the total domestic supply was imported. In those days there were many small Czech manufacturers, bus, as a Czech historian writes, they all went broke because they failed to produce a reliable machine that the rather poor populace could afford to purchase.

About that time things took a turn for the better, though, when in 1928 the Ing. J. Janecek Arms Manufacturing Company of Prague began looking about for a product to make in their modern plant. The demand for guns and other armaments had drastically declined after World War I, and the need of the company to utilize their production facilities was equalled by the rapidly expanding economy's needs.

The director of the company decided that one of the greatest domestic needs was for a good motorcycle, so in 1929 a 500cc single cylinder model made its debut. The new Jawa motorcycle was not, actually, a Czechoslovakian machine, as it was produced "under license" from the German Wanderer Company. What this "under license" part meant was that the German concern actually designed the machine and then Jawa just produced it under their own name. The name of Jawa, incidently, came from the first two letters of both Janacek and Wanderer

Produced under German Wanderer patent, this 1929 Jawa featured 500-cc ohv engine, shaft drive and pressed-steel frame.

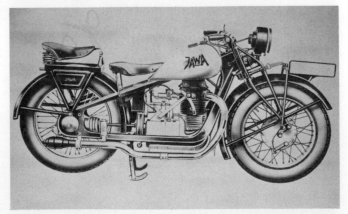

The new Jawa was a good machine that had an overhead valve engine with bore and stroke measurements of 84mm x 90mm, and the engine's output was 18 hp. The engine and gearbox were cast in one unit (and we think this is a "modern" design feature!), and the final drive was by shaft. The frame was the old pressed steel "star" type which was favored by German manufacturers at that time, and the front wheel had a leaf spring suspension. The rear wheel had no method of suspension, and the weight of the bike was 385 lbs.

It was probably wise for the infant Jawa concern to have produced their first motorcycle by using someone else's design, as the company had no experience whatsoever in the engineering of a motorbike. It was not, however, very wise to produce such a deluxe or expensive machine as very few Czechs of that era could afford one. It became obvious to the management that the rather high price would never allow a sales rate high enough to utilize the full capacity of the factory, and so the design work began on some cheaper models.

The next Jawa was a 175cc model, and it appeared in 1932. The engine was still produced "under license" (from the British Villiers Co.) but the rest of the machine was designed by the Jawa engineers. The new lightweight had a bore and stroke of 57.2mm x 67mm, and the compression ratio was 6.7 to 1. The two-stroke engine developed 5.5 hp at 3,750 rpm. The cylinder was cast iron and it featured one transfer and one exhaust port. The head was aluminum alloy, and ignition was by a flywheel magneto. The new lightweight had a three-speed Albion gearbox (British), a sheet-steel frame, and the fuel tank was beneath the top frame tube.

Within a few years the new Jawa 175 had dominated domestic sales, and the future of the factory was assured. The company did make one more blunder in their 1931 and 1932 350cc side-valve prototype, though, as the electric starter and shaft drive model proved so expensive to produce that it never got beyond the experimental stage. The management had by then learned their economics, though, and so for the future they

were destined to concentrate on producing a good machine for the man-on-the-street.

In 1934 several new models were produced with 250cc and 350cc two-strokes headlining the range. There also were 250 and 350cc ohv models for road racing, but these were produced in very small numbers. A 350cc side-valve model was also available which produced 14 hp at 4,200 rpm on a 6 to 1 compression ratio. This inexpensive side-valver proved very popular with the home folks.

During the mid-1930s the company gradually went over to their own engine designs as the engineering department's experience with motorcycles was becoming more competent. The Villiers engine was dropped and Jawa began producing two-stroke engines under the Schnurle patent in 175cc and 250cc sizes. The new 250 had a bore and stroke of 63 x 80mm and it produced 8.5 hp at 3,750 rpm. The 175cc powerplant pumped out a healthy 6 hp at 3,750 rpm. Altogether these models accounted for a production of about 5000 machines per year.

In 1937 the company decided to tap an even greater market when they produced the 100cc "Robot" model. The new Jawa featured a 2.7 hp engine that was mounted in a pressed-steel frame. A set of pedals was also fitted for starting and assistance on steep hills, and this motorized bicycle was priced so cheaply that almost everyone in Czechoslovakia could afford one. This Robot model was a smashing success, and many thousands of citizens climbed off their bicycles and onto a Robot.

During the late 1930s the factory became more sporting conscious and several attempts were made at producing competition machines. Probably the most noteworthy was the production of the special 350 and 500cc ohv speedway or "short-track" racing models. The Jawa Company also made available a parts kit to convert the 350cc side-valve model into an overhead camshaft unit, and then later a complete ohc 350 single was available for road racing. The factory even went so

Jawa's first production competition machine was 1935 speedway racer; 500-cc model had knobby tires and telescopic front fork.

far as to enter a team in the famed Isle of Man TT races in 1932, '33 and '35; best performances were an eighth and a twelfth in the 1933 Senior.

Then the country became involved in World War II and the factory was mobilized for military production. Despite the war effort, the Jawa engineering department spent a great deal of time and effort in designing some new machines for peacetime production. Working secretly in a remote store, the Czech designers drew up their plans for a new Jawa that would be competitive in the world market. Previously, the marque had been strictly a home-country product as the Jawa was not a well enough engineered machine to compete in the world market.

In the spring of 1945 the new Jawa was unveiled at the Paris show-and the worldwide response was tremendous. Designed by the engineers J. Josif and J. Krivka, the new Jawa was termed to be ten years ahead of its time by several prominent journalists of the day.

The obvious theme of the new model was comfort and styling. The 250cc two-stroke engine had a bore and stroke of 67 x 75mm, and the engine and four-speed gearbox were both in one clean-looking case. The frame was a rugged square-tube affair that had a good "plunger" rear suspension system. The front had a drop telescopic fork with a generous amount of travel. Then, for some frosting on the cake, the seat had a special torsion spring mounting that gave an extra degree of comfort.

The brilliant engineering did not end with the frame, though, as the gearshift had an "automatic" clutch than enabled the rider to shift gears once underway by just using the footshift lever. The headlight was contained in a streamlined nacelle, and the general appearance of the machine was sleek and smooth.

Probably the most noteworthy feature, though, was the smooth and comfortable ride. This was really remarkable on such a cheaply priced machine, considering the fact that most of the world's motorcycles were still using rigid frames.

The 250 model was augmented by a new 350cc "Ogar" twin the following year, and these two models were marketed all over the world. The fast growing sales and acceptance of these new Jawas were all it took for the company to expand its horizons, and so in 1951 an exciting new 500cc ohc twin was added to the range. This new twin was too expensive for the majority of riders, but it nevertheless was popular in eastern Europe as a sporting roadster.

The new twin looked very much like the other Jawa models, except it was larger and had the ohc engine with measurements of 65 x 73.6mm, and the compression was left very low at 6.8 to 1 for the dreadful gasoline that was available then. The engine had a single camshaft which actuated short rockers. The 500 twin proved to be expensive and it remained in production for only a short time, but some private owners did modify and race them with a fair amount of success.

The next Jawa milestone was in 1954 when they changed from the plunger type of rear suspension to the popular swinging-arm system. With only minor detailed improvements since then, the Jawa line remains much the same today. The basis of the current range are the 250cc and 350cc single cylinder two-strokes with measurements of 65 x 75mm and 76 x 75mm respectively. The Jawa can be had today in a variety of models including road, moto-cross, and trials trim. All models feature the rugged engine and gearbox in one case, two exhaust ports and pipes, and the "automatic" clutch.

The present day Jawa is a highly respected motorcycle all over the world for its quality of finish, fine handling, and reliability. While the engine in its present stage of tune is not producing quite as much power as some of its competitors, its smooth delivery and wide spread of torque often makes it a more desirable machine for the rider of average ability.

In the sporting sphere of motorcycling the Jawa has had some truly great moments. While the marque could not be considered as being one of the giants of the international competition scene, its record is nonetheless impressive. The only problem in examining the technical features of Jawa's racing history is the great secrecy that has surrounded their efforts since the mid-thirties. A typical Jawa tactic is to throw a cover over their mount after a Grand Prix and hustle it back to Czechoslovakia-talking to no one in the process.

The type of competition that has probably been the most rewarding to the company has been moto-cross racing. Jawa produces several machines specifically for moto-cross such as the 250 and 350cc two-stroke models and the 500cc ohv Eso. This later mount is produced by a branch company that sells four-stroke engined machines for competition only.

The most noteworthy achievement in scrambling was obtained by Jaromir Cizek in 1958 when he won the very first of the 250cc Coupe d'Europe Moto-Cross Championships. Cizek's Jawa was a special "works" model that the factory had "breathed" on, and its performance was somewhat more devastating than the standard production model.

The following year Cizek could get no higher than third place in the championship standings, as Rolf Tibblin's Swedish Husqvarna was much lighter than the Jawa and therefore had better acceleration. Since then the Jawa has gradually faded away from the winner's circle, and they have taken a greater interest in international trials.

During the late 1960s Jawa did become half interested in moto-cross again, and this time with a brutish 400cc single. V. Valek did reasonably well in 1967 with a fourth place in the 500cc championship, but in 1968 he fell to tenth place. In 1969 J. Homola finished thirteenth, and then Jawa seemed once again to lose interest in scrambling.

The 500cc Eso has done well, also, but the factory has never made a really serious attempt with top-flight works riders. The Eso continues to be popular as a production scrambler, as its light weight of around 275 pounds plus a beefy 40 hp at 6500

This clean looking 1935 ohc 350-cc GP single was not fast enough to defeat British singles that dominated classic races then.

1935 Jawa 350-cc ohv single was popular mount in its day. Girder front fork, rigid frame were accepted practice in mid-thirties.

1937 "Robot" model was Jawa that put Czechoslovakia on wheels. Inexpensive to purchase and maintain, two-stroke developed 2.7 hp.

rpm make it a fine handling machine with good acceleration.

One of the most interesting of the Jawa competition machines is the Eso speedway racer. The latest 500cc DT-6 model features an ohv engine with a bore and stroke of 88 x 82mm, and the engine churns out a mighty 50 hp at 8,000 rpm on straight alcohol. For specialized European short-track racing, a light rigid frame is used along with a tiny fuel tank, a total loss lubrication system (the oil just spills out on the track), and studded tires. This Czech racer began defeating the traditional British J.A.P. engine during the late 1960s, and by the early 1970s their single was dominating the scene.

Racing to a European means road racing, particularly in the classical Grand Prix events, and Jawa has expended a modest amount of effort in this direction. It is rather odd, though, considering the fact that Jawa has primarily been a two-stroke producer, that they have chosen the four-cycle engine for the bulk of their racing activities.

The marque's serious racing program began back in the mid-1950s when they built some 250 and 350cc twins for a works team. On these machines the venerable Frantisek Stastny has garnered many Czechoslovakian championships, and his record over the years in world championship racing is impressive. Franta has also been ably supported by Gustav Havel, and these two riders have brought a great deal of honor to both the sport and their country.

Franta's first visit to the Isle of Man TT races was made in 1957 with a 250cc twin that had gained him many a Czech championship. The little twin had a fair turn of speed, too, being capable of something like 120 mph with a full "dustbin" fairing. The speed that year was about 15 to 20 mph down on the World Champion Mondials, though, and Statsny had to settle for a twelfth place.

After the race a British journalist tested many of the works TT bikes for a comparison, and he noted that the Jawa was one of the finest handling bikes he had ever ridden around the circuit. The massive 10¼ brakes (the front was a twin leading shoe unit) were said to be exceptionally powerful and fully up to the job of stopping the 310-pound twin. The engine's 30 hp at 11,000 rpm was fed to a five-speed gearbox.

During the 1957 season Franta also garnered a fifth in the Dutch Grand Prix, but the following few years proved fruitless as the Jawa simply lacked the speed to be a winner. A great amount of development work was put into the twin and the engine was gradually expanded into a 350cc unit. In 1960 Franta appeared with a new and much lighter 305 model, and the horsepower had become great enough to trounce all but the MV Agusta Fours. In the French GP he took a second, and in the final event of the season on the fast Monza circuit he took another well-earned second place. This gave Franta enough points for a fourth place in the World Championship.

For 1961 the factory raced in the junior class almost exclusively, as the 250 model was a bit heavy and it lacked the speed to compete against the Honda fours. The best that a 250 Jawa did that year was a fifth in the Dutch event, with Stastny in the saddle.

In the 350cc class Franta had a good year, taking a fifth in the I.O.M., thirds in the Dutch and Ulster events, a second in the East German, and outright wins in the German and Swedish classics. In addition, teammate Gustav Havel took a second in both the German and Swedish events, a third at Monza, and a fourth in the East German G.P. For his efforts, Franta gained the runnerup position to the late Gary Hocking (MV) in the World Championship standings. This was and still is both Jawa's and Stastny's finest year.

The following year the marque did not fare as well; the other four-cylinder racers were getting faster and the Jawa was not. Franta took a fourth in the Dutch, a third in the I.O.M., and a second in the Ulster; and Havel captured a fifth in the Ulster. More speed was needed!

The factory racing department responded in 1963 with a new

bike that has proven to be a very good racing machine. The engine was still a twin with a bore and stroke of 62 x 57.9mm, but the head was changed over to the four-valves-per-cylinder arrangement. The lighter valve gear allows higher revs, and the 350cc engine developed 52 hp at 11,500 rpm on a 10.5 to 1 compression ratio. Ignition was by coil to four spark plugs.

The higher-reving engine had a narrower power range, and so the five-speed gearbox had gave way to a six-speed version. The frame was a tubular cradle type with a standard telescopic fork for the front wheel and a set of Girling suspension units on the rear swing-arms. The front tire was a 3.00 x 18 size, and the rear was a 3.50 x 18. Both brakes were a massive 200mm diameter, and the front brake was a dual unit. The top speed of the 350 was approximately 150mph, and the dry weight was a light 279 pounds.

During 1963 there were a lot of "bugs" to be worked out of the new design, and Jawa often failed to finish the race. Stastny garnered a third in the Junior TT plus a fourth in the Belgian, and that was about it for the new four-valver. Riding the older two-valve models Gustav Havel took a sixth in the Belgian, and fourths in the East German and German events; and P. Slavicek took a fifth at Monza.

During 1964 the works team did not fare too well, as the factory was improving the four-valve engine and the team had some rotten luck. Havel took a second place in the East German GP and a third in the Ulster for the only high notes of the year.

In 1965 the team made a great comeback. The marque even had a bash at the 250 class again with Stastny taking fifth places in both the I.O.M. and Monza events. On the bigger junior model Havel captured thirds in the Ulster, German, and East German classics. Stastny followed his teammate up with fourths in the East German and Monza events, and then Franta scored his popular last lap victory in the Ulster Grand Prix. This late season showing by Stastny was good enough to give

The 1966 factory 250-cc scrambler featured 5-speed gearbox and a potent 27 hp. Front tire is 2.75 x 21; rear is 4.00 x 18 size.

him a tie for fifth place in the World Championship standings.

During 1966 the Jawa team gained many good "places" in the classical grand prix events, and a new "overbored" 350cc model was used in the Senior class with a fair amount of success. Stastny was again the team leader, and his many second through sixth places were a great tribute to both his riding skill and the reliability of his Jawas.

In 1967 the Jawas did not do so well, so that the company began looking about for a new approach. The new bike was a two-stroke 350cc V-4, which proved to be fast but unreliable. During the 1968-71 era much was hoped for the new Czech racer, but a lack of finances or interest seems to have plagued their efforts. Perhaps, some day, they may find the combination and have a winner, but at present they seem to be destined for lesser things.

So this is the story of Jawa, the leader of the Czechoslovakian motorcycle industry. It is a splendid story of how a

The latest 500-cc Jawa-Eso speedway racer is a functional piece of equipment. It has excellent reputation as "cinder" track racer.

company has produced a really good and comfortable motorcycle for the everyday rider, while at the same time adding a distinctive flavor to the international sporting scene. Not having a really great sales volume, the Jawa factory has had to operate their racing program on a limited budget, but their contribution to our sport is still unique and colorful.

Someday, though, Frantesek Stanstny shall have to retire, and when he does a really great chapter in classical racing wil be ended. Always faithful to his homeland products, Franta has established himself as one of the smoothest and most reliable men of the Grand Prix courses. He is also a terribly popular and highly respected man and, in fact, he is often referred to as the most beloved racing man in all of Europe.

After his great victory in the 1965 Ulster Grand Prix, Franta had the traditional wreath placed around his neck by a pretty young Irish Colleen. Standing there baldheaded, by such a pretty young lass, one could not help but feel the impact of how long the old man has been racing his Jawas. Jawa and Stastny-a really great legend.

The 1966 twin-cylinder Jawa two-stroke Grand Prix machine with semi-fairing was both beautiful and fast.

Frantisek Stastny at speed on the OHC Jawa 350cc twin. Franta won the 1965 Ulster Grand Prix for the factory's only GP win.

Jaromir Cizek gave Jawa the first European 250cc moto-cross championship in 1958. The factory now concentrates on ISDT type events with great success.

LAMBRETTA

Italy, more than any other country, is known for its motor-scooters. In the movies, a photograph of Rome, or in a story about this sunbathed country, the motorscooter is an obvious feature in the Italian way of life.

The name most often mentioned when scooters are discussed is Lambretta, and the story of this marque is a study of the post-war industrialization of Italy. For the Lambretta, like many of its European brothers, is locked up and interwoven with a parent company that produces many other products in addition to its two-wheeled vehicles.

The story of this legendary scooter actually began in 1922, when Ferdinando Innocenti moved to Rome from his native Pescia for the purpose of building a factory. The product of this enterprising industrialist was steel tubing, and such ingenuity was involved that Innocenti's wares became renowned throughout Europe.

1949 Model B featured exposed 125-cc engine, twist-grip gearshift.

In 1931, Fernando moved to Milan, which had become the industrial center of Italy, and a new and much larger factory was built. In this plant, Innocenti developed a seamless steel tube for industry, and 6000 people were employed there.

Then came World War II, and the factory was reduced to a smoldering pile of rubble. After the war, Fernando was faced with the job of rebuilding, which was a formidable task because the whole Italian productive economy was a shambles. This challenge seemed to inspire the aging Innocenti, however, and the energy and vision that he manifested are today considered to be genius is stature.

The primary need, as Ferdinando saw it, was twofold in nature. The first was to begin production of industrial equipment and heavy machinery, and the second was to provide a cheap and reliable method of transportation. To effect this, the new factory was devided into two divisions-the heavy equipment division and the motor division. The motor division has since been divided into two sections-the scooter section (1947) and the car section (1960).

When Ferdinando viewed his war damaged homeland in 1946, he saw the roads torn up, cities leveled, and the populace left with little means of transportation. The answer to the transportation problem, he reasoned, was the motor-scooter-a vehicle that would feature a low production cost, be inexpensive to operate, and would offer better weather protection than a motorcycle. The wisdom of Ferdinando's decision can be judged by the fact that today 50 percent of the Italian motor vehicles on the roads are scooters-one for every 25 inhabitants of the country. Altogether, over 3.5 million Lambrettas have been produced, and 40 percent of the current 200,000 annual production is exported to all corners of the world.

The production of motorscooters began in 1947, after one year had been spent in developing and testing the prototype

Italian racer Romolo Ferri is pictured with the 1950-51 Lambretta streamliner that still holds records in the FIM book.

model. The first Lambretta was quite naturally named the Model A, and it featured a single-cylinder two-stroke engine with a bore and stroke of 52 by 58 mm. This provided a displacement of 123 cc, and 4.2 bhp was developed at 4400 rpm. Operating on a 6:1 compression ratio, the Model A delivered up to 120 mpg-a strong sellling point in gasoline scarce Italy.

The frame into which this little engine was mounted was a tubular-panel type with a floorboard on which the rider put his feet. Two seats were provided-one for the rider and one for the passenger. A leg shield at the front of the floorboard provided some protection in the event of rain, and a windshield helped protect the rest of the rider's body.

The rider's comfort was cared for by leading-link front and torsion bar rear suspension. A point to make here is that, in 1947, about 90 percent of the world's motorcycles still featured a rigid frame, and probably a half still employed the girder front fork. The 158-lb. Lambretta, therefore, was a very advanced little vehicle-at least as far as riding comfort was concerned!

The gearbox on the Model A was a three-speed unit with ratios of 4.17, 6.12, and 12.3, and gear shifting was accomplished by a heel-toe lever on the floorboard. Drive was by chain. Tire size was 3.50 x 7 in. Internal expanding brakes were used on both wheels, and the wheelbase was 48.8 in. Top speed was something like 42 mph-a speed that must have seemed very rapid when dodging all the potholes in the war ravaged roads!

The following year, the Innocenti Corporation began production of several three-wheeled scooter-truck combinations, which was an ingenious approach to the hauling of goods and supplies. Four models were built, including three closed panel models, and one open bed affair. On all four models, the cargo compartment was mounted in the front end of the scooter, and two wheels were spread wide to make the thing stable. A car type rack-and-pinion steering mechanism was used, and the gear ratios were lowered so that top speed was only 31 mph on a 6.5:1 third gear. The tire sizes also were enlarged to 3.50 x 8, and the weight was 330 lb. The hauling capacity was a suprising 440 lb., which made the truck a popular rig with businessmen.

The creative genius of Ferdinando was not content to sit still, of course, and the scooter underwent constant development. In 1949, the Model B was introduced, and this scooter was the first Lambretta to be exported in goodly numbers. The powerplant was basically identical to that of the Model A, but a new method of gear shifting was adopted that is still used today. Gear shifting on the B was done by merely twisting the handlegrip on the right handlebar, plus using the orthodox hand clutch lever on the left handlebar.

The weight of the Model B also was reduced to only 130 lb., and the tire size was increased to 3.50 x 8. Power output was listed as 4.3 bhp at 4000 rpm, and the top speed was 43 mph. The fuel consumption was no less than 110 mpg, which even today would be a remarkable rate. A small luggage compartment in the rear was available by lifting the passenger seat, and an attractive red paint job helped make this scooter a popular mount the world over.

In 1950, the Model B was renamed the Model C. The only true difference was addition of a spare wheel and tire on the back. The truck line also was continued with minor changes, and the sales of the dependable little scooters continued to expand.

During these years, the economy of Italy continued to develop, and it was only natural that the public wanted something a little more refined. In response to this, the company produced the LC model-the first Lambretta to feature a sheet metal enclosure of the engine. This bit of paneling made

Lambretta has always offered truck models with panel or open boxes.   *By 1950 Lambretta was more streamlined. Model LC still has 125 cc.*

the scooter more streamlined and modern looking, and the foreign markets were developed even farther. The engine and basic frame were the same as used on the standard model, but larger 4.00 x 8 tires were adopted. The gear ratios were 4.8, 7.0, and 13.0, and the weight was up to 187 lb.

During the early 1950's, the recovery from the war became more manifest in Italy, and several of the Latin motorcycle companies began an aggressive effort to dramatically increase their export sales. The Innocenti Corp. was one of these, and it was obvious to Ferdinando and his son Luigi that something was needed to put their name in a prominent place for all to see. Several other Italian concerns had turned to racing or record setting for publicity and prestige, and it was only natural that Moto Lambretta would give some thought to this approach.

The thought soon turned into reality, and the result certainly was and still is one of the most remarkable chapters in the story of the motorcycle. The Innocenti people decided, and wisely so, that road racing was too far removed from scooter practice for them to fully benefit from the publicity. Road racing also had developed into a very technical and expensive proposition then, and it would have taken an all-out effort to topple the giants of the racing game.

So, the challenge was to break some speed and endurance records, and the goal was to do it with the basic scooter design. To this end the factory dedicated itself, and the work began.

In order to get as much direct publicity as possible from the project, the company decided to use their basic 52 by 58-mm 125-cc engine. The simplest method of raising the power output was to add a supercharger, and this was mounted on the left side, where the magneto normally is located. For sparks, the designers used a battery-coil setup in conjunction with a set of points, and then an exhaust system was devised that would work well with the supercharger.

The cylinder, piston, connecting rod, and lower end were very similar to the production version; and the three-speed twist-grip gearbox was retained. The clutch was standard, but with another plate added to accommodate the additional torque, and the gear ratio was greatly increased in order to clock the desired speeds. The fuel used was a mixture with a methanol base, and oil was added for lubrication.

The frame was a tubular type that was quite long and very low. Standard front and rear suspension units were used, but the tires were specially built for the project and were a 3.00 x 12 size.

The really suprising thing about the Lambretta was the streamlined shell that was designed to completely encase both the bike and rider. A small windscreen was mounted in the front for the rider to see through, and a tail fin was used for

added stability. The shell had a very rounded and sleek appearance, with intake and exhaust air ducts provided to cool the engine. The fairing was calculated to have an air drag factor of only 0.0003, compared to the 0.0008 factor of a rider crouched low on a road racing bike.

Preliminary tests with the tiny streamliner provided some encouraging results, such as the 24-hour record of 63.34 mph set by the team of Brunori, Masserini, Masetti, and Rizzi at Montlehery, France. More significant endurance marks were set on Oct. 5, 1950, at Montlehery when Dario Ambrosini Romolo Ferri, and R. Rizzi shattered the 1000-km, 6-hour, and 12-hour records with speeds of 82.34, 82.59, and 82.34 mph.

During 1951, the factory kept up its furious quest for records-nailing down many marks for various distances including the 50 km at 100.0 mph, 100 miles at 98.5 mph, and the 1-hour record at 98.5 mph. Several standing start records also were broken, such as 1-km at 65.2 mph, the mile at 76.38 mph, and the 5-km at 113.643 mph. These last three marks are all average speeds.

The most magnificent of all the records set was one of the last, and for this the marque used little Romolo Ferri to do the honors. Romolo ran out on the Munich-Ingolstadt Autobahn in Germany on Aug. 8, 1951, and he recorded the amazing speeds of 124.8 and 125.442 mph for the flying kilo and mile. The blown two-stroke was said to develop 13.5 bhp and the engine was spinning to 9000 rpm. This gave Lambretta the distinction of having clocked 1 mph for every cc of engine capacity-a feat that gave the firm an enviable amount of worldwide publicity.

These records seem all the more remarkable when they are compared to some of the American marks at that time. For example, the U.S. 500-cc Class A speed mark set on a methanol-nitro fuel mixture was only 126.68; and the Class C 30-cu. in., 45-cu. in., 61-cu. in., and 74-cu. in. records were 123.69, 123.52, 131.95, and 120.74 mph, respectively. The only 50-mile endurance mark in the U.S. books was set at 117.05 mph by a 40-cu. in. Triumph, and the American 24-hour record was 76.05 mph, established by Fred Ham on a 74-cu. in. Harley-Davidson. So, the little Lambretta certainly made 123cc and 13.5 bhp appear impressive.

All this world wide publicity made the Lambretta much better known, and the company's international prestige and sales continued to grow. New markets in Asia, America, and Africa were developed, and the company prospered as never before.

The Innocenti Corp. continued to improve its product. Introduced in 1952 was the Model 125 LD that had a more powerful 5.2-bhp engine. The compression ratio had been increased to 6.5:1 to take advantage of the slightly better grade of gasoline that was available, and the more comprehensive body work had increased the weight to 204 lb. Top speed was up to 47 mph.

In 1954, the company responded to the Latin demand for greater performance by introducing a 150-cc engine with a bore and stroke of 57 by 58mm. The compression ratio was 6:1, and 6.05 bhp was developed at 4600 rpm. The engine delivered a very good 125-150 mpg, which was still an important matter in nearly all of Europe.

Two models were produced-the D and the LD. The Model D was an open style without fancy paneling to cover the engine, while the LD featured sleek styling for those who could afford the higher price. Both models had a wheelbase of 51.2 in., and both had a three-speed gearbox with ratios of 4.75, 7.5, and 12.9. Both models also used 4.00 x 8 tires, but their weights were different at 176 and 204 lb., respectively. The company continued to produce several models of the trucks.

In 1955, Lambretta made an effort to produce a truly low priced method of transportation in a 50-cc motorized bicycle. The engine had a bore and stroke measurements of 40 by 38mm, and it produced 1.5 bhp. The little bike weighed only 77 lb., and it returned up to 200 mpg at speeds up to 31 mph.

In 1957, the company made a notable improvement with its TV175 model. Other than the sleek styling, major improvements were the 170-cc engine and the four-speed gearbox. The engine had a bore and stroke of 60 by 60 mm, and it developed 8.6 bhp at 6000 rpm with a 7.6:1 compression ratio. The gearbox had ratios of 5.69, 7.3, 9.77, and 14.32. Tire size was increased to 3.50 x 10. The weight was a little heavier at 271 lb., but the four-speed gearbox provided brisk acceleration as well as a speed of 64 mph.

The truck line was also developed, with several larger boxes and beds available that were mounted behind the driver. Two wheels were used in the rear, and a new gearbox had three speeds forward plus a reverse gear.

In 1958, the TV model became a 175 with a bore and stroke of 62 by 58 mm, and this engine developed 11 bhp at 5500 rpm with a 7:1 compression ratio. This very deluxe model weighed 270 lb. and had a maximum speed of 66 mph.

Today the Lambretta line is better than ever before. The least expensive is the little 50-cc Lambrettino bicycle, with its better than 200 mpg fuel consumption. Next comes the J50 model, which is a 50-cc scooter that develops 1.5 bhp at 4500 rpm and weighs only 171 lb. Then there are two 125-cc models that provide a 140-mpg economy, with a 54-mph performance, and then the larger 150-cc X150 model that is slightly faster at 58 mph. The star of the range is the 200X Special with its 66-mph speed, disc front brake, and ultra-sleek styling. All of the scooters feature the superb finish that now is expected from Lambretta, and all provide the wonderfully smooth and comfortable ride that only Innocenti can produce in his scooters.

There is one other interesting chapter in the story of Lambretta, and that is the tale of their would-be racer that never did make it to the classical grand prix circuits. Designed in 1951, by Ing. Salmaggi, the 250-cc Moto Lambretta was certainly unique, as well as being one of the most beautiful racing bikes ever built.

The engine was a four-stroke 90-degree V-twin set transversally in the frame. It had a bore and stroke of 54 by 54 mm. The drive to single overhead camshafts was by vertical shafts and bevel gears, and no less than three coil springs were used on each valve.

The crankcase contained the roller bearing lower end and oil tank, with fins cast on the lower half to aid in heat dissipation. The crankshaft was in line with the frame, so it was only logical to mount an in-line gearbox behind the engine and then use shaft drive. The gearbox was a five-speed unit, and a

One of the most beautiful small-displacement racers ever built was this 1951-52 model Moto Lambretta 250.

Modern Lambretta is a good looking scooter, available with engines from 50 to 200 cc. This 1962 TV175 featured an 8.75-bhp engine.

typically Latin heel-and-toe shift lever was used. The magneto was mounted under a cover at the front of the crankcase.

The frame used was quite unorthodox for those days, with a large diameter backbone, and the engine serving as part of the frame section. An orthodox swinging-arm rear suspension was used in conjunction with a telescopic front fork, but the drive shaft was contained in the left side swinging-arm tube. Huge air-cooled brakes were used that were located in deeply finned full width hubs, and tire sizes were 2.75 x 21 front and 3.00 x 21 rear. The first prototype built featured an unusual torsion bar rear suspension and a dry sump oil system, but Salmaggi quickly changed this to the above specifications after preliminary tests.

Painted a deep red and with all the polished alumunum, the Moto Lambretta was a beautiful sight to behold. It was also a potent performer, with its 28 bhp output comparing favorably to the 27 bhp that the all conquering Moto Guzzi 250s produced. The 5.8-gal. fuel tank was gracefully contoured for the rider's arms, and the twin carburetors and long megaphones added a touch of styling that made the bike appear fast even at rest.

In 1955, company introduced the 49-cc, 200-mpg Lambrettino.

The exotic 250 never made it to the race track, though, probably because the record attempts with the streamliner had succeeded so admirably in bringing the company the desired publicity. With some development, plus a good rider, the Twin could have certainly been a winner, but it faded away until it is now just a beautiful bit of history in the Innocenti museum.

So, this, then, is the story of the Innocenti Lambretta-a delightful post-war story that has had a great deal to do with putting Italians on wheels. Italians are colorful people with a great zest for life, and the sight of a boy and girl whirling around the town square and fountain on their scooter is a sight that is typically Roman. With a smile on his face and hair flying in the wind, the Lambretta rider typifies a way of life that many others around the world can envy.

MATCHLESS

There have been many hundreds of motorcycle manufacturers since the turn of the century. Some of these companies have carried on their business in an ostentatious manner-winning all sorts of competitions or producing fabulous models of great classical stature. Others have been more modest, producing well designed bikes that perform reliably and gain many friends, but which fail to make the big headlines.

One of these marques that has been rather quietly successful is Matchless-a British concern whose history is woven ever so closely with the basic history of the motorcycle. It is not that the Matchless has failed to produce many good designs or successes in international competition, for the firm's history is spiced with honorable achievements in both areas. Rather, it is a case of the marque never having managed a string of truly magnificent successes that make headlines the world over.

The philosophy of this legendary British concern has been to produce a good, sound motorcycle for the common man. In this, Matchless has succeeded admirably.

The story of this Anglo-Saxon pioneer began in 1878 when H.H. Collier began to produce his Matchless brand of bicycle. Collier senior soon was joined by his two elder sons, Harry and Charles, and these enterprising men tried to fit a Continental-made engine over the front wheel of one of their bicycles. This setup proved not to be the best, so they next tried mounting the engine behind the seat tube. This didn't work very well either, so then they mounted the 2.75-bhp De Dion Bouten single-cylinder powerplant centrally in the frame. These belt-driven and pedal-assisted models proved to be fairly reliable for their day, and both of the Collier boys won a goodly share of the races in the vacinity of London.

The Collier brothers proved to be good inventors, and they

The 1932 Model CS was a 500-cc "sloper" with three-speed handshift gearbox. Rigid frame and girder fork were standard practice then.

1933 Silver Arrow was luxurious mount, with pivoted-fork rear suspension. Engine was narrow 26-degree 400-cc transverse V-twin.

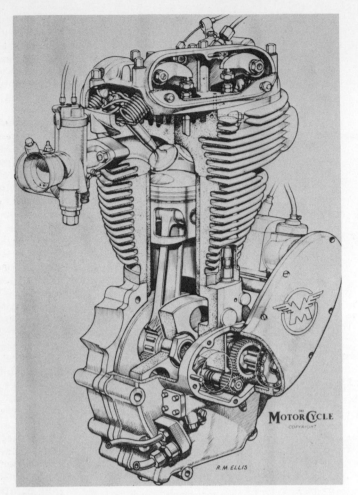

Designed in 1936, the "G" series Matchless engine has proven to be exceptionally reliable. The cylinder and head are alloy on this 1960 engine.

had some remarkably progressive ideas for those early days. In 1903, they added a pillion seat to their Single, so that a passenger could be carried and, in 1904, they produced a Tricar which was fitted with a chain drive in 1905. In that same year, the company also produced a powerful V-twin model that had a JAP engine. This twin-cylinder model featured a leading-link front fork and an experimental swinging-fork rear suspension- and all this in 1905.

The Collier brothers were great competitors. In 1905, Harry represented his country in the International Cup Race that was contested in France. In 1906, the two brothers both qualified, with Charlie riding to a 3rd place-the only British machine to finish. The boys were dissatisfied with the rules that favored the Continental bikes-big engines in tiny frames, and a 110-lb. maximum weight limit. So, they joined with others in organizing a race on the Isle of Man for touring or production motorcycles. The Marquis de Moisilly of St. Mars, who was a friend of the Collier family, agreed to donate a trophy, and thus was born the glorious tradition of the "TT."

The first TT race was staged in 1907, and Charlie Collier won at 38.23 mph. The following year Charlie came in 3rd on his Single. Then, brother Harry won the trophy in 1909 at the fantastic speed of 49.0 mph. That same year, Harry set up a new 24-hour record of 32.3 mph. to prove how reliable the company's products were. All this publicity helped establish the reputation of the tiny concern.

These early thumpers used a JAP pushrod-operated ohv engine, which returned no less than 94.5 mpg fuel consumption in the race. The frame was rigid, with a leading-link front fork that had a single coil spring, and a single-speed belt drive was used. By 1908, magneto ignition had been adopted, and the marque also produced a beastly

racing model with a 120 by 120-mm JAP V-twin engine that punched out 24 bhp.

The Collier brothers continued to race with great success- C.R. winning the 1910 TT, with H.A. in second place. Charlie also lapped Brooklands on a 976-cc JAP-powered model at 80.24 mph, and then he clocked a top speed of 84.92 mph. The following year, the Indian factory sent over some potent models with chain drive and two-speed gearboxes, and these models placed 1st, 2nd and 3rd in the Senior TT ahead of Harry. This led to the challenging by the Matchless Co. of Jake De Rosier for a match race at Brooklands to save England's honor, but the American won and the British began to switch to chain drive and two-speed gearboxes. Charlie did salvage some degree of honor when he clocked a sizzling 91.37 mph on his big Twin, which stole the world speed record away from De Rosier.

After those early days of glory, the name slowly faded away from the Isle of Man, with Harry's 3rd place and Charlie's 4th place in 1912 being somewhat of a swan song. The brothers had decided to concentrate on improvement of their production models, because those were the days when the motorcycle was undergoing very rapid development. This design work was manifest in several three- and six-speed drives that were tried, with rear hub gearboxes and adjustable belt pulleys in use. In 1912, the marque also started to produce its own engine-an 85.5- by 85-mm bore and stroke Single that delivered 3.5 bhp.

In 1913, the company went "foreign" for engines-using a Swiss Motosacoche V-twin that had a bore and stroke of 64 by 77 mm. This overhead valve engine featured the now common hemispherical combustion chamber, which historians regard as the first use of this type of design. A Motosacoche inlet-over-exhaust-valve V-twin was also used to power the Model 8B, which featured a three-speed gearbox and all-chain drive. This model also displayed a kickstarter and an internal expanding rear brake, instead of the previous caliper type brake on the wheelrim.

Then came World War I, and the factory concerned itself with producing war materials and aircraft parts. After the war, the company lost all interest in racing and concentrated on improvement of the standard production models. The whole range was comprised of V-twins, with both side-valve and ohv engines being used. In 1923, a 350-cc side-valve Single was added to the range, which had chain drive and hub brakes. These models were sound and reliable, but there was nothing about them that made headlines or won races.

This 350-cc Single underwent continued development in 1926 with installation of an ohc valve system, but its appearance in the Isle of Man Junior TT was doomed to failure. A 600-cc low compression ohv Single was then introduced for the burgeoning sidecar market, and this was followed by a 250-cc side-valve Single. By 1927, the range of models included a 250-cc side-valve Single, 500-cc ohv sports Single, 600-cc ohv Single, and 1000-cc side-valve and ohv V-twins.

In 1926, H.H. Collier Sr. died, and the concern was renamed Matchless Motorcycle Co. The elder Collier had been busy,

The 1937 side-valve 1000-cc V-twin was a popular mount for sidecar owners. These old flatheads were known for their low-speed power.

before his death, in design of the new models, and these were introduced in 1928. The main features were modern saddle type fuel tanks that went over, instead of between, the top frame tubes, two-exhaust-port single-cylinder engines, and a new standard of reliability. The gearboxes were still three-speed affairs with a clumsy hand shift and foot clutch. These models were very reliable, and they saw the company through the depression years that wiped out so many of their competitors.

By 1930, Charlie Collier was beginning to make felt his design ability. With introduction of the 400-cc "Silver Arrow," the company embarked on a new approach at catering to the more sophisticated rider who wanted a luxurious motorcycle. The Silver Arrow was knicknamed the "whispering wonder," by reason of its ultra-quiet, smoothrunning, side-valve two-cylinder engine. The Silver Arrow was very comfortable for its day, with a pivoted-fork rear suspension, which was in the era when the rigid frame was still standard practice.

In 1931, the company introduced an even more sophisticated mount in the "Silver Hawk." This model featured a narrow V-four engine set transversally in the frame. The 593-cc powerplant featured ohc valve operation. The deluxe specifications included such things as a chromed fuel tank and an instrument panel. A fully sprung sidecar was available. This V-four sold at a price that was actually not terribly far above the ohv 500-cc Single's price, but the scarcity of pounds in those depression years prevented the sales figure from ever attaining a commerically profitable rate. The Four was dropped from production within a few years-the verdict being excellent engineering, but unsound business practice. Today, the Silver Hawk is prized as a collector's item, and as a great classic, but few are known to exist.

In 1931, the Matchless Co. bought the A.J. Stevens concern, and thereafter the AJS and Matchless began to acquire similar specifications. During the early 1930s, the fashion in England was for "sloping" Singles, and Matchless responded with 500-cc side-valve and ohv models that were quite light. With a rigid frame, girder front fork, and three-speed gearbox, the side-valve machine weighed only 220 lb.

The big side-valve V-twin had been redesigned in 1929, and this model, called the Model X, was produced until World War II. The market for the husky 1000-cc V-twins was substantial during the prewar days in England, since the sidecar owners loved the low-speed power, reliability, and low maintenance expense that these chuggers possessed.

In 1936, the amalgamation of the AJS and Matchless was apparent when the "G" series was introduced. These 350-cc and 500-cc Singles featured pushrod-operated ohv powerplant, a four-speed footshift gearbox, a rigid frame, and a girder front fork. About the only difference between the AJS and Matchless in later years was the location of the magneto-which was in front of the cylinder on the AJS and behind the cylinder on the big "M." These thumpers were known as exceptionally rugged bikes, and their handling and performance were up to the high standards that motorcylists had come to expect during the late 1930s.

These G models were soon followed by the Clubman and Clubman Special models, which were more highly tuned Singles for the sporting minded riders. The Clubman Special model could be purchased in competition trim with a 21-in. front wheel, knobby tires, upswept exhaust, and special gear ratios. These Singles were used in trials and scrambles events with great success during the late 1930s, and this publicity helped further the marque's export sales.

During these years, the international road racing scene had taken on great stature, with many companies fielding works teams on everything from fine handling ohc Singles to exotic watercooled and supercharged Fours. The Matchless name (under the company name of Associated Motor Cycles, after 1938) was quietly absent from this grand prix game, preferring instead to develop a range of bikes for the man on the street. In all fairness to the marque, it should be stated that the firm conducted an intensive racing program under the AJS banner, which was a policy that was continued after World War II.

During the war, the factory once again was switched over to wartime production, only this time it was for military motorcycles. The model produced was the G3L-the ohv 350 thumper that was exceptionally reliable. Altogether, no less than 80,000 bikes were produced during the war, and even today one can occasionally see the trusty little Singles thumping down the country lanes of England.

After the war, the marque narrowed its range down to the G-3 (350-cc) model and G-80 (500-cc) model-both with "iron" engines and the new hydraulically dampened telescopic front fork. The design was cleaned up a little from the prewar days, but it remained the basic design that was laid down in 1936.

The company also produced some trials mounts, which were mainly 350s set up with 21-in. front wheels, knobby tires, upswept exhaust, wide ratio gears, and alloy fenders. These were superb little trials mounts, and men such as Hugh Viney and the Ratcliffe brothers established a splendid reputation with these machines. The 500-cc model was used extensively in motocross racing, and Basil Hall scored many wins on his factory model.

It was during these immediate postwar years that the company greatly expanded its export market, with the United States figuring prominently in this expansion. The fine Singles were especially loved by California desert riders, because handling, traction, and reliability were better than any of the others for cross-country and scramble races of that era. Indeed, AJS and Matchless riders were the most successful of all the riders until the late 1950s, and it would take a story in itself just to cover all of the victories racked up by riders such as Dutch Sterner, Del Kuhn, Julius Kroeger, Guy Louis, Aub LeBard, Earl Flanders, Don Bishop, Rod Coates, Ralph Adams, Lee Carey, Dalton Holliday, Vern Hancock, Bud Ekins, Butsy Mueller, Dick Dean, and Fred Borgeson.

In 1949, the marque made another great step forward when the new "Super Clubman" model was introduced. The new Matchless was a 500-cc Twin with a bore and stroke of 66 and 72.8mm. It featured a three-bearing crankshaft, alloy head, and a comfortable dual seat. The Twin displayed an additional

The 1959 trials 350 was cobby looking 306-pound mount with 10-inch ground clearance. This model won many important trials in Europe.

Prototype Matchless Twin was unveiled in 1951, featuring a modified roadster pushrod engine. AJS fuel tank was from a 7R racer.

A model many old-timers will remember is 1952 G-80CS. These great singles were nearly unbeatable in California desert races.

1960 Matchless Twin with 500- or 600-cc AMC powerplant was not an especially good design, dropped in favor of Norton unit.

characteristic--the new swinging arm rear suspension. This new frame was a major contributor to rider comfort and road-ability, and it was available on all of the models.

During the next several years, the range of models expanded to include mounts for trials and motocross riders, and these fine Singles established a great record on both sides of the Atlantic. The 1952 catalog listed a total of nine models-one Twin and eight Singles. This also was the year that the AJS and Matchless Singles became virtually the same bike, with the magneto being mounted in front of the cylinder on both makes.

Serious touring riders loved the G-9 500-cc Twin for its comfort, 90-95 mph performance, and sporting appearance. The Twin had a four-speed gearbox with ratios of 13.35:1, 8.8:1, 6.4:1, and 5.0:1. A favorite with everyday riders was the 350-cc Single-a reliable model with brisk performance. The G-3L model was built around a rigid frame; the G-3LS had a spring frame. Next came the G-80 and G80S models-both 500-cc Singles in rigid and spring frame trim. An improvement to the Singles that year was the alloy head, which helped the engines run cooler and allowed higher compression ratios to be used. These 85-90-mph thumpers were known for their reliability and low maintenance expense, and they proved popular with riders the world over.

The 1952 catalog listed four competition models-two rigid frame models (350 and 500 cc) for trials and two spring frame models (350 and 500 cc) for motocross. The engines were considerably modified on these competition mounts, with alloy cylinders and heads, special cams, high compression pistons on the two motocross models, and a heavier gearbox with wide ratio gears on the trials bikes and close ratio gears on the scrambler models. Both the trials and scrambles versions were delivered with 3.00 by 21-in. front tires and 4.00 by 19-in. rear tires. Both models were fitted with small 2.25-gal. fuel tanks. The wheelbase was a short 52:5 in. on the competition models, and alloy fenders, sports solo seats, and upswept exhaust systems were fitted.

The next significant chapter in the history of the marque began in 1951 when a racing department was established to develop the 500-cc Twin. The idea was to determine if the standard G-9 Twin showed potential as a road racing model, with the long range goal being to produce a pukka racing machine at a cost well below that of an ohc Single. The Twin first appeared in the 1951 Manx Grand Prix in the hands of Robin Sherry, who proceeded to garner a 4th place with the machine behind the famous Norton Manx Singles. Justifiably encouraged, the factory continued to develop the Twin in preparation for the 1952 Manx GP. Derek Farrant rode the Matchless prototype that year, and he led from start to finish-setting up race and lap records at 88.65 and 89.64 mph.

This sensation virtually required the factory to start production of the Twin, which appeared in 1953 as the G-45 model. The G-45 was produced for five years, during which time it underwent detailed improvements. By 1956, the 66 by 72.8-mm Twin was producing 48 bhp at 7200 rpm on a 10.0:1 compression ratio, which provided a level road speed of 120 mph without a fairing. The G-45 had a four-speed gearbox with ratios of

8.57:1, 6.19:1, 5.0:1, and 4.58:1; and the wheelbase was 55.25 in. A deep, knee-knotched 6-gal. fuel tank was used, and the dry weight was 320 lb. Tire sizes were 3.00 by 19-in. front and 3.25 by 19-in. rear, and both brakes were a huge 8.25-in. size with an air scoop and twin leading shoe arrangement being used on the front brake. This Twin was a beautiful thing with its massive alloy cylinder and head, plus the pair of 1.094-in. GP carbs, and it attained a splendid record in the hands of private owners the world over.

This range of models remained much the same until 1956, when a new 600-cc Twin was introduced that had a bore and stroke of 72 and 72.8 mm, respectively. Gone were the rigid frame models, with the catalog down to only seven machines-the 500- and 600-cc Twins, the 350- and 500-cc road Singles, the G80CS scrambler, the G-45 road racer, and the new G-3LC trials model.

This new trials model was a direct result of the works mounts that had done so well in 1954 and 1955 (Artie Ratcliffe won the 1954 Scottish Six Days Trial), and it had the swinging arm frame for the first time. A trim and fine handling Single, the G-3LC ran on a 6.5:1 compression ratio and pumped out 18 bhp at 5750 rpm. The bike weighed a light 320 lb. and had gear ratios of 21.0:1, 16.0:1, 10.3:1, and 6.6:1. Very few of these superb trials models ever made their way to this country, but they achieved a great number of outstanding successes in British and Scottish trials.

The range of machines continued much the same until 1959, when the G-45 Twin was dropped and the G-50 ohc Single was introduced. The G-50 also was derived from a previous model-this one the 350-cc 7R AJS racer. The big Single had a bore and stroke of 90.0 by 78.0mm, and it pumped out 47 bhp at 7200 rpm on a 10.6:1 compression ratio. The Single breathed through a huge 1.50-in. GP carburetor, and it was known for being able to power a very high gear ratio. The Matchless was slightly slower than the double-knocker Manx Norton, but its simple chain-driven single-cam engine was easier to tune and less expensive to maintain than the Manx. With a top speed of 125 mph, plus good handling, the G-50 proved to be especially popular with the private owners.

Other notable changes in 1959 included the increasing of the 600-cc Twin's stroke to 79.3 mm, thus making it a full blown 650. The trials 350 also was improved by chopping the weight to 306 lb. and increasing the ground clearance to a whopping 10 in. The trials mount continued to be the finest bike of its type in the world.

During the early 1960's, the international motorcycle scene underwent a great change with the arrival of the Japanese models on the market. This had a profound effect on the British scene, and especially upon the Matchless. In 1956, AMC purchased Norton Motors, Ltd., and within a few years the standardization began within the AJS-Matchless-Norton range of machines. The first to go were the Norton Singles in favor of the AMC design, and then the AMC Twin went by the board in favor of the big 650- and 750-cc Norton powerplants. The lusty G-50 racer also was dropped at the end fo the 1963 season-a fact that saddened motorcycle sportsmen throughout the world.

Early 1960s saw this 500-cc Single fall from favor with world's riders. Virtues were low cost, reliability and fair performance.

1964 G-80CS had robust 500-cc engine, good handling and moderate performance. Current edition is still known for its reliability.

During these years, the design progress seemed to stagnate at the factory, with the only new model being the G-85CS scrambler. This 500-cc Single was produced in 1966 and 1967 as a fire breathing motocross mount with a 1.375-in. GP carburetor, Metisse type frame with the central frame tube serving as an oil tank, light 300-lb. weight, and 42-bhp engine. The red hot two-strokes already had taken the play away, though, and this expensive scrambler faded from the picture.

During 1967, the company was known to be virtually bankrupt, and it appeared that the famous name would dissapear. At the last hour, a new company was formed when Manganese Bronze Holdings bought out the Norton-Matchless Co., plus the old Villiers concern.

In 1969 the production finally ceased on the venerable old 500cc G80CS scrambles model, which had had its bore and stroke changed to 86 x 88 mm in 1956. The basic design was much the same as it was in 1952, or even 1936 for that matter! With the passing of the heavy but reliable single, an era was ended at the factory. Perhaps it shall never return. Today, no Matchless models are being produced, and one more great name has thus passed into the history books.

During the 1947 to mid-1960 era the Matchless singles were the model to beat in the western desert races. Fred Borgeson is shown here with the 1961 Greenhorn trophy. In 1962 Matchless produced some "street legal" G50 racing singles to meet the American racing rules. Dick Mann used a bike similar to this prototype to win the 1963 American championship.

MONTESA

It is said that Spain is a poor country and that life is tough. Lacking in natural resources and sufficient rainfall for agricultural purposes, it is no wonder that the industrial age was very late in coming to this Mediterranean country.

All this is beginning to change, though, as huge reservoirs have made it possible to irrigate large areas of formerly arid desert, and the bustling cities are becoming manufacturing centers from when products are shipped all over the world. Along with this industrial revolution has come the desire of the Spanish peon to park his burro and begin traveling on wheels-particularly two wheels.

In this setting the name of Montesa comes to light, for Montesa was **the** company to put Spain on wheels. It is also true, even though Spain was nearly 50 years behind western Europe in developing its own motorcycle manufacturing industry, that today their standard production machines are some of the finest in the world.

Early Montesas were simple two-stroke singles of 100- and 125-cc. Features were three-speed gearshift and girder front fork.

In 1944 Montesa started what was destined to become Spain's oldest and largest motorcycle manufacturing company. The year spent in designing their first motorbike-a prototype they displayed in June of 1945 at the Barcelona International Trade Fair, where public response was so enthusiastic that Montesa immediately began production. The initial product had a 100cc two-stroke engine, but this was soon changed to a 125cc powerplant. The bike itself was of straightforward design with a three-speed hand gearshift, 19-in. wheels, and a girder front fork.

Sales rapidly expanded during 1946, and in 1947 the infant company became a corporation. The problem had been in obtaining parts which were not produced in Spain, such as tires, magnetos, and brake linings; as a full fledged corporation the small company was in a better position to finance these needed imports.

Production continued to expand so much that in June of 1950 a move was made to a larger, more modern plant. With these new facilities it was possible to develop improved designs, a prime necessity if Montesa was ever to sell their machines outside of their country.

A vastly improved new model was introduced in 1951, called the D-51; it had a telescopic front fork with a now familiar offset front axle plus a plunger suspension on the rear wheel. The engine, of course, was a 125cc two-stroke. The D-51 proved to be a very popular little bike, winning many production machine races plus two medals in the International Six Days Trial held in Italy. As an everyday transportation machine the model established its reputation, though, for it proved to be a most reliable mount with a comfortable ride over the usually rough roads.

By 1953, Montesa had some definite ideas about expanding their sales throughout Europe, and so the new Brio-90 model was exhibited at the Geneva International Motor Salon in

Switzerland. This was the first time the Spanish flag had ever been flown at the Salon-another milestone in the history of Spanish industrialization. The Brio-90, built as a "sports" machine, had a deeply finned and rather peppy engine, a fine finish, and husky finned brakes.

Montesa made another great step forward in 1954 when they displayed their whole range at the famous Earl's Court Show in England. This was a bold bid for International sales, and it was eminently successful as orders came in from all over Europe. In fact, sales expanded so much that it was necessary to move the administrative offices from the plant to make room for increased production.

In 1956 some additional new models were introduced-the Brio-81, Brio-82, and an improved Brio-90. These were supplemented the following year by the Brio-91 and Brio-110. Engine size had been pushed up to 175cc and buyers could choose between a cheap utility bike, a sports model, or an outright road racing machine.

For 1958 Montesa made another big change when they went to a swing-arm rear suspension. By then the Brio-110 had become a truly fine motorcycle with a sleek dual seat, massive brakes, an excellent finish, and a really spirited two-stroke engine. With its low overall weight, good handling, and such niceties as alloy wheel rims, it is no wonder that Montesa acquired a splendid reputation.

In 1962 it was obvious that Montesa was out to garner their share of the world-wide markets, and for publicity a team of three riders was selected to cross the continent of Africa on a new prototype model. The expedition, called "Impala," proved such a success that for 1963 the new sports road bike was given the same name. Also produced was a new Moto-Cross model which has subsequently become very popular in this country. The new Montesas, first produced with 175cc engines, were soon pushed up to 250cc units.

A completely new factory was also built in 1963, for production had far outstripped the capacities of the old facility. The new plant was another great industrial chapter in Spain, as the

Front view of "Sprint" model which Marcello Cama raced so successfully in 1956. Full dustbin fairing gave good air penetration.

Dynamic Spanish rider Marcello Cama is shown on his incredibly quiet ride into second place in the 1956 ultra-lightweight TT.

stroke was 78 x 73.5 mm (351cc), and a four speed gearbox was used. The Telesco (Ceriani type) suspension was superb, and this 245 pound bomb won many track races in America.

In 1970 a new improved trials model called the Cota was introduced, which has a 250cc engine that produced 19 HP at 6500 rpm with remarkable low speed power. The gearbox was a new five speeder, and the dry weight was only 205 pounds. This model achieved a great deal of success in classical European trials, and it was to become exceptionally popular with private owners all over the world.

While Montesa is best known here for their potent 250cc scrambler, in Europe the opposite is true, as road racing achievements are considered to be the most significant. Right from the beginning the company's philosophy was to prove the merits of their equipment in long distance road racing. While Montesa has not chalked up many outright victories in world championship events, their achievements are nevertheless noteworthy and interesting.

At first the factory was content to race only the standard production machines with minor alterations to make them race-worthy. In this trim they were quite successful in local races, being perennial Spanish 125cc Champions plus taking a few places in minor Grand Prix races.

During 1951 a more serious effort was made with some special "works" racing machines. While the marque did not score any resounding international victories, they did estab-

One of several Montesa Brio models introduced in 1956 was this type 80/56. Engine size of two-stroke singles went up to 175 cc.

lish a reputation as a very reliable mount by taking fifth and sixth places in the 125cc class in the Isle of Man TT races plus a fifth in the Spanish GP. The little two-stroke had a quite standard looking single exhaust-pipe engine, but its average speed in the TT was over 11 mph down on the winning four-stroke Mondial of Cromie McCandless. More research would obviously be needed!

So it was home to the race shop and chief race engineer, Francesco Bulto, went to work. In June of 1955 his efforts recieved world acclaim when an experimental 175cc model carried off the 24-Hour Barcelona race over a field of much larger machines. This magnificent victory really helped the expanding sales effort of the 10-year-old company, as the Barcelona 24-Hour classic is truly a rugged test of endurance.

Montesa's greatest hour came in 1956, when they took an official works team to the Isle of Man TT races. The factory had four little 125s entered, with the accent on "little" as each bike weighed only 154 pounds. The engine was a two-stroke with piston controlled ports, and both the head and cylinder were of aluminum alloy. Bore and stroke were 51.5 x 60mm, and two exhaust pipes used very standard looking mufflers which made the machines unbelievably quiet. A 30mm Dellorto carburetor was fitted; ignition was by a flywheel magneto.

The gearbox, a six-speed affair, was bolted up to the back of the crankcase. The clutch was a standard chain-driven unit, and the final gear ratio was 5.34 to 1. The frame featured a plunger rear suspension with hydraulic damping; the front end

Coming from a country with a hot climate, Montesas have liberal engine finning. Here factory rider Pedro Pi shows motocross form.

modern machinery and equipment were the finest in the land.

Another new model was introduced in mid-1963--this one a scooter. It was with this scooter that Montesa finally broke with tradition and built a four-stroke engine. The small scooter has proved popular in the homeland, combining low maintenance expense and good gas mileage.

By 1966 the Montesa range had a model for everyone. There were inexpensive utility models, sports roadsters, scramblers, and enduro models-all with lusty 250cc two-stroke engines. The company also periodically produced a small batch of 125cc road racers, but very few of these ever left Europe. One or two made their way to America and were used with success in some of the East Coast events.

In 1968 the company made a big hit with their new Trial model-a 250cc single that weighed only 210 pounds. The 72 x 60 mm engine put out 18 HP at 5500 rpm, and the wide ratio gearbox had ratios of 8.4, 13.4, 16.2, and 21.7 to 1. The ground clearance was a whopping 14.0 inches on this bike, and it performed credibly wherever it was used.

In 1969 the range was expanded to include a 360cc Cappra GP model, which was a wicked scrambler that churned out 38 HP at 6500 rpm on a 10.0 to 1 compression ratio. The bore and used standard Montesa hydraulic telescopic forks with offset front axle. The massive brakes had steel drums shrunk into conical magnesium-alloy hubs.

Covering the front half of the bike was a sleek, full "dustbin" fairing, and this Montesa racer must certainly have been the lowest-built bike ever raced in the TT. The wheels were also quite small with 2.50 x 17 inch tires, and even a normal sized rider loomed unusually large above the bike.

The riders were John Grace of Gibraltar, and Spaniards, E. Sirera, F. Gonzales, and Marcello Cama. Mounts of the first three had engines with part-spherical heads and an 11.5 to 1 compression ratio, while Cama's engine had a squish-type head and 14.5 to 1 compression ratio. Horsepower was listed as 17 at 8,000 on the lower compression engine; 18 at 8,000 on Cama's model.

With six-speed gearboxes the bikes were capable of 40, 67, 73, 84, 92, and 98 mph at 8,000 rpm through the gears. The experimental high-compression engine was noted as having better acceleration than the others, and Cama could squeeze 8,200 revs out of it on the level for an even 100 mph.

Lubrication was provided by mixing S.A.E. 40 mineral oil with the gasoline at a 1 to 25 ratio. An auxiliary oil tank fed castor oil into the carburetor intake at 10 drips per minute for extra upper lubrication. Fuel consumption was 40-45 mpg.

In the race itself the Montesa team had formidable opposition from the MV Agusta, F.B. Mondial, and CZ. Reliability had its day though; one by one the faster Italian machines dropped by the wayside until Cama came home second at 65.24 mph behind Carlo Ubbiali who won at 69.13 mph. Gonzales and Sirera brought the other Montesas in third and fourth, and John Grace retired with clutch trouble. The balance of the season saw a few more "places," then Montesa decided to quit GP racing and concentrate on production racing-bike development.

Later that year the company began limited production of the 125cc "Sportsman" model- a pukka racer that established an enviable reputation for reliability at speed. The Sportsman differed little from Cama's old 1956 works bike, except that the compression ratio was 12 to 1 and a smaller 27mm carb was used. The model also had an improved expansion box exhaust system which helped pump out the 18 hp at 8,000 rpm. A modern swinging-arm frame was fitted, and the brakes were housed in beautiful full-width alloy hubs.

Since the factory has decided to concentrate its efforts on developing "over-the-counter" competition machines, their international racing record has become impressive. The 1956 and 1963 Barcelona 24-Hour races went to Montesa, as well as many 125cc, 175cc, and 250cc Championship events in France, Chile, Mexico, Paraguay, Uruguay and Spain. It is in the endurance events that the Montesa continued to shine, and in 1964 the marque took third in the Barcelona classic behind a works 285cc ohc Ducati and a 600cc BMW. The 250cc Montesa won its class by no less than 29 laps over its nearest competitor that year-a true measure of reliability.

In June of 1965 the company wanted very badly to win the 24-Hour Barcelona classic again, since 1965 is Montesa's twenty-year anniversary. A team of factory riders mounted special "prototype" models, and high hopes were voiced that the larger engined bikes could be worn down on the twisty 2.35-mile long Parque de Montjuich course.

The race was led early by a works 650cc Triumph, but it dropped out and the two 250cc Montesas of Jose Busquets/ Cesar Gracia, and Jorge Sirera/E. Sirera came to the lead ahead of the Norton, Triumph, Velocette, and BMW teams. At the thirteen-hour mark Jorge Sirera punctured a tire and fell, injuring his arm and breaking the handlebar. After a one-hour stop he was back in the race.

At the fifteen-hour mark Busquet's Montesa came into the pits, also for a one-hour stop. This put a 650cc Dresda/Triton (a Triumph engine in a Norton chassis with Oldani hubs) into the lead which it held to the end. A privately entered 250cc Montesa came second-only three laps behind, and Montesa also took the first three 250cc places. A gallant effort by a courageous little factory!

For the 1966 event the Spanish factory made a supreme effort to win their home country classic, and they were rewarded with a magnificent victory. After the two hour mark their two-strokes surged ahead, and finish had two little Montesas in the first two positions ahead of all the big bikes entered. The leader board, gentlemen, of the 1966 Barcelona 24 Hour Grand Prix d'Endurance:

1. Busquets/Villa, 250cc Montesa ....646 laps

By 1966 Montesa had comprehensive range of models – roadsters, scramblers and enduros – all with lusty 250-cc two-strokes.

2. J. Sirera/E. Sirera, 250cc Montesa ....637 laps
3. Phillips/Croxford, 500cc Velocette ....624 laps
4. Degans/Butcher, 650cc Triumph ....616 laps
5. Iglesias/Petras, 250 Ossa ....608 laps
6. Lawton/Carr, 650cc Triumph ....607 laps

After that Montesa lost interest in road racing and concentrated on improving the foreign sales of their roadsters. In 1968 they became interested in "dirt" competition, and especially so in trials events.

The company had a great deal to learn about how to build a good trials bike, but the only way to learn was to plunge into the game. Don Smith was their best rider that year, and he rewarded them with a sixth place in the European Championship plus a fourth place tie with Lawrence Telling (also Montesa) in the British Championship.

In 1969 things looked up with a new works bike that really performed. In the famous Scottish Six Day classic, Smith finished fourth, Gordon Farley sixth, and Telling ninth. In the European Championship Farley staggered the experts by trouncing the field, which included Sammy Miller and his supposedly invincible Bultaco. In 1970 Farley finished second with Telling in third, and Smith in sixth. In the Scottish Rob Edwards gained a second, Farley an eighth, and Telling a ninth. By far the most remarkable achievement in 1970 was Farley's winning the coveted British Championship-a defeat that ended Sammy Miller's reign of eleven consecutive years.

Farley repeated his Championship in 1971.

Since then Montesa has emphasized and developed their "dirt" bikes. The cota 250 has become one of the best and most popular trials bikes in the world, with many championships being won on these fine handling bog wheels. In 1973 Montesa added another Cota to the range-- this one a cute little 125 with a six speed box that weighs only 154 pounds. The performance in a "tight" trial is impressive.

So this, then, is the story of Mostesa, an industrial pioneer in sunny Spain. It is the saga of putting a nation on wheels, and of building a motorbike that is one of the very best in the world today. Just think of the obstacles to overcome in bringing forth such an outstanding machine in such a short period of time from a country so poor as Spain. It is like starting to race when you don't even have your engine running and the other fellow is already doing 100 mph-and you want to catch up and then pass him.

It is beautiful to see a country turn green from irrigation, and a people go from poor to well fed and full of life. In all of this Montesa has played a big part; no wonder Spain is smiling. Look again at the Barcelona Endurance Race results-then reflect that 28 years ago there was not a single bike being manufactured in Spain. Some of the best from Europe and Japan have run at Barcelona and many of them had a 50-year head start.

The 1970 Capra 360 was a fast moto-cross mount for the skilled rider. The big two-stroke had 38 HP and weighed 245 pounds.

The 1968 Scorpion 250 was a fine enduro-type bike with 21 HP and a weight of 225 pounds. The Scorpion is still in production.

The 1975 Cota 125 trials bike has a six-speed gearbox, 13 HP at 7000 rpm, and a weight of only 154 pounds.

1958 Ariel 1000cc Square Four

1973 Bultaco 250cc Alpina

1957 Ariel 500cc HT

1964 Honda 50cc CR110

1960 Norton 500cc Manx

1957 Matchless 350cc G3LC Trials

1939 BSA 500cc S.V. M20

1960 Norton 500cc ES-2

1959 Matchless 500cc G80CS

1964 Velocette 500cc MSS

1939 Velocette 350cc Mk VIII KTT

MOTO GILERA

The story of Moto-Gilera is a study of one man-Giuseppe Gilera, born in Zelobuonpersico, Milan, Italy, in 1887. Giuseppe at an early age displayed the mechanical genuis that was to make his name known over nearly all the world, for the name of Gilera was destined not only to become revered by Grand Prix racing fans, but the very invincibility of his fabulous fours was to put fear in the hearts of his competitors.

As a young man Giuseppe showed great interest in the internal combustion engine, and by the early nineteen-hundreds he had become known as a prominent mechanic on motorcycles. This in itself was an outstanding achievement, because motorcycles were still not common in Italy. The country was poor and lagged well behind the more western European nations in industrial development.

By 1909, Giuseppe had completed several years' training with an engineering firm named Bucher and Zeda, and he felt the time was ripe to launch the production of his own machines. In a little shop in Milan he designed his first motorcycle, a single cylinder model that proved to be most reliable.

With his reputation established sales began to climb, and Giuseppe was forced to move to larger quarters at Arcore. During the first World War, the company received a prestige boost when the Italian Army officially used their machines. After the War the expanding economy boosted sales, and Gilera became one of Italy's leading machines, fielding a range of models from 125cc to 500cc.

Gilera was still largely an Italian motorcycle, but during the 1930's the company began to expand their distribution to other European countries. After World War II the concern expanded even further, adding a production plant in Argentina (Gilera of Argentina), and establishing distributors in several North African, Oriental and South American countries. The Gilera production is still sold mostly in Italy, although in a recent year the U.S. did receive an authorized distribution of their machines.

The present factory facility is very modern, featuring its own steel and smelting plants, production line, and test track. Cavaliere del Lavoro Giuseppe Gilera was chairman of the board and exercised a competent control of all engineering and technical matters until his death in 1971.

The current range of Gilera motorcycles includes models of 98cc, 124cc, 150cc, 175cc, and 350cc, all with pushrod operated OHV engines. In addition, there are the two new scooters, also OHV, with cylinder capacities of 50cc and 80cc. Most are built to "pavement riding" specifications.

Single cylinder engines power the full line, except for the 350cc model which is a vertical twin. A beautifully engineered swinging arm frame, telescopic front fork, full alloy hubs, and an engine-gearbox in unit are other notable features. Other technical specifications that appeal to the enthusiast are the

"La Prima," first motorcycle produced by Giuseppe Gilera, made appearance in 1909. It established reputation for reliability.

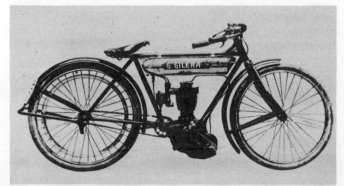

The 1935 side-valve 500 had a three-speed handshifted gearbox, a rigid frame, and a girder front fork. The quality was good.

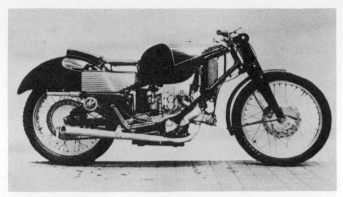

First of many Grand Prix championships for Gilera was captured by Dorino Serafini on this supercharged 1939 four-cylinder Rondine.

Much revered Gilera Saturno model established enviable record as road racer (shown) and scrambler; Saturnos are rare in U.S.

High-speed all-enclosed shell with small windows and large tailfin was built for speed record runs; note bulge for rider's head.

alloy engines, the bore that is equal to or greater than the stroke to hold down piston speed, and alloy wheel rims on some "sports" models.

It is another sphere of motorcycling activity that Gilera is more famous though, and that is competition, particularly Grand Prix road racing. Early in his career Giuseppe decided that competition was the best way to find out just how good his engineering was, and within obviously tight financial limits he accomplished wonders. The great contribution to motorcycle engineering that Gilera has made is impossible to accurately assess, but Moto Gilera's accomplishments on the great racing courses of the world are already a legend.

Giuseppe himself started the company's competition program rolling by competing in Italian races in the period prior to World War I. The first great International victory came much later though-in 1930 at Grenoble when the works team of Miro Maffeis, Rosolino Grana, and Luigi Gilera captured the coveted International Six Days Trial Trophy. To prove the quality of his machines Giuseppe again entered the trial in 1931, held that year at Merano, and again the team took home the trophy. The models used were selected from the standard production range.

During the 1930's the Gilera concern was expanding its sales market, and it was only natural that they began to cast their eyes upon the great classical road races of the day. During that era Grand Prix racing became a leading international sport with hundreds of thousands of potential motorcycle customers viewing each event.

It was in this atmosphere that Giuseppe decided to shoot for the top-the Senior Class World Championship. The problems were almost insurmountable. To have a chance at defeating the supercharged AJSs, BMWs, NSUs, and the fine handling Nortons and Velocettes, Gilera would have to design and build a genuine "works" racer, since a standard production model would be far too slow. In addition, a really top flight rider would have to be engaged if Georg Meier and his BMW were to

be dethroned. The really big problem, however, was money, as Gilera was still unable to expend as much capital as the giant European manufacturers.

Undaunted, Giuseppe tackled the problem with ingenuity and determination to succeed. The Rondine factory was approached, as they had a small four-cylinder engine with a double overhead cam head, water cooling, and supercharging. Giuseppe reasoned that if he could take advantage of an already developed high performance engine, he could save both the time and movey involved in developing one himself. Furthermore, it would take all of Gilera's financial resources to develop a machine capable of handling the phenomenal horsepower and speed that the supercharged engines of the day were capable of producing.

During 1936 the first machine was assembled, and the result was certainly an impressive piece of raceware. The 500cc Rondine engine was mounted partially laid down in the frame with the compressor on top of the crankcase. Since the model was liquid cooled, a radiator was mounted on top of the head between the two front down-tubes of the frame. A gear train drove the two overhead camshafts, the supercharger, and the transmission. Final drive was by chain.

The frame was most unusual. Described as a duplex cradle frame, the top and bottom tubes were very wide and extended to the outside of the transversely mounted engine. The front end had a pressed steel girder fork with friction dampers, and the rear suspension was by an unusual pivoting fork with horizontal spring units. Massive full width brakes and a four-speed gearbox were used.

The performance figures were kept quite hush-hush, and a great amount of secrecy always surrounded the machine. Reliable sources said the Rondine produced 90 hp at 10,000 rpm for a top speed of over 150 mph. Anyone who ever saw the monster in action never doubted that performance rating.

During the spring of 1937 the Gilera was given its first airing and reportedly attained 157 mph. Piero Taruffi was the first to put the new challenger in the news when he upped Jim Guthrie's one-hour Norton record from 114.092 to 121.23 mph.

Development work continued on the racer during the summer, as the handling left something to be desired. Gilera felt his machine was ready by the season's end, though, and Giordano Aldrighetti scored the first big victory by winning the Gran Premio d'Italia at Monza. Aldrighetti followed this up in 1938 by winning the 1200 km. (745.2 miles) Milano-Roman-Napoli-Bari-Taranto race at 73.278 mph, a record which to this day has not been broken.

Giuseppe was grooming another man for the championship circuit, though, a brilliant newcomer named Dorino Serafini. For 1938 young Serafini was merely to learn how to handle the colossal performance of the Rondine and to become familiar with the great classical Grand Prix courses. In championship racing that year a third place in the Dutch GP was the best obtained. Taruffi showed the world what was due the following spring when he upped his one-hour record to 127.5 mph and recorded an all-out speed of 170.15 mph, a new record that stood only a few months as Ernst Henne added 3.53 mph to it with his BMW.

In 1939 the fabulous Gilera came of age, and Serafini won the World Championship with victories in the Grands Prix of Sweden, Ulster (Ireland), and Germany, Taruffi closed out the year for Gilera by placing 23 world records in the books, and the concern also captured the Italian championship. Then came the War.

In 1947 racing resumed again, but the classical superchargers were not to be seen. The Federation Internationale Motocycliste decided that the blower would have to go, and in its place was a formula that specified pump gasoline and atmospheric induction. Italy, like most other European countries, was engaged in rebuilding a war ravaged country, and so Gilera's first post-war competition efforts were quite modest.

In 1946 the pre-war 500cc single was reintroduced called the Saturno, and it was available in either road, moto-cross, or road racing trim. The new thumper was a success in racing as it possessed good brakes, was very light (300 lbs.), and had good acceleration. For the 1946, '47, and '48 seasons the factory team of Nello Pagani, Carlo Bandirola, O. Clemencich, and M. Masserini raced the Saturnos, winning a few Grands Prix but generally having to take a back seat to the faster Nortons.

For the 1949 season a fabulous new 500cc four was fielded for the works team of Nello Pagani and Alberto Artesiani. Designed by Pietro Remor, the new Gilera was air-cooled, and the DOHC engine was mounted transversely in the frame. Girder type forks were used at the front end, and a pivoting-fork suspension at the rear. The final drive was by chain, and the gearbox had four speeds.

During the 1949 racing season the fours proved fast, but improvement was needed in the handling qualities. Pagani did win the Dutch and Monza events on a four, but on the "tighter" courses the fine handling Saturno was also used. For 1950 Umberto Massetti was signed to the team, and he rewarded the factory with the World Championship after a terrific struggle with Geoff Duke.

In 1951 Duke and his new "short-stroke" featherbed Norton got the better of the fours, but in 1952 Massetti was back on top. Duke joined the factory team in 1953 and Gilera became invincible. A master racing technician, Duke provided the knowhow to improve the Gilera's roadability. An orthodox telescopic front fork and swinging arm rear suspension were adopted, a five-speed gearbox used, and great improvements were made in the suspension, brakes, and cornering qualities of the machine. Geoff was World Champion in 1953, '54, and '55, and then sat out half the 1956 season due to an injury and a suspension by the F.I.M.

For 1957 Gilera fielded a superb racing 500cc, and a new stablemate 350 as well. By then the 500 model was producing 70 hp at 10,500, and the 350 churned out 50 hp at 11,000 rpm. Top speeds were about 170 and 150 mph on the two models. Full dustbin streamlining was used (this had been progress-

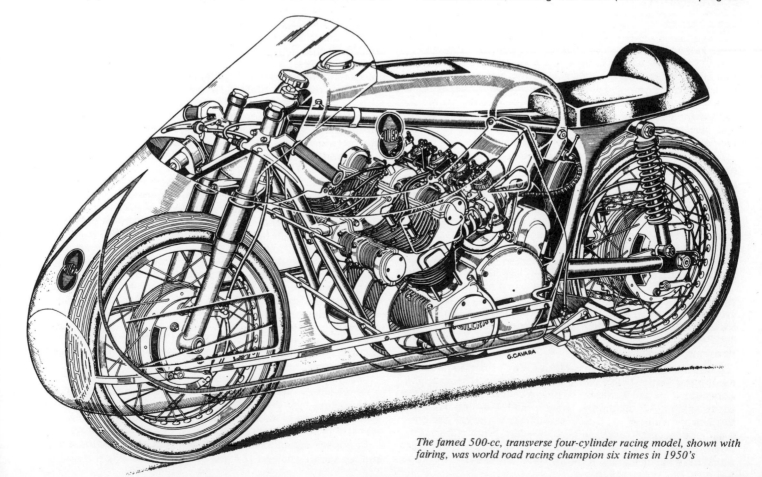

The famed 500-cc, transverse four-cylinder racing model, shown with fairing, was world road racing champion six times in 1950's

Racing's immortal Geoff Duke, left, fits a member of his 1963 racing team behind windscreen of "borrowed" four-cylinder Gilera.

ively developed since 1954) and several sizes of fuel tanks and brakes were available to suit the various courses.

There was no stopping the works team of Bob McIntyre, Libero Liberati, Bob Brown, Geoff Duke, Alano Montanari, and Alfredo Milani. Bob McIntyre started off, in what was destined to be the finest year of post-war Grand Prix racing, by winning both the Junior and Senior TT races, and in the latter he became the first to lap the Isle of Man at over 100 mph.

Every race that year was a fantastic battle with the fully streamlined MV Agustas, Moto Guzzi singles and V-8s, BMW twins, and the Norton and AJS singles all in the show. In the end, the brilliant newcomer Liberati took the Senior class championship, but the Guzzi of Keith Campbell proved too much in the Junior.

To crown a really outstanding year, Gilera then went to the

Benedicto Calderella is shown just prior to 1964 U.S. Grand Prix at Daytona; Argentine rider went out with gearbox troubles.

banked Monza International circuit and set no less than 32 world records. Romolo Ferri was the first to score, and he pushed 123.0 miles into one hour with a 125cc model at a time when the absolute one hour mark was held by the 500cc Norton streamliner at 133.71 mph. Bob McIntyre then took out the 350cc four and upped the hour mark to 141.37 mph, and Albino Milani attached a sidecar and did another hour at 134.4.

The standing start kilometer records were the next to fall, and Alfredo Milani used the 350 and 500 fours to average 96.5 and 106.77 mph for the distance. With sidecars attached Milani clocked 87.0 and 95.0 mph. To climax the week, a new 175cc twin was rolled out and it averaged 129.5 for one hour.

Then it was over-a golden era had come to an end. The F.I.M. imposed severe restrictions on streamlining, and Gilera, along with Moto-Guzzi and F.B. Mondial, retired from the racing game. For 1963 Geoff Duke was lent several of the fabulous fours by the factory, and for a while it looked like the world championship was again destined for Arcore. Derek Minter and John Hartle beat defending champion Mike Hailwood and his MV Agusta into third place at Imola, and halfway through the season Gilera was leading MV in the championship race. Gilera's only real chance at beating Hailwood lay in Minter though, and he was injured early and did not return to top form all season. Mike kept his championship.

For 1964 Gilera depended solely on Benedicto Caldarella, a newcomer from Argentina, who spent the year learning the GP circuits. Benedicto has great talent, but any real chance at a world title will take a determined effort by Gilera-an effort all true motorsportsmen hope the company will make.

MOTO GUZZI

In the great saga of international motorcycle racing there are many colorful chapters, but for pure nostalgia and exotic machinery none can equal the story of the Moto Guzzi. Not a common machine in the Americas, this Italian marque has its home on beautiful Lake Como in northern Italy, and the story of its life is one of the most colorful and intriguing in all the world.

Italy has traditionally been a rather poor country, and the benefits of the industrial revolution were rather late in coming to its people. When mechanization finally came, though, it was carried on with such fervor that Italy's motorcycles became pre-eminent on the European classical road racing courses, as well as being some of the finest in the world for day-to-day transportation. An important part of this rise in industrialization was the legend of the Guzzi-a story that put the Italians on wheels, made the company the best seller in the land, and brought home the prestige of many world championships.

This great legend all began way back in the days of World War I, when Giorgi Parodi and Giovanni Ravelli were flying airplanes in defense of their country and the two flyers' planes were serviced by a young technician named Carlo Guzzi. This particular mechanic could talk about nothing except his dream of building the finest motorbike in all the world. In off-duty hours, Carlo would sketch out his design while the two flyers listened. And Ravelli, being an experienced motorbike racer, voiced the opinion that the design had great merit.

So, after the war, Carlo Guzzi and Giorgi Parodi got together on the project and laid plans for the new G & P motorcycle. The emblem selected for the new make was a Condor with its wings spread wide in flight. This was out of respect for brother Ravelli, who had lost his life in action.

The first problem was to raise the capitol to begin operations, so Parodi went to his father who was a man of some means. The necessary finances were duly obtained (some 2000 lire), and the elder Parodi promised more if the experiments proved successful.

Later, with a few employees, a waterwheel powered lathe, and a lot of determination, the two young industrialists went to work. Their course was quite clear then as Italy produced virtually no motorcycles and her export business was non-existent. In this atmosphere one would think that chief engineer Guzzi would have stuck to orthodox or proven design principles, but this was not the case, and his approach was to be a really fresh one to the problem.

In the December 15th issue of **Motociclismo** the new machine was announced publicly, and the name had been changed to Moto Guzzi. The specifications were rather advanced for those early days, and also very different, but on this design the infant company was to stake its future. The frame and fork were quite standard for those early days, but the single cylinder engine was mounted horizontally in the frame. Not only was that unusual, for the flywheel was mounted outside of the crankcase instead of inside.

The valve gear was the inlet-over-exhaust arrangement, which meant that it had an "overhead" inlet valve and a "side" exhaust valve. The engine capacity was 500cc, and a hand shift and chain drive were featured. The front wheel had no brake and the rear wheel used an internal expanding brake.

One of the principles that has historically been associated with Guzzi has been that racing improves the breed, and so this "La Prima" model received an early baptism. Aldo Finzi is the name that the history books mention with a win at the famous Targo Florio circuit, but it was really the amazing stamina of this new machine that impressed the public.

Not content to sit on his laurels, Carlo kept at his design work, and in 1923 he produced a new overhead valve engine, as well as a production racing machine to go with the standard road model. This new 500cc model also featured the horizontal

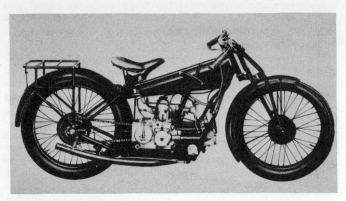

Moto Guzzi "La Prima" – a 1921 model. Engine was inlet-over-exhaust-valve type that proved to be very reliable for its day.

A cobby looking racer was the 1935 wide-angle twin which won the Senior TT. Horsepower was 44 and top speed about 112 mph.

Seldom seen and never raced was 1940 Guzzi 500-cc "three." The war halted development of this potent double-overhead-cam mount.

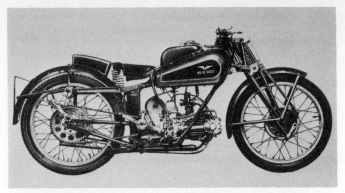

The 1947 Albatross was a very successful 250-cc racer. Note the spring box for the rear suspension mounted beneath the engine.

The 1952 Gambalunghino 250-cc model was the father of the 350-cc models that won world championships in 1953, '54, '56 and '57.

engine with the tiny crankcase and outside flywheel and it, too, was soon entered in the great homeland races to prove the brilliance of its design. And it won, taking trophies at Concorso Di Consumo, Giro d'Italia, Pinerolo-Costagrande, and Del Lario.

These early successes went a long way in proving the genius of this young Ing. Guzzi, and public demand for his products rapidly increased. Once again new designs came off the drawing boards, and this time a 250cc single joined its 500cc older brother. The new engines featured a bevel-gear-driven overhead cam, and four valves were used along with two exhaust pipes. The girder fork was retained on the front and an internal expanding brake was still used on only the rear wheel. The frame was the old "vintage era" type with the gas tank between two top frame tubes and the oil tank mounted on top of that.

These 1924 models were raced with great success in Italy. Then, in September, the Guzzis were prepared for their first international race-the Grand Prix of Europe at Monza. Despite the really fierce opposition from all the leading factories in Europe, the marque scored a smashing victory. Guido Mentasi took first, E. Visioli garnered second, and Pietro Ghersi captured third-a truly remarkable achievement for such a tiny factory.

This great international victory put the company firmly on the map and sales rapidly expanded. For 1925, a new "Peoples Sport" model was introduced which had the I.O.E. type of engine, lights, and a three-speed hand gearshift.

A few years later, in 1928, the engineering progress was really manifest when the 500cc "Sport 14" and "Grand Turismo" models were announced. The engines were a new ohv design with a hemispherical combustion chamber, and much larger fins were used to dissipate the heat. A dynamo was fitted for the lighting system and a magneto was used for ignition. Lastly, internal expanding brakes were finally fitted to both wheels, which made the bike much safer to ride.

A definite attempt was also made to improve rider comfort as a more modern girder fork with both compression and rebound springs was used. It was the Grand Turismo model that really made the news for rider comfort, as it included a method of rear suspension in its specifications. The springing was effected by having a triangulated rear sub-frame which was pivoted at its top joint to the main frame and with the lower arm connected to a long springbox that ran completely underneath the engine. This was probably the first really successful spring frame on a motorcycle, and it was truly a great milestone in engineering progress.

The following year, the factory again made great strides in producing a good machine for the public. Use of the motorcycle for both sport and transportation was on the increase, and the public demanded a more reliable mount that was capable of genuine touring. Guzzi responded with a new range of 250 and 500cc models for 1929, and one of the most notable changes was the new triangulated cradle frame that had the "saddle" type gas tank mounted over the top frame tube with the oil tank beneath the gas tank.

That same year Carlo Guzzi manufactured his first motorcycle-truck combination--a type of machine that is still produced today. The idea was sound, since Italy was still a rather poor country, and this inexpensive method of hauling materials was just the ticket for the businessman.

The furious design improvement pace was maintained, and during the early 1930s many new models were introduced. The 1931 "Sport 15" model proved to be particularly popular; its clean lines were a big improvement over the earlier models. By 1934, a customer had his choice of a 175, 250, or 500cc Guzzis in standard trim, with a spring frame, or to road racing specifications.

The 500cc replica racing model achieved many successes during the late twenties and early thirties in continental grand prix events and national championships, but the marque had failed to score any really big victories that would enhance export sales. The traditional oversquare ohc 500cc single with measurements of 88 x 82mm bore and stroke was pumping out only about 97 mph in 1930, so the factory decided to put more emphasis on some new designs that would set the racing world on fire.

In 1933 the work began on a new 500cc twin that was destined to usher in an exciting new era for the company, as well as take them to the summit of motorcycle racing--the Isle of Man TT. It was not until 1935 that they actually got there, and that year happened to fall in the middle of the era when anyone with any sense at all left the all-conquering Norton strictly unchallenged.

Norton had a famous Scot by the name of Jim Guthrie who piloted his singles with such skill that he simply squashed the opposition into embarrassing second places. Realizing full well that it would take a truly great rider, plus a mighty fast Guzzi, to upset this reigning world champion, the factory hired one Stanley Woods to do the coupe de grace. Stanley was, in his own right, a formidable contender, having won more races and TTs than anyone else, but to trounce the Norton on its home ground was asking quite a bit.

The new Guzzi, though, was quite a racing machine. The basic design was a wide angle (120-degree) V-twin, which was rumored to have offset cranks so that it fired at 180 degrees.

Bevel gears and shafts drove the single overhead cams, and hairpin valvesprings were used. The engine produced about 44 hp at 7,500 rpm for a maximum of 112 mph, which was about equal to the Norton single.

The front fork was an orthodox girder type, but the rear wheel had a very unusual feature for the race track--a type of pivoted-fork suspension. The fork was a triangulated affair similar to that used on the 1928 GT model, but the spring boxes were mounted beneath the rear fork so that the spring unit moved with the fork. A springer had never won a Senior TT, and it was generally agreed that the handling would never be good enough and the whole plot would be unstable at speed. This suspension, incidentally, could have its damping altered during the race by simply moving a lever on the left side of the bike.

The other specs on the twin were equally impressive. A massive brake was fitted to the front wheel which had twin leading shoes, a four-speed footshift gearbox was used, and straight pipes were used instead of megaphones. Another innovation was alloy wheelrims--a move to cut down unsprung weight as well as lessen the revolving weight that the brakes must stop.

And so it was. The race began as everyone thought it would, with Guthrie leading Woods by 28 seconds. On the second lap the margin was 47 seconds, and on the third lap it was 52. Then, on the fourth lap, Stanley began to creep up and the clocks showed only 42 seconds difference. On the fifth it was 29 seconds, and on the sixth it was 26. Still, 26 seconds was a very substantial margin to make up on such a brilliant rider as Guthrie, so it looked like another Norton win.

At the end of the seventh lap Guthrie wheeled in to be acclaimed the winner, the wreath was placed around his neck, champagne was uncorked, and the Island's Governor gave Jim his congratulations. Guthrie, by virtue of his starting number one, was the first to finish, while Woods was well back in the pack on a much later starting interval. So, all there was for Jim to do was to watch Stanley's clock and see just how bad he had him beat.

Then began the drama. Into the last lap went Stanley, his

The 1953 four is shown on record-breaking ride in Hockenheim classic. Note the leading link front fork and shaft drive. The four proved to be unreliable.

torso glued to the top of the tank and the V-twin turned up to a noticeably higher speed. Faster and faster he went, and the revs mounted to 8,000. From curb to gutter the Guzzi was flung and the seconds were slowly pegged back--one by one. Silently in his pits, Jim Guthrie watched as Stanley and the Guzzi gained. Soon he came into sight and screamed past the checkered flag.

It took a few minutes to calculate, but then came the announcement that Stanley had smashed the lap record by nearly four miles per hour on his last lap and so had won the Senior TT by four tiny seconds. Overnight the marque became famous, as Stanley had also won the Lightweight TT on his little single. A new era was born.

Back in Italy, the factory expanded its plant facilities to keep pace with the demand for their products, and soon the roadsters were featuring such race-proven features as footshifts, powerful brakes, speedy ohv engines, and superb roadholding.

In the race shop the midnight oil was burned and many brilliant designs were produced. Probably the most successful was the ohc 250cc single which won many races, as well as setting a speed mark of 132.2 mph in the hands of R. Alberti, and a standing start kilometer record of 25.45 sec. (88.18 mph average) by G. Sandri. This little 250 featured a supercharger, which is one of the few blown singles to ever be successful, and it even scored an astounding first and second place in the 1939 German Grand Prix when Nello Pagani and Sandri trounced the reigning world champion DKWs.

Another blown Guzzi was the 1940 three-cylinder model, a 500cc beast that never saw many races because of World War II. Probably the prettiest of the lot was the 1939 Condor, a 500cc production racer that established a splendid reputation in the hands of private owners. The Condor featured the pivoted-fork rear suspension pioneered on the 1928 GT model--one of the first uses of a spring frame on a production racer.

Then came the war and all motorcycle racing and most motorcycle production was halted in Italy. After the war, the factory was soon into production; and many new street models were produced in sizes ranging from 65cc on up to 500cc. Scooters, motorcycle-trucks, 250cc roadsters, 500cc roadsters, and replica road racers were all manufactured, and the marque's sales hit a new high as exports spread all over the world.

Probably the most popular Guzzi was the 250cc Airone Sport, a race-bred model that provided a spirited 80 mph top speed combined with powerful brakes and a good suspension. The Airone featured an ohv engine with bore and stroke of 70 x 64mm, and the powerplant acquired a reputation of being unburstable.

The 500cc models were the Astore (touring) and the Falcone (a sports model), and these Guzzis were known for their excellent roadholding and tireless high cruising speeds. The Falcone was clocked at 98 mph in European road tests, but few ever made their way to America.

Fabulous 1957 Guzzi V-8 without its streamlined fairing. Despite bulk, weight was only 320 pounds. Horsepower was 75 at 12,000.

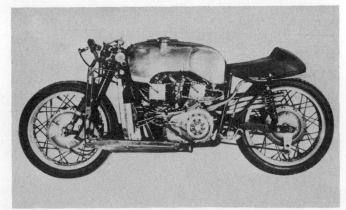

In the late 1950s, the horizontal singles were phased out and new, more modern looking vertical-mounted engines made their debut. These new scooters and bikes up to 250cc have maintained a healthy sales figure and have continued the Guzzi reputation of quality engineering. Realizing that perhaps something was lost when the big singles were dropped, the factory began production in 1965 of a 700cc V-twin, which was originally intended for police use.

The big 700 was enlarged to 750cc in 1969, and a deluxe roadster called the Ambassador was introduced. This luxurious roadster developed 60 hp at 6,500 and ran 115 mph, and its 545 pound weight gave it a very comfortable ride. The quality was exceptional on this model, and it has become a favorite of serious touring riders all over the world.

In an effort to produce an even better "super bike," for 1975 the Italian concern pushed their V-twin out to a brutish 1000cc-a move that made the Guzzi one of the fastest roadsters in the world.

The Ambassador is much too heavy in stock form to be a great performer, but the factory did want to display its good engineering by setting some long distance speed records. They were successful, too, and in June of 1969 Vittorio Brambilla set new 750cc 10 and 100 kilometer marks at 125.6 and 131.9 mph. A one hour mark of 132.9 mph was also established.

In October the team again returned to Monza and set more 750 and 1000cc records--both solo and sidecar. The most impressive were the six and 12 hour marks at 125.76 and 111.53 mph. The sidecar records included the one and six hour marks at 115.64 and 86.99 mph--not bad for a standard pushrod engine!

The marque also resumed racing activities after the war and their successes reached a new high. A new 250, the Albatross, made its debut in 1945, and the model was also sold as a replica racer. The Albatross was a cobby looking little bike with its traditional ohc horizontal engine, unusual pivoted-fork rear suspension, and the girder front fork. The engine turned to 8,000 revs and produced 24 hp, good enough for a speed of 102 mph.

The 250's bigger brother was the Dondolino, a 500cc model that also was available to the private owner. A really great classic of a racing bike, the big single never did achieve the aura of invincibility that surrounded the Albatross. The 250 literally dominated its class in 1947 and 1948, with the 500 scoring a few victories such as the 1947 Swiss and 1948 Ulster classics.

For 1949, the marque once again introduced new singles, both as works and production racers. The new 250 was called the Gambalunghino and the 500 was named the Gambalunga, which meant simply "little long leg" and "long leg." These two bikes continued the Guzzi tradition of winning races. Also raced in those early post-war days was the old V-twin, which had undergone a great deal of development. The twin's power was down to something like 42 at 6,800 rpm, though as the post-war switch from petrol-benzol fuel to just plain "pool" gas forced a drastic lowering of compression ratios.

The twin did not fare too well in those days, as the reliability was not up to the standard of the singles. In the 1948 Senior TT, for instance, Omobono Tenni had a big lead at the end of the fourth lap until one cylinder failed and he toured home in ninth position. Then, in 1949, Bob Foster was way out in front with only a lap and half to go when the clutch gave up. The development work went on, however, and in 1952 the engine was producing 48 hp at 8,000 rpm for a top speed of 129 mph. The twin did gain many good "places" in those years, but the factory decided that the one win in the 1951 Swiss GP was not enough to keep the model in the lineup.

The little 250 single did much better, and its reputation as a winner was sealed with such victories as the 1949, '51, '52 and '53 Lightweight TTs, the World Championship in 1949 (Bruno Ruffo), 1951 (Ruffo), and 1952 (Enrico Lorenzetti), and many hundreds of minor grand prix events. The Gambalunghino, by 1952, was producing 27 hp at 7,500 rpm on its 8.7 to 1 com-

Keith Campbell on his way to victory on 350-cc single in 1957. It weighed only 216 pounds, the 500 only 235. Speeds were 145 and 160 mph.

pression ratio, and this was good enough for a 109 mph top end. The little racer was noted for its fine handling, its unique feature of the gas tank being streamlined for the rider's arms, the leading-link front fork, a massive front brake, and the horizontal engine with its outside flywheel.

About that time the leading designer at the factory, Ing. Giulio Carcano, decided to join the Italian trend to four cylinders--only with a difference--as the Guzzi four had the engine mounted in line with the frame. Shaft drive and water-cooling were adopted, as was a partial "dolphin" type of fairing. The new four had a very advanced dohc head with fuel injection, and four short straight pipes were used. The four was very fast and it won its first race at Hockenheim in 1953 when Lorenzetti romped home at an average speed of 107.8 mph. After that initial success the four turned out to be totally unreliable and it was soon dropped.

A far more successful chapter was the quest of the 1953 World Championship in the Junior (350cc) Class. Fergus Anderson was on the team then, and, after his record breaking rides in the 1952 and 1953 Lightweight TTs, he urged Carcano to scale up his 250 into a 350. The first step was to increase the 68 x 68mm engine to a 72 x 80 mm size, which gave 320cc. This move was eminently successful and Fergus garnered a third in the Junior TT and then a win at Hockenheim.

Justifiably encouraged, the factory enlarged the engine in mid-season to a 75 x 79mm 350, and power was thus raised from 28.5 at 8,400 rpm to 31 at 7,700. The weight of this Junior model was very light 264 pounds, and the maximum speed was an amazing 130 mph. This terrific speed on only 31 hp was due to another great Guzzi engineering achievement--streamlining. The racers that year showed the results of many hours spent in the wind tunned on airflow studies, and the full "dustbin" fairing gave excellent air penetration. On this speedy 350, Fergus Anderson easily won the World Championship.

For 1954, the valve sizes were increased to 37mm for the inlet and 32mm for the exhaust, a 35mm carburetor was fitted, and the compression ratio was 9.5 to 1. Power output was 33.5 at 7,500 rpm. Anderson was again successful and one more World Championship came home to Mandello del Lairo.

In 1955, the brilliance of Ing. Carcano was once again manifest when the racers appeared with a new and very light "space" frame that was designed to fit the dustbin fairing. The engine was also modified to a 80mm bore and a 69.5 stroke, the valves enlarged to 41 and 36mm, and the carburetor increased to 37mm. The head featured two spark plugs, battery ignition replaced the magneto, and the compression ratio was 9.4 to 1. And then, lastly, the head was modified to a double overhead cam setup; all these improvements helped boost power to 35 at 7,800 rpm.

Bill Lomas was the first-string rider for 1955 and 1956 and he easily won the 350cc world titles, but on the tighter courses the new engine had actually lapped slower than the old long stroke engine. Ing. Carcano once again made some changes for 1957 when he went back to the 75 x 79mm measurements with 39 and 33mm valve sizes. One spark plug was used and ignition was by a magneto. Power output was up to 38 at 8,000 rpm and the medium speed torque was much improved. The weight of these racers was fantastically light, with the 350 weighing only 216 pounds and a larger 500 model just 20 pounds more.

Carcano's genius, however, did not end here, for he was hard at work designing the fastest road racing motorcycle that the world had ever seen. First raced in 1956, it was not until 1957 that the world found out just how fast this new 500 was. The basic design was a dohc 90-degree V-8 with the tiny measurements of 44 x 41mm bore and stroke. Eight 20mm carburetors were used as were eight short exhaust pipes, and water-cooling was also employed.

The engine was mounted transversely in the frame and chain drive was used. The frame was similar to that used since 1953 on all Guzzi racers, with a swinging-arm rear suspension and leading-link front fork. Massive brakes were fitted to cope with the colossal speed. The weight was actually quite light at 320 pounds, but the sheer bulk of the bike made it appear much heavier.

It is only natural that many teething troubles cropped up on such a complex machine, and lap records, rather than race records, fell to the V-8. The horsepower in 1956 was listed as

62 at 12,000 rpm, which provided a 162 mph top end on a 6.1 to 1 gear ratio. This speed, however, was with the dolphin-type of streamlining, and it was not until one year later that the fabulous eight was to truly show its speed.

The venue was the beautiful Spa-Francorchamps course in Belgium, which is terribly fast with its 100 mph corners and long straights. Keith Campbell, fron Australia, was the first-string rider that year, and his skill was never in doubt, as he had already trounced the best in the 350cc class. But would the new V-8 hold together long enough to actually win a race?

The flag fell and away went the field with such stars as Libero Liberati on his Gilera, John Surtees, MV Agusta; and Walter Zeller, BMW. It was soon apparent that the 75 hp the V-8 developed, combined with the full dustbin fairing, gave Campbell the speed he needed to sear through the field and take the lead. On and on Keith rode, smashing the lap record again and again, until he turned in his finest hour with a 118.56 mph lap. Then, just after he was clocked at a fantastic 178 mph on the fast Masta straight, Campbell came to a halt with gear-box trouble.

And so ended the last great chapter of the fabulous Moto Guzzi V-8, for little did the half-million spectators know that an era was ended. For at the season's end, the beloved racing Guzzis, along with their World Champion brothers, the 125 and 250cc Mondial and 500cc Gilera, announced that they were withdrawing from racing. It seemed impossible at first that Guzzi could really mean this, for their heritage of racing since 1921 was one of the greatest and certainly among the most colorful, that has ever existed.

We realize now, of course, that the real cause for thier decision was not within their control. As Italy prospered in the post-war economy her people switched from motorbikes to cars, and this does not help a motorcycle company's profits any. It takes great sales and huge profits to design a modern-day racing bike and then take it all over the world to do battle.

Sadly, it all came to an end. The men, the great races, and the romantic machines--it is all just a legend now. But while it lived it was one of the really fascinating stories of our century, and the uninhibited engineering and beautifully exotic racing bikes will probably never be equaled.

From 1921 through 1957--a truly remarkable record. For their honor, I list it below:

International Racing Victories	3,329
World Speed Records	134
Italian Championships	47
National Championships	55
TT Victories	11
World Championships	14

In 1952 Gino Cavanna sped to a 137.38 mph sidecar record with this sidecar rig in which the passenger rode behind the driver. The blown 250 developed 38 HP at 7800 rpm.

This 1965 Stornello 125cc single was typical of the new look of the Guzzis in the 1960s. Every inch a quality product.

The 1945 Dondolino 500cc OHV racing single was a cobby looking 110 mph model. Notice the outside flywheel and unique rear suspension.

The 1952 Falcone 500cc single was known for its fine handling and powerful brakes. The 90 mph single is now a collector's item.

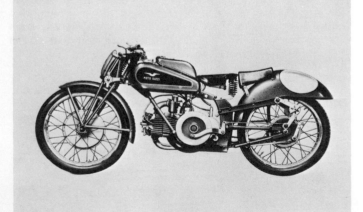

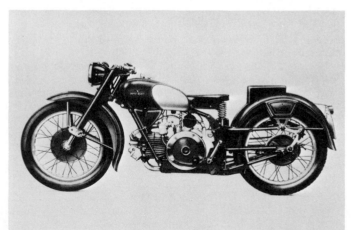

NORTON

James Norton started his company very humbly in 1898, but it was not to stay that way for long as the name was destined to become the very symbol for excellence in motorcycle design. Winner of 34 TTs, many hundreds of major Grands Prix, and literally thousands of local races all over the world, the Norton is certainly the greatest name in the history of motorcycle racing.

Born in 1869 in Birmingham, England, James Lansdowne Norton was one of the truly great pioneers of the motorcycle industry. For the first twenty-five years of this century his genius at engineering and production methods helped put the British industry at the very top, and when he died in the spring of 1925 his company was destined to help carry on British supremacy of international sales and racing competition throughout half the century.

Norton launched his little company in 1898, and for the first few years he concentrated on making a 1-⅓ hp single, and a host of propietary parts for other motorbike manufacturers. Norton did not build his own engines in those early days, but relied instead on the French Clement, the Moto-Reve from Switzerland, and the V-twin French Puegeot. It was on one of the latter that Norton scored their first TT win, with Rem Fowler up in 1907 in the twin-cylinder class.

"Pa" Norton was hard at work on his own engine design though, and in 1908 the "Big Four" was introduced--a single of 633cc with a bore and stroke of 82mm x 120mm. This side-valver was later stable-mated with a 500cc model with measurements of 79mm x 100mm--measurements which were to become legend with Norton.

These early thumpers proved very popular. They were one of the most reliable motorbikes on the road, and the reputation of Norton was sealed. The models were steadily improved, and several gearboxes were tried as Norton was a great advocate in those days of two and three-speed countershaft gearboxes. All this, remember, was at a time when nearly everyone else used only a single speed belt drive.

It was apparent to James Norton that the real future lay with the over head valve engine design, and in the years just prior to World War I he drew up the plans for his new OHV engine. The factory still relied on their 500cc side-valve models for racing after the war, however, for it would take a few years to prove the merits of the new engine. The 1920 side-valve TT machine was no slow poke either, as it was by then capable of 75 mph at 4,300 rpm on its 5.25 to 1 gear ratio.

In 1922 the OHV engine was given its first airing, and the 500cc model retained the same 79 x 100mm measurements of its forebearer. In 1923 the new model hit the headlines with two records: the one hour mark at 82.67 mph, and the flying kilometer at 89.22 mph. From then on the OHV engine was used exclusively for racing, although the side-valve model stayed popular many years as a roadster.

Pride of "Pa" Norton, 1910 single was the machine that made the reputation of the young company. Reliability was exceptional.

The original CS 1 model of 1927 with Alec Bennett in the saddle.

Harold Daniell on his 1938 Norton after winning Tourist Trophy.

Development work on the OHV engine became intensive, and for 1924 a "works team was signed on to race. Alec Bennett handsomely rewarded the factory with the Senior TT trophy at the record speed of 61.64 mph. Alec's mount featured an engine with a 6 to 1 compression ratio that was capable of nearly 100 mph on its 4.2 to 1 gear ratio. The bike had a three-speed gearbox and all-chain drive (the belt drive had been dropped in 1914). Complete with fuel and oil it weighed 315 pounds.

From 1923 through 1926 the OHV models were well nigh invincible on the local tracks, and they also scored many international racing victories. This racing fame plus the top flight engineering and workmanship of the Norton put them into an enviable sales position. The concern expanded rapidly during the twenties and exported machines all over the world.

The depression of the early thirties slowed things down a bit, but by the mid-thirties sales were climbing again and Norton became one of the world's leading machines. By 1936 the concern produced no less than 13 models, from 350cc to 633cc. The models all had rigid frames, girder forks, and one-cylinder engines.

For general touring at a low initial cost the side-valve models in 500 and 633cc sizes were available and these bikes were particularly popular for sidecar work. For more spirited riding there were six OHV models in 350cc, 500cc and 596cc sizes. These OHV models used the same basic engine design laid down by James Norton in 1913, and this design was retained until 1964-a tribute to his engineering genius.

A special trials model was also devised with an upswept exhaust pipe, a special frame for more ground clearance, a folding kick starter, wide ratio gearbox, smaller gas tank, and narrow fenders. This trials model established a great reputation and on many occasions some members of the victorious British International Six Days Trial team were mounted on Nortons.

The models that really excited the sporting man were the four overhead camshaft machines, two for racing and two for high speed roadwork. The 350cc C.J. and 500cc C.S. 1 models had been introduced in the early thirties, both featuring a single OHC engine which had a cast iron cylinder and head. The cycle parts were built to a "sports" specification for fast touring which, along with the higher cost, meant that these fast roadsters were for the experienced rider,

The 384cc and 490cc International models were intended for racing, although lights were fitted, and either bike was as fine a racing mount as was then available. Bore and stroke dimensions were 71 x 88mm on the 350, and 79 x 100mm on the 500. A large 3-¾ gallon fuel tank was used and the oil tank was also much larger than standard. The engine could be purchased with an alloy cylinder and head, and the carburetor and magneto were of the TT type.

The gearboxes were close ratio, the 500 being 4.4, 4.9, 5.9, and 7.8 to 1. The 350 model had ratios of 5.2, 5.7, 6.8, and 9.2 to 1. A special racing rear seat was included, and the handlebars, seats, footpegs, brakes (7 in. x 1-¼ in.), fenders, and controls were all designed for road racing.

The International was continuously developed; in 1938 it acquired a plunger suspension on the rear end, and in 1947 a hydraulically dampened telescopic fork was used on the front. After the War the C.J. and C.S. 1 models were dropped, the International became the high speed roadster, and the new Manx model became the pukka racer.

In 1949 Norton introduced their twin--a sleek 500cc model with a plunger frame and telescopic front fork. The 500 was developed into a 600 during the early 1950s, and then on into a full 650 in the middle 1950s. The twin grew some more in the early 1960s to a fast 750, which has endured to this day. In 1969 the now famous Commando was introduced with its rubber mounted engine, and this beast has done well in production model and endurance races due to its stamina and speed.

During the 1950s the OHV and OHC 350 and 500cc singles were very popular--the former for their reliability and the later for their speed, stamina, and fine handling. With the introduction of the swinging-arm frame in 1953, the OHC International model became a superb mount for the sportsman, and it won many Clubman and production model races.

Norton failed to improve their "Inter", though, and by 1958 other sports models had a definite superiority. Norton decided to drop their classical single rather than fight back, and a great era came to its end. The pushrod thumpers were continued into the 1960s, but then they, too, were dropped from production. Norton then tried a 400cc electric starter model for the sophisticated rider in the middle 1960s, but this proved to be a dismal failure. After a financial failure at the factory, the company was purchased by the huge Manganese Bronze

J. H. "Crasher" White at speed in 1939 Senior TT. Note massive finning of cylinder and head, early non-hydraulic telescopic fork.

Holdings concern and renamed Norton-Villiers. The Commando soon followed, and sales once again were on the rise.

The real story of Norton is not its roadsters though, but rather the history of its racing team. The real pulse-throbbing saga of Norton is racing, so let's go back to 1927 during the golden era of International Grand Prix racing when Walter Moore decided that an overhead camshaft engine was the only answer.

The new engine had a single camshaft which was driven by a vertical shaft between two sets of bevel gears, one set on the mainshaft and one set on the camshaft. The bore and stroke remained at 79 x 100mm, and the engine was mounted in a new cradle frame.

During 1927 and 1928 the OHC engine was used alongside the pushrod model, but the cammer proved the better of the two. Alec Bennett took the Senior TT in 1927, and Stanley Woods made a record lap at 70.99 mph. Woods also won the Grands Prix of Belgium, Holland and Switzerland, finishing second in the German, and third in the Ulster. Bert Denly garnered a whole lot of records that year, including the classic hour mark at 100.58 mph and the 500cc flying kilometer at 109.22 miles per hour.

The successful 500 was joined by a new 350 in 1928, with a bore and stroke of 71 x 88mm. Norton's fortunes declined sharply for a few years then, as a great amount of development work was needed on the camshaft engines, and also because Rudge and Sunbeam were reaping their rewards of years of development on their OHV racers.

Things looked up in 1930 when Arthur Carroll took over the racing department after Walter Moore went to NSU. The exhaust pipe was moved from the left side to the right, the lower bevel gear chamber was redesigned to a box affair, and the cylinder and head were improved. Woods won several GPs that year, while the design work went on.

For 1931 the carburetor was down draft slightly; a 14mm spark plug was used, a four-speed gearbox replaced the three-speed version, and the semi-slipper type aluminum piston made its appearance. Nortons began their ascendancy of championship racing that year with Stanley Woods and Tim Hunt winning no less than ten GP events, plus Hunt's double in the TT.

In 1932 with the fuel tanks enlarged, the full seven laps of the Isle of Man could be covered with only one refueling stop,

and the girder front forks carried a new method of damping, using two small auxiliary springs instead of the usual friction dampers. Nortons really came into their own that year winning seven out of eight of the classic races in the senior class, and five of eight in the junior class.

More improvements were made to the works bikes for 1933; most notable was the adoption of an aluminum alloy cylinder and head. The cylinder had a cast iron sleeve and the head had the alloy fins cast onto a bronze "skull." The team that year consisted of Woods, Hunt, and Jimmy Simpson, who between them won just about everything, with Woods taking the Junior-Senior TT double for the second year in a row.

By 1934 the engines had hairpin valve springs, megaphone exhausts, two spark plugs, twin-spark magnetos, and "bolt through" fuel tanks. The team that year was Walter Rusk, Jimmy Guthrie, Jimmy Simpson and Walter Handley, and they took just about everything except the Senior class Ulster and Swedish GPs.

The 1935 models differed little from the previous year, and Rusk, Guthrie, and J.H. White kept up the winning pace. The only disappointments were in the Senior TT when ex-team member Woods on his Moto Guzzi beat Guthrie by four tiny seconds, and several Junior class events which went to their arch rival, the Velocette. Guthrie capped the year by setting a new one hour record of 114.092 mph at Montlhery.

It was during those years that Grand Prix racing was truly in its golden era, and understandably the Norton was having to face increasingly tougher opposition. Spurred by this, Norton made some major design changes in their 1936 works bikes. A new frame was used which had the plunger type of rear suspension, the remote float chamber was rubber mounted, and the cylinder bore was increased to bring the engine up to 499cc.

A brilliant newcomer named Fred Frith joined White and Guthrie that year. Between them they captured nearly all the Senior races, losing only the Swedish to BMW. In the Junior class they were not quite as successful as in previous years, but the team still was able to win five out of the nine classic events.

The spring of 1937 revealed more design changes on the works bikes, with the most notable being the engine. A new head featured double overhead camshafts was used, which had a train of five gears to drive the cams from the upper bevel gears. The dual spark plugs were dropped, the finning of the head and cylinder increased, and the valves and springs were still left exposed for cooling.

The Nortons that year proved fast, and Frith, Guthrie and White dominated the TT races with Frith turning his last lap at 90.27 mph. This was the first time the course had been lapped at over the 90 mark. The team fared less well on the continent, picking up only three out of nine Senior class events, but still gaining sufficient points to edge out BMW for the Championship. In the Junior class they finally went under to the Velocette, and Norton was destined not to win this back for fourteen years.

Engineering effort then became intense, and for 1938 there were many splendid technical improvements. The most noticeable was the fitting of a telescopic fork at the front which had main and rebound springs but no hydraulic damping. Massive conical wheel hubs were cast from magnesium alloy with ribbed brake drums, and air scoops were provided for cooling.

In an effort to obtain greater rpm and horsepower, the stroke was shortened from 100mm to 94mm on the five hundred, and from 88mm to 77mm on the 350. The bores were opened up from 79 to 82mm and 71 to 76mm on the two engines. The finning was again increased on the head and it acquired that square look which was so appealing to the technical minded. Larger bore carburetors were fitted, with the 500 having a 1-15/16 inch venturi. The Senior mount was said to produce 50 bhp at 6,800 rpm for a top speed of 120 to 125 mph. These were truly magnificent racing machines for their day, but then they had to be because their supercharged competition was crowding 150 mph.

For the Senior TT that year Harold Daniell had joined the team. He carried off the trophy at 89.11 mph, and set a 91.0 mph record on his last lap that was destined to stand for 12 years. On the continent the team was faced with rather fearful opposition, as Georg Meier had nearly double the horsepower in his supercharged BMW. The Britishers fought back valiantly, but in the end Meier's speed proved too much. Their only continental victory was in the Swiss GP where better handling paid off on the torturous corners of the course.

There was little change in the 1939 machines, but Frith's 350 had a bore and stroke of 73.3 x 82.5mm and these dimensions were adopted for the post-war works 350s. Norton failed to win the TT races that year, and on the Grand Prix trail they took a bad drubbing from the blown Gilera and BMW in the Senior class and from the Velocette and supercharged DKW two-stroke in the Junior.

When racing was resumed after the war supercharging was abolished, so the Nortons were again back in contention. Pre-war machines were used with small design improvements. In 1948 the front brake was modified to a twin leading shoe assembly, and in 1949 the riding position was lowered by using 19 in. wheels and shortening the front forks.

Despite the antiquity of the bikes, they returned to their winning form of the mid-thirties, and Harold Daniell, Ernie Lyons, Johnny Lockett, and Artie Bell were the men to beat in the Senior class racing. Daniell carried off the Senior TT in 1947 and '49, and Bell took the Senior in 1948. Irishman Artie also dominated the 1947 and '48 Grand Prix scenes and won the Championship for Norton. In the Junior class their 350 was not fast enough and they generally had to be content with runnerup positions to the Velocette.

While it is true that Norton won the 1949 Senior TT, the rest of the season was a different story as the AJS "Porcupine," the new Gilera fours, and the Guzzi simply outsped them. In fact, in the season's final race over the fast Monza course the team could not even get into the first six places!

It was obvious that the old veteran works bike was obsolete, so for 1950 an entirely new mount made its appearance. The famous Irish racing brothers, Cromie and Rex McCandless, had been successfully experimenting with a swinging arm frame for their Nortons, and so they were duly invited to help Joe Craig design the new racer.

The swinging-arm frame "Featherbed" Norton was born, and so successful was it that it was used on the 1951 production Manx model. The mechanical genius of Joe Craig plus the brilliant riding of newcomer Geoff Duke began to make itself felt, and Norton swept the first three places in the Junior and Senior TT's. On the continent the opposition was a bit tougher. Duke was edged out by Umberto Massetti (Gilera) for Senior Class honors, but the team did manage to win the manufacturer's championship.

By 1951 there was just no stopping Duke, and he won nine out of a possible sixteen races in the Junior and Senior

The immortal Ray Amm on the last of the factory Nortons, this one equipped with one of the "ant-eater" fairings. Norton won the Senior TT in 1954.

Last of the "Garden Gate" Manx Nortons, the 1950 model.

This 1964 650-cc Norton twin won British Thruxton 500-mile race.

classes. It was in 1952 that more changes were made to the racers with the engine receiving the most attention. Bore and stroke were changed to 75.9 x 77mm on the 350, and to 85.93 x 86mm on the 500 with much larger valves and carburetors fitted. These modifications were subsequently adopted on the production Manx, except with measurements of 76 x 76.7mm and 86 x 85.6mm on the two models. Nortons again swept the TT races, but on the continent they had to settle for only the Junior Championship (Duke) as the 500 Gilera was just too fast that year.

In 1953 Geoff Duke left Norton for Gilera, and a new team comprised of Ray Amm (Southern Rhodesia), Ken Kavanagh (Australia) and Jack Brett (England) carried on the battle. The dogged oourage of Amm pald off in both of the TT races, but for the balance of the season the Gilera and Guzzi proved much too fast. The factory did have the satisfaction of a world record though, when Amm used their low streamlined "kneeler" to set a one hour mark of 133.71 mph.

It was obvious that more speed was needed if Norton was to have a chance, so a completely new engine was designed. The 500 and 350 became oversquare with a bore and stroke of 90 x 78.4mm and 78 x 73mm on the two models. The connecting rod was shortened, and an outside flywheel used. The engine coupled to a new five-speed gearbox, and several types of fairings were used depending on the course.

On these superb racing singles Amm won the Senior TT in appalling weather conditions and also set a Junior lap record of 94.61 mph before retiring. In the Grand Prix chase he put up a courageous battle, taking the Ulster Junior and Senior and the 350cc German GP. It was too much to defeat Gilera and Guzzi in their heyday though, and Ray was forced to settle for a lesser spot.

Then it was announced in 1955 that Norton was officially withdrawing from genuine works Grand Prix racing. The reason given was that the pukka GP bikes were getting too far removed from production practice, and Norton would concentrate only on their standard Manx model. This was a pity, because although Joe Craig was still full of fight, his horizontal single and, yes, even his drawing board four had to be shelved. Truly, an era was ended.

The factory had a team for a few more years which was mounted on the standard 500 and 350cc Manx models with a bore and stroke of 86 x 85.8mm and 76 x 76.85mm. The Manx continued its great reputation as the best production junior and senior mount available, and the marque was even to win two more TTs in 1961 when the lone MV Agusta in each race retired.

In late 1963 it was announced that production of the Manx had ceased, and the factory's only interest in competition was the production machine class where the big 650-750cc twins have established a fine reputation.

Something has been lost though, and maybe it shall never return. The lusty bellow of the Manx in full flight on the drop down to Creg-ny-Baa, the luster of such names as Woods, Guthrie, Frith, Daniell, Duke, Amm, McIntyre--this is real history, the kind that just fills the cup full of nostalgia. They say the single is dead, which may or may not be true, but while it lived it was great.

This 1947 500cc International has an "iron" engine, but an alloy cylinder and head were optionally available. The top speed was 95-100 mph.

The 1960 ES-2 was a sleek 90 mph 500cc single with an engine similar to the 1935 model.

NSU

Sawdust, plaster of paris, and sewing machines may not seem to have much to do with the motorcycle industry, but nevertheless these commodities had a great deal to do with the early days of the German NSU concern. The story began way back in 1873 when two engineers, Christian Schmidt and Heinrich Stoll, joined forces to manufacture and repair sewing and knitting machines.

On a small island in the Danube River by a little town named Riedlingen, they set up shop with an old English made lathe and a waterwheel to provide the power. The little business produced a good "Strickmaschinen" for the local "Hausfrau," and the company prospered to such an extent that a move was made in 1874 to a larger factory at Reutlingen. Here, the partners parted company, Heinrich remaining with the original

This sturdy looking NSU is typical of the larger German bikes of the thirties. A 500-cc side-valve model, it dates from 1935.

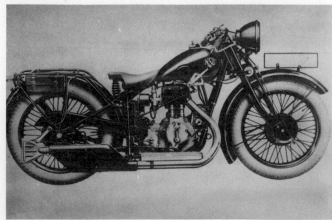

sewing machine and Christian going on to Neckarsulm. Schmidt located an old plaster of Paris mill, which had also been a sawmill, and here he settled down to produce his own sewing machine.

Schmidt had another goal, however, and this was to produce a bicycle, as the two-wheeled craze was sweeping the country. Christian never lived to see his dream come true, for he died just four years later after getting his NSU concern on its financial feet. It was then left to his brother-in-law, Gottlob Banzhaf, to bring out the new NSU bicycle in 1886.

The following years, Gottlob got the factory humming and the NSU bicycles and parts sold abundantly. About the turn of the century there was much excitement over the internal combustion engine being applied to transportation, and Banzhaf was caught up in the fever. Already in the bicycle business, it was only natural that he would have a bash at producing a motorbike. This he did in 1900 by attaching a Swiss-made 1¾ hp engine to his bicycle. Altogether, about 100 of these crude motorbikes were produced.

The improvement of their product began immediately, and in 1902 a heavier frame was adopted to cope with horsepower instead of human muscle power, and a spray-type carburetor replaced the earlier drip-feed unit. Another NSU first in that early year was a reliable magneto ignition, a device which enabled an NSU to cover the surprising mileage of 1,600 miles without a breakdown.

In 1903, the company produced an all NSU machine with a 2 hp engine designed by Christian Schmidt's son, Karl. The new model proved reliable and production soared to 2,228. This model was followed in 1905 by a water-cooled 4 hp NSU, and then some V-twins of 3, 3½, 5, and 5½ horsepower. Sales expanded and so did the factory.

The next innovations of note were the trailing-link front fork in 1905, which gave a much softer ride than the previous rigid

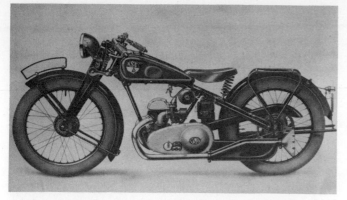

A lighter two-stroke, this 200-cc 1934 NSU was known for its reliability. Power output was 7 hp and top speed was 53 mph.

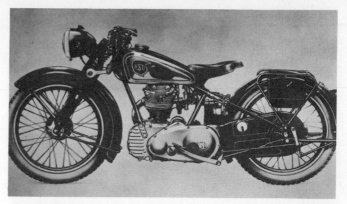

The NSU 251 OSL touring machine first came on the market in 1936. Power output was 10.5 hp. Development continued for many years.

forks; then a telescopic spring dampened leading-link fork in 1906; and lastly, a two-speed engine hub assembly that provided a gear for both hills and level road. In 1906 the company also entered the "light" car field with three- and four-wheel vehicles of 10 and 24 hp.

In 1907 the first Isle of Man TT race was held, and the factory sent Martin Geiger over to uphold homeland honors, as the British were good customers of NSU motorbikes. Geiger had a trouble-free run that day and finished in fifth positions--NSU's first racing success. The following year the concern sold its first production racing machine, a rigid forked lightweight model with an astounding 1½ hp to propel it!

In 1908 the factory also brought out some V-twin engines of 2½ hp on up to 7½ hp. On one of the larger jobs a fellow by the name of Liese recorded a speed of 108.5 kph (68 mph) which was claimed to be a world record for its day, although no official records were kept in those early days of the sport. The following year Otto Lingenfelders clocked his NSU at 124 kph (77.5 mph) on a road near Los Angeles, California, and the NSU folks once again claimed the title of world's fastest.

With an expanding export business, the factory was encouraged, and they listed a 4 hp single in 1909 with a bore and stroke of 82 x 105mm. A two-speed rear hub was used which contained an internal expanding brake. This brake deserves particular note, as the British did not generally adopt this method of stopping until the middle 1920's.

With a continued expansion of export sales, the NSU factory proceeded to introduce many new models with fine engineering achievements. In 1911, a method of rear suspension was produced, and a 6 hp V-twin had all chain drive with a three-speed gearbox and plate clutch. For 1912 the pushrod and rocker type of overhead valve engine was introduced, a truly great milestone in European engineering history. Then, in 1914, the "ultimate" NSU was available with a powerful 1,000cc 9 hp engine that provided speeds to 60 mph and with a total weight of only 300 lbs.

Then came the Kaiser's war and the NSU factory was converted to military production. During the war the factory produced a 1½ hp lightweight called the "Pony," and this model formed the basis of a 2 hp utility mount after the war. The effect of war on NSU was extensive, and it was not until 1922 that the factory really got back on its feet again when 3,000 people were employed. The models produced were basically the pre-war machines until 1924, when a completely new "unit-construction" line came off the drawing boards. The first model was a 2 hp side-valve single that was available with either a two or three speed gearbox and belt drive. A four hp twin was next, and then an 8 hp twin, and these sleek speedsters had all-chain drive.

Aiming for the utility market, the "Kriegspony" was next produced, and this inexpensive lightweight featured such niceties as a clutch, a weight of only 160 lbs., a top speed of 38 mph, and a gas mileage of over 100 mpg. In 1929, the company pioneered "line" production in their factory, and the sales once again began an expansion. Walter Moore also joined NSU that

year, and this Englishman is the man who designed the original overhead camshaft racing Norton. Was this a hint of things to come from NSU?

The answer was not long in coming, and almost overnight the NSU folks were "smack dab" in the middle of the racing game. The first racing model off More's drawing boards was the overhead-cam single, produced in 350, 500, 600, and 700cc sizes. The new racer was a cobby looking model, with a single cam actuating a pair of rockers. Hairpin valve-springs were used for valve control, and the Amal racing carburetor had a slight downdraft angle. The cam drive was by a vertical shaft and bevel gears, and ignition was by a Bosch magneto.

The engine was mounted in a single-loop cradle frame, and the girder fork at the front was the only method of suspension. A footshift gearbox was used, and the brakes were husky units with aluminum alloy hubs. The wraparound oil tank was similar to that used on the British Nortons, and the long fuel tank was hand-hammered aluminum alloy.

The works racing team consisted of Britisher Tommy Bullus and German Heiner Fleischmann. The new NSU racer proved to be fast, but not quite fast enough to challenge the top British marques. About the only really significant success attained was by Bullus in the 1930 Grand Prix of Italy, where he scored a suprising victory.

Then followed the worldwide economic depression, and this catastrophe hurt Germany more than most other countries. Always practical, NSU turned their efforts from playing with expensive racing machines to produce a cheap utility motorbike. The first was the 63cc Motosulm, which might be considered to be the ancestor of the 1965 Quickly model. The little two-stroke engine was mounted on the front fork and it drove the front wheel through a clutch and chain. Car production ceased at NSU and the full plant facilities were turned to producing this popular little motorbike.

Sleek 250-cc Max is still popular in Germany because of 80-mph performance and reliability. Overhead cam is driven eccentrically.

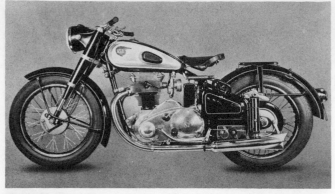

The 1957 NSU 500-cc single was a clean looking model with plunger frame. The 80 x 99-mm engine developed 21 hp at 5200 rpm.

The next new NSU was a Walter Moore designed moped in 1936. This little jewel, named the "Quick," sold no less than 235,000 units. As Germany recovered from the depression it was only natural that larger, more expensive models would be produced, and so during 1935 and 1936 the range of NSUs that were produced rapidly expanded. One of the most popular models was the ZDB, a 200cc two-stroke of unfailing reliability. The ZDB produced a healthy 7 hp for a 53 mph top speed. The little two-stroke had a rigid frame and girder front fork.

The next, more expensive NSUs were the 350 and 500cc Tourensport models. These sportsters had single-cylinder ohv engines with a bore and stroke of 75 x 79mm on the 350 and 80 x 99mm on the 500. The horsepower was 18 and 22 on the two models, developed at 5,200 rpm on a 6 to 1 compression ratio. The gear ratios for the 350 model were 15.4, 10.2, 6.9, and 5.8 to 1; and on the 500 model they were 13.2, 8.8, 5.9, and 4.95 to 1. Gear shifting was done by hand; this was common practice on the European continent in the middle 1930s.

Then, for the sidecar enthusiast, there was the big 600cc side-valve model which produced a beefy 16 hp with lots of low speed torque. There also was available a 500cc model which developed 12.5 hp. The bore and stroke of the larger motor were 87.5 x 99mm and the 500 had the same measurements as the ohv version.

In 1938, the range was expanded to include a brutishly powerful 600cc ohv model, which developed 24 hp on a 6 to 1 compression ratio. The big 600 still had no method of rear suspension, though, and the girder fork was retained at the front. As with the other NSU models, the engine and gearbox were in one unit case, making for a clean looking design.

It was during the mid-1930s that NSU again became interested in racing, probably because it was the first time since the depression that they could afford to participate. Their old single was sadly lacking in speed, compared to the all-conquering Nortons and Velocettes, so a new engine was produced. During 1937 a double-overhead-cam single was raced by Heiner Fleischmann, which was actually just the older engine with a twin cam head and other improvements. The single proved to be too slow to have any chance at victory, and so a new design was thought up.

In the Spring of 1938 the new racer came forth from the race shop, and what a speedster it was. The major feature was a supercharged double ohc twin in 350cc size, but a 500cc model was soon added to the stable. The horsepower claimed was fantastic, with 65 hp at 8,500 rpm being wrung from the 350 and 90 hp from the 500 at 8,000 rpm. The bore and stroke of the two engines was 56 x 70.5mm and 63 x 80mm.

The double cams were driven by two vertical shafts with bevel gears, and the heads were cast of aluminum alloy with shrunk-in valve seats. Both pistons rose and fell together, and the lower end featured roller bearings throughout. The finned crankcases were vertically parted on the centerline of each cylinder, and a central main bearing was used on the crankshaft. The centric type supercharger was driven by chain.

The rather massive engine-gearbox unit was housed in a duplex cradle frame which had a boxed plunger rear suspension. The front fork was a girder type, and massive air-cooled brakes were housed in alloy hubs. The fuel tank was a huge alloy affair that had a high hump to clear the engine. The weight was naturally rather high at 440 and 486 lbs. on the two models, but a lot of this weight was fuel; the models gulped the petrol-benzol at a fantastic rate. The actual dry weight of the 350 was rumored to be only 369 lbs., which gives an idea of the fuel load.

Out on the grand prix courses the results were not very rewarding. The weight plus the high center of gravity hurt the handling and roadability, and the sheer complexity of the new racer caused a lot of teething troubles which had to be worked out. The speed, however, was never lacking, with the 350 clocking over 130 mph on the faster courses and the 500 hitting around 150. The end result was a great deal of precision engineering and lots of speed, but few trophies.

Then came the war and the factory at Neckarsulm was virtually destroyed. During the immediate post-war years the factory was rebuilt, and Walter Moore was replaced as chief engineer by Albert Roder. One of Roder's first triumphs was the 100cc Fox model, introduced in 1948. This 6 hp ohv model set a new trend in styling, comfort, and performance for a lightweight, and sales rapidly expanded.

The little Fox model had a square bore and stroke at 50mm, and it developed its horsepower at 6,500 rpm on a 7.8 to 1 compression ratio. With a maximum speed of 55 mph, the performance was spirited enough to capture the hearts of the public, yet the price was low enough for the wartorn Europeans to afford. A leading-link front fork and a torsion-arm rear suspension made the Fox a comfortable mount.

The rigid frame 125cc ZDB two-stroke remained in production as a cheap utility bike, and the 200cc LUX model was also added to the range. The policy at NSU was to produce small bikes that the poor populace could afford, and any racing would have to be on a very slim budget.

Racing runs deep in the German blood, however, and history records the deeds of a fellow by the name of Wilhelm Herz. Wilhelm built up a 350cc racer from the ruins at the factory, and then later a 500cc model. At first he contented himself with competing only in German national races, as Germany was on "probation" by the FIM until 1951 and could not compete in international racing. Using his blown twins, he racked up a list of impressive home country victories, but the urge for something really big gnawed away inside.

Finally Herz could stand it no longer and he approached the company executives about his plan to capture the world motorcycle speed record. Surprisingly, the upper echelon agreed, and Herr Roder went to work to prepare the bikes. By fitting a vane-type blower instead of the original impeller unit, it was possible to increase the horsepower to 70 and 105 on the two engines. The next step was to design a fully streamlined shell to cover the bike and rider, and then everything was pronounced ready.

On April 12, 1951, the quiet dawn of the Munich-Ingolstadt Autobahn was shattered by the ripping roar of the 500cc supercharged twin. Wilhelm rode well that day, for the speed record took a thrashing. The new speed was 180.065 mph--NSU was in the news!

Meanwhile, Roder was not sitting still. Off his drawing boards came some new road racing designs and some roadsters. The most exciting of the roadsters was the 250cc Max, which featured a unique connecting rod and eccentrics method of driving the single overhead cam. Introduced in 1953, the Max was followed by a 175cc version called the Maxi, and a refined 250cc version called the Super Max.

These ohc models were produced until the late 1960s, and they featured a clean looking pressed-steel frame with a leading-link front fork and a standard swinging-arm rear suspension. With top speeds of 68 and 80 mph, the two NSU cammers have proven to be smooth and comfortable.

The best brain child of chief engineer Roder has probably

All-conquering 1954 NSU 125-cc of Rupert Hollaus was one of earliest "dustbin" streamlining attempts. Shell is hand-hammered aluminum.

been the 50cc Quickly model, a two-stroke moped introduced in 1953. This has become NSU's best seller, with as many as 95,000 units being sold in one year. The specifications of the Quickly include a bore and stroke of 40 x 39mm in its little engine, which is mounted in an "open" type of bicycle frame.

Then there were the 350 and 500cc Konsul models which were introduced in 1954 and produced for a few years. These ohc sport singles were designed as a high speed or "clubman" type of sports bike, and the 500 had a maximum speed of around 100 mph. A clean looking mount, the Konsul featured a telescopic front fork and a plunger rear suspension. The two models were known for their fine workmanship, but they failed to catch the public's fancy and so they were later dropped from production.

Sales of NSU products continued to climb until, in 1955, a total of 342,583 machines were produced. Then two-wheeled sales began to fall in Europe as the countries had recovered so fully that the populace could afford the luxury of an automobile. NSU responded by introducing the Prinz light car in 1958, with a 600cc engine which was virtually a double-up of the Max design.

Since then, the NSU folks have gained a great deal of fame with their Prinz car and their new Wankel-engined Spyder car. The company no longer produces motorcycles, but cars are taking an every increasing share of production as the standard of living in Germany continues to rise.

cycles includes only the Quickly; carrying forward the goal of reliable transportation for the man on the street.

This, however, is not the end of this story of NSU, for the really greatest chapter in the marque's history was in the 1953 to 1956 era when the company made a full-fledged attack on the world's great racing courses. Albert Roder, in 1952, began this chapter, when he designed new 125cc and 250cc grand prix racers. It took a year to get all the bugs worked out of his new design and develop some championship riders, but when

This is the NSU Sportmax, a 250-cc 4-stroke racing single.

this was accomplished there was no doubt whatsoever that Herr Roder and equipe were the finest racing technicians in the motorcycle business.

The new 125cc racer was a single with measurements of 58 x 47.3mm, and a vertical shaft drove the set of spur gears on the double overhead camshafts. The 250 was a twin, with slightly different measurements of 55.9 x 50.8mm. Both racers featured a six-speed gearbox, a swinging arm frame, and a leading-link front fork.

The new NSUs were first raced late in 1952 and Werner Haas obtained a significant second place in the Monza Grand Prix. During the winter, the models were refined and a sleek dolphin shell made its debut. The hand-hammered aluminum stream-lining gave a notable increase in speed and earned the factory

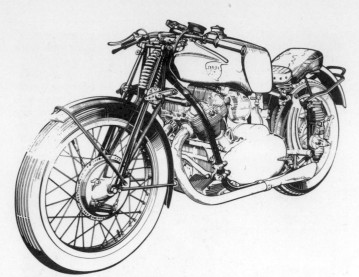

1939 NSU Grand Prix racer was a potent supercharged twin. Double-overhead-camshaft engine was produced in 350- and 500-cc sizes.

the reputation for progressive thinking.

In the Isle of Man TT races, Werner rode both his racers into second place behind the 250 Guzzi and 125cc MV Agusta. In the Dutch event, the little Bavarian reversed the tables and from there he sped on to capture a first in the 250cc German classic, a second in the 125 event, a win in the 125cc Ulster event and a second in the 250 class behind teammate Reg Armstrong, and then another 250 second at Monza plus a win in the 125 class. This splendid record gave Werner both the 125cc and 250cc World Championships--the first-ever German "Doppelweltmeister."

The 1953 successes were just a hint of things to come, for in the Spring of 1954, the NSUs were considerably quicker than the previous year. Development work by Roder during the winter had hoisted horsepower from 31 to 42 hp on the 250 model, and from 17 to 20 hp on the 125. With the dolphin fairing Haas was clocked at 123 mph--which was a truly fantastic speed in those days.

In the June 250cc TT race Werner Haas, Rupert Hollaus, Reg Armstrong, H.P. Muller, and Hans Baltisberger took first, second, third, fourth, and six places to simply crush the opposition. Werner's record speed was 90.88 mph, a truly remarkable increase over the 84.73 average of only one year earlier. In the 125cc class Rupert Hollaus took the win, with Baltisberger in Fourth position.

The rest of the 1954 season was strictly an NSU walkover, except for the Monza classic where the team did not race due to the death of Rupert Hollaus in a practice lap crash. Hollaus, however, had garnered sufficient points to become 125cc World Champion, with Haas again taking the 250 title. After the Ulster GP, the NSU dolphin fairing had been replaced with a full dustbin type and the improved air penetration provided a speed of 136 mph from the 250 twin--a truly remarkable achievement.

For the 1955 season the factory announced that they would retire from the pukka works team racing, but that H.P. Muller would ride a factory prepared 250cc Sportmax single in the classics. The idea, no doubt, was to give some publicity to the new production racer, which was based on the standard Max model. Another factor may have been that the post-war economic boom was allowing the German citizenry to switch from motorcycles to cars, and NSU was beginning the switch to follow their new market.

At any rate, no one really gave Muller much chance at the world title that year. The season proved, however, to be full of suprises, mostly due to the lack of reliability on the part of the Italian factories who were in the process of developing new engine designs. With a rather mediocre but reliable record, Muller garnered enough points by the season's end to capture the World Championship. The following few years the NSU Sportmax continued to acquit itself admirably, being the consistently best placed 250cc production racer until 1960, when better, more modern designs overwhelmed it. Two names, in particular, who established great reputations early in their careers on Sportmax models were John Surtees and Mike Hailwood.

Then followed the swan song of the NSU concern in international competition--the fabulous 1956 speed records set at the Bonneville Salt Flat. Exhibiting the usual NSU type of technical excellence, the team arrived with a 12 hp supercharged 50cc model, a 15.5 hp unblown 100cc model, the 20 hp 125cc and 42 hp 250cc unblown models (the 1954 works road racing engines), and the fabulous 75 and 110 hp 350 and 500cc models. The smaller engines were all mounted in the long and low "flying hammock" chassis developed by Gustav Baum, and the 350 and 500cc models were basically the pre-war road racers with an elongated frame and a full shell.

For one whole week the NSU team screamed across the flat, and when it was over no less than 54 new world records were put into the books. Probably the most noteworthy was the 210.64 mph clocking by Wilhelm Herz in the 500cc model--the first time the "double ton" had been exceeded on two wheels.

The Baumm II screaming across Bonneville Salt Flat in 1956. Gustav Baumm developed shape, used by all recent record contenders.

The 350 model attained 189.5 mph, the 125 set a 150.3 mph record, the 100cc unit clocked 138.0, and even the little 50cc projectile did 121.7 mph. The 100cc and 250cc unsupercharged models ran on 80 octane gas, and the other engines used a diet of straight methanol. The runs, however, did have one big failure, and that was the 180 mph crash of Herz in the 250cc projectile when a gust of wind suddenly hit. It had been hoped that the 250 model might attain the magical 200 mph mark, but the model was too badly bent to make further attempts. Herz, miraculously, was unhurt in the crash.

This is the story, then, of the NSU--one of the great prides of the "Herrenvolk." It is a story of typical Teutonic technical development and success. For the present the company is concentrating on their small cars instead of motorcycles, but maybe someday this will again change and we will hear the howl of NSU exhausts over the world's great racing courses.

In 1952 NSU appeared with this 500cc four, which was soon dropped to concentrate on the 125 and 250cc class.

The 1965 Quickly was a tiny 50cc two-stroke moped that sold by the millions in Europe as an inexpensive mode of transport.

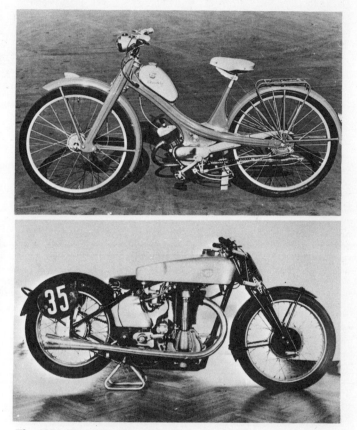

The 1951 Fox was a peppy four-speed 125cc two-stroke with the unusual rear suspension that is quite similar to current moto-cross practice.

The 1930 NSU 350, 500 and 600cc OHC racing singles were an impressive looking model but not fast enough to defeat the AJS, Norton or Velocette singles.

OSSA

Ossa is a relative newcomer to the international motorcycling scene, but, in just four years, this Spanish marque has established an enviable reputation among the world's sporting-minded riders. The story of this innovative concern is a fascinating tale of remarkable men who love the sport, and they, perhaps more than the technical excellence of their wares, are a most interesting aspect of Ossa's history.

The story of Ossa actually began in 1924, when Manuel Giro bought an American-made Cleveland 270-cc two-stroke Single. Giro quickly fell in love with motorcycling. Even today, the 64-year-old company boss thinks in terms of two wheels and an engine--especially in its more sporting forms.

Giro spent the early 1920s as a merchant marine officer. After he married, he founded his own small business, and raced motorboats in his leisure time. His company, Orpheo Sincronic, S.A., produced movie projectors and related types of cinema equipment. The name "Ossa" was later to come from the initial letters of the words in this company name, but that was in the future.

The innovative genius of Senor Giro was first demonstrated in his boat racing activities. He designed his own engines, named Soriano, and these outboard motors powered him to several world speed records.

Giro's interests soon returned to motorcycles, however, in the early 1930s, he purchased an ES2 model Norton, an outstanding bike for the time. The ohv 500-cc thumper, with its hand-shifted, four-speed gearbox, carried Giro about the Spanish countryside in regal style. By then, his tiger instinct had developed, so Giro decided to race. Luck was with him, for he convinced Norton ace Percy Hunt to sell him his works ohc CS1 model after the Spanish Grand Prix. The pukka racer had a rigid frame, foot-shift cog box, and 100-plus-mph performance--as well as a reputation for winning races all over Europe. The beastly power proved to be the undoing of Giro.

He proceeded to slide down the road on the seat of his britches in the six or seven races he entered.

During the middle 1930s, Giro changed to a 500-cc BMW Twin, but this underpowered model didn't improve his race record. The answer was more power, so he mounted one of his Soriano outboard motors in the BMW chassis. The six-cylinder ohc Soriano powerplant displaced 998 cc, and had a big, wicked looking supercharger.

The power output was a devestating 112 bhp at 6,000 rpm-- nearly three times that of other bikes. But the old BMW had a rigid frame and girder front fork--hardly equipment to hold 112 bhp steady down a winding stretch of road! The result usually was a searing screech of rubber laid down each straight, followed sooner or later by a crash at a corner.

After this unsuccessful racing career on two wheels, Giro turned to the sidecar class and won a Spanish championship. Then Giro concentrated on expansion of his cinema enterprise, which today produces 80 percent of all Spanish movie projectors. His final fling at the motorbike game before World War II was the designing and building of a 125-cc single-cylinder prototype. Giro later gave this engine to Montesa. He now ruefully recalls that this engine powered the first road racing Montesa to many Spanish championships.

After the war, Giro's primary interest was to design and produce a good motorbike. He was motivated by his affection for motorcycle sport, and the excellent business opportunity that existed then. In the late 1940s, Spain was entering an era of increased affluence because of the industrialization and irrigation of the country. Thus, the people could park their burros and begin to ride motorbikes.

Giro's first model was advertised in 1949. This first Ossa, the 125, proved to be an exceptionally sound design that established a fine reputation for workmanship, reliability, and performance. The 125-cc Single proved that Manuel Giro had a

The first Ossa, a 125-cc two-stroke single, was produced in 1949. Three-speed gearbox and telescopic front fork were featured.

1954 model B was first Ossa to have modern swinging-arm frame with oil-spring shocks. 125-cc engine gave 6.5 bhp at 5000.

Ossa has produced two-speed mo-ped for many years. Inexpensive 50-cc models, which get nearly 200 mpg, sell well in Spain.

real talent for motorcycle design. Profits from 80,000 models sold from 1949 through 1952 gave the infant company a sound financial base.

The first Ossa was very advanced for the time. A swinging arm rear suspension was controlled by large rubber bands. The use of the swinging arm principle in 1949 is noteworthy; this was the first year that Royal Enfield and AJS-Matchless pioneered the idea on their production models.

The bore and stroke of the two-stroke was 54 by 54mm, and a peppy 5.0 bhp was produced at 4500 rpm. This was a respectable output for those days, and it provided a 47-mph speed. The Ossa weighed a light 154 lb., and a three-speed footshift gearbox was used. The front fork was a telescopic type, but no oil damping was used on rebound. Tire size was 2.75x19, and a 3-gal. fuel tank was fitted. Very comfortable in those days of rigid frames, the handsome red bikes soon filled the Spanish countryside.

Ossa's next model, the Moped 50, was designed to provide the Spanish populace with a cheap, easy-to-ride motorbike. The moped featured a 42- by 36-mm two-stroke engine that developed a lively 1.2 bhp at 45 rpm. The 49-cc engine was mounted in a "girls type" bicycle frame, and lights, powered by a generator, made the bike suitable for night riding. The moped was produced through 1956, at which time it was dropped due to the demand for more power and speed.

In 1954, the company produced a much more modern looking bike, the 125-B. Vastly improved by Giro's increased technical knowledge, it offered the luxury and performance which Spanish riders could by then afford. The model B had the same bore and stroke as its predecessor, but an increase in compression ratio to 6.5:1, plus more sophisticated porting, pushed the power output to 6.5 bhp at 5000 rpm. The maximum speed through the three-speed gearbox was 56 mph, which was really stepping for 1954.

The model B's frame was completely new, with a modern swinging arm rear suspension that used spring-oil shock units. The front fork was a new telescopic type that had oil-dampened rebound control, and a beautiful pair of alloy hubs with deep ribs helped dissipate the brake heat. The tire size was still 2.75x19, but the weight had risen to 198 lb. With a comfortable dual seat and a sleek finish, the Ossa proved to be a popular mount, and the company continued to grow.

In 1958, the marque enlarged the 125 to a 150-cc mill by going to 58- by 56.4-mm measurements. Named the Comercial model, this two-stroke produced 8.0 bhp at 5000 rpm on its 7.0:1 compression ratio. In an effort to make the model more satisfying for the tourist, the rear chain was completely enclosed, thus keeping the bike and rider clean. The comercial model remained in production until 1963.

In 1959, the sporting 125-C was introduced. The engine was basically the same as the B model, but an increase in compression ratio to 7.0:1 provided livelier acceleration. The most significant change was the new duplex cradle frame, which provided greater rigidity and improved handling. Wheel sizes were reduced to 2.75x18, and the 5.6-in. diameter brakes were very powerfull. With narrow sports type fenders, a sleeker dual seat, low handlebars, and trim accessories, the model C was the first indication that Giro might return to the sporting use of motorcycles.

The model C was followed in 1960 by the model C-2, which was a refinement of its predecessor. But the next model introduced was a real innovation; Ossa left the two-stroke field and produced its first four-stroke model. Called the Gran Turismo model, the new 175-cc Single had a bore and stroke of 60 by 61 mm. The power output on the 8.3:1 compression ratio was 12 bhp at 7000 rpm, which provided a speed of 75 mph. The engine and the new four-speed gearbox were contained in one case. The gearshift lever was mounted on the right side, the opposite of previous practice.

The Gran Turismo's frame also was unique in that it resembled so closely the famous Metisse frames produced by the Rickman brothers in England. The GT model was produced as a sports mount, and its large alloy engine finning, 22.5-mm carburetor, 160-mm brakes with an air scoop in the front brake, and sports fenders, seat, and handlebars made it popular with pseudo-racers in Spain. The 242-lb. weight gave the GT a stable feeling, and it soon became known for its fine handling and powerful brakes. The GT was produced through 1963, at which time it was dropped from production. The marque evidently felt that the two-stroke had a better future in Spain, since its production cost was lower.

During the middle 1960s, Ossa sales suffered because, by that time, more Spanish people could afford to purchase small cars. But the firm benefited from the arrival of Eduardo Giro, Manuel's 28-year-old son. Eduardo is a natural engineering genius, and it is he who is responsible for the current success of Ossa in sales and competition all over the world. Eduardo first demonstrated his talents at age 15, when he designed and

The 1959 model C was first Ossa with duplex cradle frame. This 125-cc model was very reliable, and popular with Spanish riders.

1960 Gran Turismo was beautiful 175-cc ohv single producing 12 bhp at 7000 rpm and capable of 75 mph. Note big air-cooled brake.

Santiago Herrero warms up Ossa GP 250 prior to test run. Powerful single has immense engine fins, monstrous expansion box.

built an 18,000-rpm model airplane engine. Since then, this studious young man has applied himself to motorcycle design.

Eduardo's first designs were the 160 and the 160 Turismo—both 160-cc models with a bore and stroke of 58 by 60 mm, a compression ratio of 8.5:1, and a power output of 10.3 at 5750 rpm. The only real difference between the engines was that the kickstarter and gearshift were on the right side on the 160 and on the left side of the Turismo model. Both models had four-speed gearboxes and ran 65 mph, and both models featured powerful 40- by 158-mm brakes. The 160 had the air scoop on the front brake on the right, while the Tourismo had the scoop on the left. They are still in production.

By 1965, it was obvious that Ossa would have to develop an export business if it were to survive the decreasing demand in Spain. At that time, Ossa was little known outside of Spain. The problem was how to become known all over the world, and the answer was not long in coming. With Manuel's love of racing, plus the technical genius of Eduardo, the only logical approach was competition.

With this in mind, Eduardo designed the prototype model, which was to compete in the classical Barcelona 24-hour race. This great endurance event is for standard production models, although there is some leeway in the rules for prototypes by the factories. Since a team of two riders takes turns for the full 24 hours, the bikes must have full lighting equipment. The exhaust systems can be modified for more power, but pukka racing models are not allowed. The idea is to race standard production models with only those modifications that a private owner could make, and the premium is on reliability.

The bike that Eduardo designed was a 175-cc Single with a bore and stroke of 60.9 by 60 mm. The compression ratio was a rather high 11.5:1, and the power output was 19 at 7200 rpm. The four-speed gearbox was shifted from the left side, and 2.75 x 18 tires were mounted on alloy rims.

The optomistic factory entered a pair of these prototypes in the Barcelona classic, and they garnered a 1st and 2nd place in the 175-cc class over the highly favored Bultacos and Montesas. Pedro Millet and Luis Yglesias racked up a total of 584 laps in the 24-hour grind, compared to 631 for the winning Dresda-Triton (650 Triumph in a Manx chassis) and 559 laps for the fastest 175-cc Montesa.

The Ossa managers were so enthused by this stunning upset that they decided to enter a foreign race, the British 500-miler at Thruxton. The Millet-Yglesias team came home 6th in the 250-cc class on their 175 Single. These two fine showings in 1965 made Ossa better known throughout Europe, and created a new demand for the machines in the export market.

Ossa was quick to take advantage of its newfound reputation in 1966 by producing the 175-cc model for export. The new Single featured a 27-mm carburetor and pumped out 21 bhp at 7500 rpm, good enough for a top speed of 85 mph. The gearbox had ratios of 15.9, 10.7, 7.97, and 6.51:1. Dry weight was a light 207 lb., and wheelbase was a short 52.5 in. With powerful brakes, extra fine handling, and outstanding performance, these Ossas made many friends around the world. The 175 is still in production, but very few made their way to this country in 1966.

In 1966, the company again had a bash at the classical Barcelona event, this time with a new 230-cc prototype model. The marque did quite well, taking a 3rd in the 250 class behind Montesas, and a 5th overall with two Montesas, a 500-cc Velocette, and a 650-cc Triumph ahead of Yglesias and Petras.

This fine performance brought the company more publicity, and the company responded by producing the 230-cc model for 1967. The new Single had a bore and stroke of 70 by 60 mm, a compression ratio of 11.0:1, and a 32 mm-carburetor. Peak power was 25 bhp at 7000 rpm, which provided a speed of 87 mph.

This rugged engine was mounted in an excellent duplex cradle frame, and a Telesco front fork provided 4.75 in. of travel. The accent of the 230 is definitely sporting, with such features as a knee-notched 3.9-gal. fuel tank, narrow sports fenders, sports seat, low handlebars, high performance exhaust system that pushes the noise level to the legal limit, and powerful brakes, as effective as they are beautiful. The wheelrims are alloy, and the tire size is 3.00x18. The 230 became popular with sporting-minded street riders all over the world, and the export market flourished as never before.

In 1967, the company increased its activity in the production model racing game to a fever pitch, partially because of its desire to become better known, but also because of increased interest in this type of racing throughout Europe. The model used was the already proven 230-cc Single, modified by using the optional race kit that anyone can now purchase for this model. The kit includes such goodies as an expansion box exhaust system, huge 5-gal. fuel tank, racing seat, tachometer, racing tires, clip-on bars, and a rearset footpeg-gearshift-brake kit. With the kit installed, the Ossa is a kissing cousin to a pukka racer, and the top end is pushed to over 100 mph.

The first big event that year was the first of the Isle of Man production model TTs. The lone Ossa entry, in the hands of Trevor Burgess, got off to a poor start when the kickstart lever broke on the starting grid. Trevor eventually got away in last position, but managed to finish 11th at 77.98 mph, which was over 10 mph slower than the Bultacos.

The other big event in 1967 was the rugged Barcelona classic, and the Carlos Giro-Luis Yglesias team gained the marque a tremendous amount of prestige when they romped home the winner over all the big bikes entered. Ossa also took 1st and 2nd in the 250-cc class, and its 662 laps in the 24 hours was a record that stood for many years. This stunning victory brought the marque a great deal of publicity, and the export

events, winning a Gold Medal in the 1967 International Six Days Trial in the hands of Englishman Mick Andrews. The British ace also gained the marque great recognition by taking 3rd place in the 1968 Scottish Six Days Trial. Other Ossas placed well throughout the field.

In 1969 Mick Andrews displayed a superb style in the rugged Scottish classic with a solid second place on a vastly improved bog wheel, and then in 1970 he scored a magnificent win that really established the reputation of the company. All of this research was applied to production practice, and for 1971 new five-speed trials and enduro models were introduced. Andrews once again won the classic Scottish Six Days Trial, as well as the prestigious European Championship, and then in 1972 he scored his third consecutive win in the classic Scottish event.

In 1968, the company once again featured prominently in the international production machine racing game. Ossas took 4th, 5th, and 7th in the Barcelona grind, as well as 2nd, 3rd, and 4th in the 250 class. Perhaps the marque's greatest hour came in the IOM production class TT, when Trevor Burgess trounced the 250-cc field on his 230-cc thumper at 87.21 mph. This speedy performance would have given him a 4th place in the 500 class and a 6th in the 750-cc class--not bad for a 230-cc Single with a bolt-on kit!

This success in production model racing and trials competition brought the company a further boost in prestige and export sales, but to the brilliant Eduardo this was not enough. Eduardo believes the greatest glory is reserved for the fire-breathing grand prix machines and that success in this field is the very summit of achievement for an engineer. With this in mind, Manuel gave his son blessings to produce a genuine grand prix racer.

Most successful rough-stuff Ossa has been the trials model. This 250-cc single took 3rd place in 1968 Scottish Six Days Trial.

The 1964 model 160 was first modern Ossa with excellent suspension, powerful brakes, sleek appearance and peppy performance.

market continued to grow.

In 1968, the company expanded its roadster range by offering new 160- and 175-cc models in both touring and sports trim. The 160 Sport pumped out 10.3 bhp and ran 65 mph, while the 175 SE model developed a wicked 21 bhp and ran 87 mph. The 50-cc moped also was produced, mainly for the European market.

In 1967 the company made a significant move in entering the rough-stuff game by producing trials, motocross, and enduro models. All of these models use the new 250-cc (72- by 60-mm) engine, but differences in tune distinguish them. The trials model, for instance, ran on a 9.0:1 compression ratio and developed 16 bhp at 6000 rpm. Carburetion was by a small 24-mm carburetor, and an extra wide ratio four-speed gearbox was used. The motocross model used a 33-mm carburetor on a 12.5:1 compression ratio, and it pumped out 32 bhp at 7000 rpm. The enduro model ran on an 11.0:1 ratio and developed 20 bhp at 6800 rpm. The enduro model was equiped with lights, and was produced especially for the American market.

The trials model has been fairly successful in European

Eduardo began the design work in 1966, bearing in mind that his small company could not afford to finance exotic multis or a vast works team. The goal was maximum performance on a modest budget; Eduardo chose the trusty old single-cylinder design.

By late 1966, the engine was completed and on the test bed, and early in 1967 the completed bike was given its first test runs. The specifications of the Ossa GP are rather unique, and technical aficionados are facinated by it. The engine featured a rotary valve, since Eduardo found that a disc valve would better charge the crankcase than a conventional piston-controlled port. The exhaust system must be the largest expansion box ever built, and the gearbox was a six-speeder. Ignition was by a unique transistorized setup, and the engine finning was immense.

The frame was totally unorthodox with its monocoque chassis. Made from alloy sheet, the frame was extremely light, yet very strong. Probably the most unusual specs were the oleo-pneumatic front and rear suspension units, throwbacks to the old KTT Velocette air-oil shocks. The advantages are that

A beautiful shot of the contemporary Ossa Pioneer, a 250-cc 2-stroke enduro machine with a 4-speed gearbox.

the air pressure and/or oil flow can be quickly adjusted to suit local track conditions, and the large reservoir of oil does not overheat or aerate--thus changing the suspension characteristics during a race.

With an impressive 45 bhp on tap, the Ossa was considered the fastest 250-cc two-stroke Single on the grand prix circuit. The new Ossa's first race was the 1967 Spanish GP, in which Carlos Giro took the bike to 6th place. More work obviously was needed.

In 1968, the GP model reappeared in the hands of 1967 and 1968 Spanish 250 champ Santiago Herrero. Many minor changes had been made to improve the handling, suspension, and reliability. The first race was the German event at the Nurburgring, where Santiago took a 6th place. In the Spanish GP over the twisty Barcelona circuit, Santiago actually led the 70-bhp Yamaha V-4s until his engine blew, but Carlos Giro

saved company honor by finishing 4th. By then, the racing world was astounded at the sheer speed of the disc-valve Ossa Single.

In the famous TT races, the Spanish ace could fare no better than 7th, but the 37.75-mile island course **does** take a bit of learning. In the timed section on the drop to Sulby, the Ossa was clocked at a cool 121.6 mph, the fastest by a single-cylinder 250 in the race.

Santiago then proceeded to take a 6th in the Dutch, 5th in the Belgian, and a 3rd in the Monza GP. Despite missing several races that season, Santiago finished in 7th position in the 250-cc World Championship, and Ossa garnered 4th in the manufacturers' championship. In races he finished, Santiago was never headed by another single-cylinder model.

In 1969 Santiago finished a close third in the 250cc championship after a torrid season of racing. The dynamic and popular Spaniard won three grand prix events that year--a tremendous achievement for a single. Tragedy struck in 1970, though, for Herrero crashed in the Isle of Man and died later from his injuries. This so saddened the company that they withdrew for the rest of the season, but recent development work suggests that they have not lost their love of racing.

And so ends this tale of Ossa--a story of fascinating personalities, brilliant engineering on a modest budget, and a typical Spanish love for competition. Currently one of the most interesting makes on the market, the Ossa surely must have a great future ahead of it in international motorcycle sport. Unknown until recently in this country, the company nevertheless has a colorful history that began when Manuel Giro pointed his Soriano-BMW down that winding Spanish road. A rigid frame, 112 horsepower, and a girder front fork--the screeching of rubber and then a horrible crashing of metal. That was just the beginning.

The Mick Andrews Replica is a superb 250cc trials model with three Scottish wins to its credit. The weight is 210 pounds.

PUCH

One marque about which little is known in America is the Puch--an Austrian concern that has never courted the American market with the fervor displayed by other manufacturers around the world. Instead, Puch has chosen to concentrate on an eastern European market, where its philosophy of producing unspectacular but sound machines has met with great success. The company also has an unspectacular but significant sporting history, and this story is virtually unknown to American motorcyclists.

The story of Puch began a very long time ago when Johann Puch set himself up as a bicycle mechanic in 1889. In 1891 Johann began the actual production of bicycles, but in 1897 he sold out and retired. However, Johann's restlessness demanded an outlet, and in 1899 he again entered the bicycle production and in 1903 the production of a true motorcycle began. This business prospered so much that in 1910 Johann had the necessary capital to allow the designing of a small automobile.

This first Puch was, naturally, a rather primitive device compared to modern machines, but it did follow accepted design principles of those days and proved to be as reliable as any of the undependable motorcycles that were produced then. The powerplant was the then common inlet-over-exhaust valve type of engine, which was a single-cylinder model that developed 2¾ hp. Larger 3¼-hp and 3½-hp models were also available, all of which had the engine mounted centrally in the frame. These early Singles used a magneto for ignition, and lubrication was provided by a hand-operated pump.

Transmission of power was accomplished by a belt on these 1903 Puchs, and pedals were used for starting and on hills. Only one brake was fitted, which was a band type on a dummy rim on the rear wheel. In two years Johann produced 750 of these Singles, which helped get the tiny company on a sound

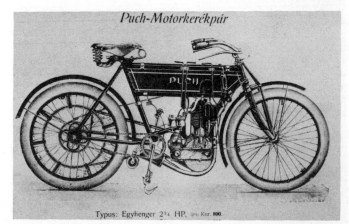

Puch-Motorkerékpár

Typus: Egyhenger 2¾ HP. ára: Kor. **800**.

First Puch motorcycle was produced in 1904 and had an inlet-over-exhaust-valve engine. Note belt drive and pedal gear.

financial basis.

In 1905 and 1906 Puch produced his first Twins--3½-, 5-, and 6-bhp models that were otherwise quite similar to the Singles. The engine was an I.O.E. V-Twin, and 1900 of these models were soon on the Austrian roads. Puch also began production of automobiles then, and all of this activity made him a leader of the early motoring industry in Austria

The 1930-31 Puch 250 split single GP model won many races, but is probably more noted for ugly appearance. Gearbox was three-speed.

The next few years Puch expanded his production and improved his machines, sticking with the four-stroke design and making it more reliable. Most of these models were Singles, but a few Twins were produced that had up to 6 hp. A few of these Twins were ultra-deluxe mounts for the connoisseur of fine motorcycles; however, they were a rarity, as only 50 of the model II and ten of the model MM were ever produced. Then came World War I, and the Puch Werke was forced to halt all production from 1917 through 1923.

After the war, some new brainpower was brought to Puch in the person of Ing. G. Marcellino (Johann had died in 1914), and under this man's guidance the Puch Werke was destined to become a major European producer of motorcycles. The first of Marcellino's new designs appeared in 1924. This unique model featured a split-single, two-stroke engine in which two pistons used a common combustion chamber. Both pistons worked from a common split connecting rod, but the transfer ports were located in the rear cylinder and the exhaust port was located in the front cylinder. The idea was to obtain a cleaner running engine with less loss of the fresh fuel charge out the exhaust port, since those were the days before loop scavenging when a raised edge on the piston crown was used to prevent the incoming fuel charge from traveling out the exhaust port.

Another peculiarity was the crankshaft placed parallel to the frame. This required that the tranmission convert the power from parallel to a right angle with the rear axle, since chain drive was used. The two-speed gearbox was contained in the rear hub, and the pedal gear was dispensed with. This new model, called the LM, had a 122-cc engine that pumped out 2 hp, and internal expanding brakes were used for the first time.

By this time European motorcycle manufacturers were producing variations of their basic models to suit different needs, with Puch producing the LM model in the man's, woman's and sports model. The sports model featured a lower set of bars, a central plug head, and an open exhaust, just in case an owner wanted to go racing. A few of these sports models were even produced with an outside flywheel. The top speed of this Puch was about 35 mph, and the split-single design went a long way toward improving the spark plug fouling that was so common

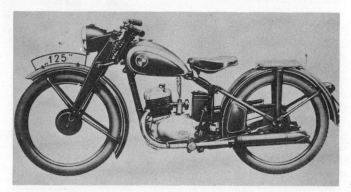

An exceptionally clean looking Puch was 1939 125-cc split single that put out 5.2 hp with one carburetor or 7.5 hp with two.

then on two-strokes.

The LM model was followed in 1925 by a 175-cc version which pumped out 3 hp. In 1926 the 220-cc model made its debut with a 4.5-hp output. This last Puch was a tremendous success; 12,000 of these 220s were sold during a three-year period. This split Single, a three speed, would do about 48 mph. Puch's next model was a big 10-hp, 500-cc Single, which used the side-valve JAP engine produced in England. This model didn't sell well, so the company dropped it after one year to concentrate on developing their split-single design.

In 1929 the marque introduced the 250-cc model T, and by 1932 no less than 13,200 units were on the roads. This 6-hp (at 3000 rpm) model was followed by the 8-hp 250 Special in 1931, and by the 500-cc Z model in late 1931. The Z, a 14-hp vertical Twin, never sold as well as the smaller 250s, which had a bore and stroke of 45 by 78mm and gear ratios of 15.73:1, 7.69:1 and 5.16:1

In 1933 the Puch had a more modern appearance with its fuel tank mounted over the top frame tubes instead of between them, but it still looked about 10 years behind the British bikes which were setting the style and sales pace in those days. Two of the most popular Puchs then were the 250-cc Tourenmodell and the 250-cc Sportmodell, both of which had the split-single

In recent years Puch has built fast works road racing bikes like this 125-cc single, which had unusual radially finned engine.

1960 Gelandesport model was 250 produced for such enduro classics as International Six Days Trial. Rugged model performed well.

engine and the crankshaft set parallel with the frame.

The parallel crankshaft created a few power transmission problems, and consequently these Puch models of the early 1930s had some very unique design features. Foremost of these peculiarities was the location of the clutch in the rear hub. The three-speed gearbox was mounted directly behind the engine, and it had a right-angle output shaft so that chain drive could be used. The gearbox was shifted by hand and there was a hand clutch lever, which was common continental practice then. These 7-hp models sold reasonably well, due to such features as internal expanding brakes on both wheels and improved reliability. The frame was rigid on these Puchs and the front fork was the girder type, so rider comfort was still questionable.

In 1934 Puch introduced a vastly improved S4 model that had a more modern appearance. The S4 was a 10.5-hp, 250 split Single, and a cleaning up of the external bits and fittings gave it a more purposeful appearance. The basic design was much the same as the earlier models, but a four-speed gearbox provided a more spirited performance. Perhaps the most suprising thing about the S4 was the new lubrication system, which consisted of a mechanical pump and oil tank system that delivered oil under pressure to the intake port. This dispensed with the messy gas/oil mix, and it also shows us that a lot of our "modern" designs aren't quite as new as we think they are.

The next milestone in the Puch's history occurred in 1938 with the introduction of the 350-cc Grand Sport. This 12-hp split Single was designed to satisfy the needs of the growing number of sporting minded riders during the late 1930s. It was intended as a fast roadster or an off-road machine. The frame was a tubular twin-loop cradle type that featured a coil-spring rear suspension. The travel was rather limited on this swivel-link suspension, but then those were the days when spring frames were in their experimental stage. The new Puch also featured, for the first time, a foot gearshift.

The Puch 350-cc GS also had a raised exhaust system and a substantial ground clearance. Deeply valanced fenders and a nicely shaped fuel tank gave it a more modern appearance.

These GS models became very popular with Austrian riders, and they proceeded to perform creditably in the enduro type trials that were held then in continental Europe.

During the late 1930s Europe had recovered from the economic depression of the early '30s to such an extent that a market existed for a luxurious roadster. Puch attempted to satisfy this demand in 1936 with a beautiful 800-cc opposed Four. Not much technical data is available today on the fabulous 800, mainly because of the damage done to the factory during World War II, but it is known that only 550 of these prestigious machines were ever built. The Puch Four was not an exceptionally brilliant design, though, and it was dropped after 1938.

The last Puch to be designed before the war was the 125-cc T, a clean looking split Single that pumped out 5.2 hp. The T model was also available with a two-carburetor cylinder that had "sports" timing on all the ports. This bomb churned out a very respectable 7.5 hp. The Puch was equipped with a unit-construction engine-gearbox design, and the gearbox had three speeds. The frame was rigid and had pressed girder front forks. Dual exhaust ports and pipes were used on the T model, but the clutch was finally moved to the gearbox mainshaft end.

This new T model, produced from 1939 to 1952, established an excellent reputation as an attractive, peppy and reliable lightweight. Indeed, historians now consider the Puch T to be a classic in design evolution, as it well represents the excellence of small motorcycle design during the late 1930s.

There are several other interesting items about the pre-war Puch history that are notable, one being the merger with the giant Daimler corporation in 1928. After that came the amalgamation with Steyr in 1934, thus merging the motorcycle end of the business into a huge steel factory, armament and automobile industry. Then came the war, and 960 bombs rained out of the sky onto the main works at Steyr. After the war it naturally took a few years to rebuild from the rubble, but by 1949 the factory was humming and some totally new models were produced.

The first of these new Puchs was the 250-cc TF model, a superb machine that was as modern as anything on the continent. The TF model was available in either standard or sports tune, which was a one or two carburetor option that allowed 12 or 15 hp to be produced. The engine was still the, by then classical, split Single, and it featured two exhaust ports and pipes. The powerplant also had unit construction and a four-speed gearbox.

The frame was new on the TF model, featuring a plunger rear suspension that contained coil springs but no hydraulic dampening. The front fork was a hydraulically dampened telescopic type, and the rest of the bike had exceptionally clean lines. The TF proved to be a good bike as well as pretty; even today it would seem to be a modern design.

In 1951 Puch made another great stride forward when they produced the 125-cc SL model and the 150-cc TL model, both of which had the modern swinging arm rear suspension. The 125 had a bore and stroke of 38 by 55mm, while the 150 had a 40-mm bore. The 125 used two carbs and pumped out 7.5 hp at 5500 rpm on a 6.5:1 compression ratio, while the 150 developed 6.5 hp at 5000 rpm on the same ratio. The maximum speed of the two models was 65 and 60 mph respectively, and both had four-speed boxes.

Perhaps the most significant thing about these new lightweights was the styling, which was ultra-modern and included a sleek pressed-steel frame. The accent on styling, comfort and protection from the elements made Puch a leader in Europe.

The next improvement came in 1953 when the 125-cc SV and SVS models came out with full-width hubs cast in alloy. The one or two carb theme was carried out on these two models as well, with 6.5 or 7.6 hp being produced. These Puchs had deeply valanced fenders and a spring loaded and hinged seat, which went a long way toward improved riding comfort.

During the late 1950s Puch became interested in entering a works team in such rugged classics as the International Six

Shown competing in 1968 International Six Days Trial is this 175-cc Puch; radial engine fins can be easily seen in this view.

242, 245, and 306 lb., which certainly indicated how ruggedly these bikes were built.

During the early 1960s Puch continued to market these venerable old designs, but by 1965 the company realized that some new designs were needed, especially for the smaller sized bikes. In response to this demand for a true lightweight, the company designed a 50-cc two-stroke engine that had an orthodox single cylinder and a bore and stroke of 38 by 43mm. This engine was then mounted in a wide variety of frames, from scooters to roadsters and scramblers. The accent was on a low initial cost plus a modest maintenance and operating expense. Today these tiny buzz bombs can be seen scampering all over the Austrian roads.

The new design trend soon resulted in a larger 125-cc Single with a bore and stroke of 55 by 52mm. The power output is a solid 12 hp at 7000 rpm on an 11.5:1 compression ratio, and a 1.03-in. bore Bing Carburetor is used. This new Puch, called the M-125, was introduced in 1966. The chassis is orthodox but rather racy looking, and the new engine has an unusual radially finned head. A four-speed gearbox is used on the 125, the factory has produced the new 100, 175, and 250 models--all of which are Singles except the 250, which is a twin.

In recent years Puch's interest in the trials and enduros that are held all over Europe has inspired it to produce many special works models for these events. The marque has been highly successful, too, and the factory museum now holds hundreds of trophies, gold medals, and silver medals that have been won in these events.

This competition activity naturally led to the marketing of some production comp models. At present a range of 50, 100, 125, and 175-cc bikes are produced, all superb trials or enduro machines. The 50, 100, 125, and 175 Sportmodelles pump out 9.3, 14.8, 18.1, and 20.9 hp at engine speeds of 9200, 8400, 8000, and 7300 rpm. The weight has been dropped to 177 lb. for the 50-cc model and 207 lb. for the larger models.

For those who like more power there are the 125-cc and 250-cc Rennmodelles that pump out 21 hp at 10,000 rpm and 40 hp at 10,000 rpm respectively. The gearboxes have six and five speeds on these two bombs, and top speeds are 105 and 124 mph. These road racing bikes are currently produced only in limited numbers for selected works riders. The bore and stroke on the 125 Single in 55 by 52mm; the 250 Twin has the same measurements. The Single has one 30-mm Dell Orto carburetor, while the 250 has a pair of 30-mm units. Not much else is known about these two-stroke grand prix machines, but they are rumored to have a competitive performance. Hopefully, the factory will continue to develop this beautiful grand prix bike.

Perhaps the most interesting 1970 Puch was the pukka trials model, a 125 that had a six-speed gearbox in ISDT trim and a wide-ratio, four-speed box in English trials trim. The enduro version came with lights and a 16 hp at 8800 rpm engine, while the pukka trials model was stripped to the bone and had a 12 hp at 7000 rpm powerplant. Both models had 2.75x21 front tires and 4.00x18 rear tires. The trialster weighed only 156 lb. and had ratios of 47.0:1, 28.0:1, 18.75:1, and 15.0:1, which made it a superb bog wheel in rugged going. These newest Puchs have performed remarkably well, as was proven by Scot Ellis who won the prestigious 1969 Welsh Three Day Trial without the loss of a single mark.

Puch's recent interest in competition is unique in the company's history with but one exception, and for this chapter we must go back to the early 1920s when Ing. Marcellino decided that the best way to gain some much needed prestige and publicity was to go road racing. This was a logical move for many companies then, since motorcycle sales were rapidly expanding, and a successful racing campaign helped a company obtain its share of this market. In those days road racing also provided a tremendous amount of technical knowledge that could be immediately incorporated into improving thier standard roadsters, since road racers then were normally only tuned-up roadsters.

The saga of Puch grand prix machines began in 1925, when Rupert Karner and Hugo Hobel garnered 2nd and 3rd places in

Days Trial and other endurance trials popular in Europe. This, of course, required a suitable machine, so the factory organized a competition shop to build a good comp model.

One of the first of these new works competition machines was the 1960 250-cc Gelandesport. The 20-hp, two-carb bike performed in an exceptionally good manner in the ISDT that year. It featured a special frame that provided 10 inches of ground clearance, knobby tires and an upswept exhaust pipe. These cobby looking enduro models with a split-single engine proved to be both reliable and rugged. A modest number were also produced for the private owner.

Another interesting Puch about which little is known is the 1951 speed record model that set a 250-cc, 24-hour mark of 74.7 mph. The bike, a 250 split Single, was ridden by the French father and son team of Georges and Pierre Monneret and two men known only as Moury and Weingartmann. Its fine record is still standing in the FIM record book.

By 1961 Puch had a good range of models that were selling well in Eastern Europe, and they decided to court the American market by contracting with the huge Sears Roebuck Co. to sell their wares under the Allstate brand name. The models then were the 125 SV (6.5 hp at 5800 rpm), 125 SVS (8 hp at 6100 rpm), 175 SV (10 hp at 5800 rpm), 175 SVS (12.3 hp at 6200 rpm), 250 SG (14 hp at 5400 rpm), and 250 SGS (16.5 hp at 5800 rpm). All of these models had the split-single design laid down by Ing. Marcellino 40 years earlier. The 250-cc models had the oil injection system that dispensed with the gas/oil mixing.

These Puchs were very strong and reliable, virtues that the east Europeans dealy love in their motorcycles. The performance was not spectacular, but it was certainly adequate for a day-to-day transportation machine. The maximum speeds for the 125-cc models were 50 and 55 mph, while the 175-cc models would clock 62 and 69 mph. The big 250s would run 65 and 76 mph, and fuel consumption was about 75 mpg. The dry weights of the 125-, 175-, and 250-cc models were listed as the Monza 250-cc race with a pair of 125-cc LM models that had been fitted with an open exhaust and central-plug head. The company also had some 175-cc models to use then, one of which had a bronze cylinder and head.

That same year Puch won their first race when Karner won the 175-cc class of the Austrian Grand Prix with a special supercharged works model. The factory could not provide any technical data on this unique split-single two-stroke, but one old photo does show that the blower was mounted in a small case on the right side of the crankcase. The supercharger appears to be a piston pump similar to those made famous by DKW. The top speed of this model was listed as 55 to 62 mph, and the output was 5 to 6 hp.

In 1926 the marque raced their standard split-single engine with its parallel crankshaft with great success, taking a 1-2-3 in the Austrian GP 175-cc race. These works models had a three-speed gearbox with the clutch in the rear hub. The roadsters were still using the two-speed rear hub.

In 1927 Puch came out with its 220-cc model, but the company continued to use a standard 175-cc machine for racing. A new racer was designed later that year that had two exhaust pipes and ran 80 mph--a fantastically fast bike then. Rudi Runtsch won the Austrian TT 175-cc race, easily outspeeding the fast 250-cc model, but the reliability was not up to the speed potential. The engine had a bronze head and produced 11 hp.

Puch also tried an ohv four-stroke in 1928, which was a JAP V-Twin that was slotted into a Puch chassis. This model proved to be a failure, so Ing. Marcellino went back to developing his two-strokes.

In 1930 the marque decided to go all out and produce a genuine grand prix machine to trounce the fast British 250s. This model proved to be one of the most unique and, perhaps, the ugliest road racers ever built. The basic design was a 250-cc, split-single two-stroke with the crankshaft parallel to the frame. The three-speed handshifted gearbox drove through a rear hub clutch. This racer featured a piston-type compressor that helped suck the incoming fuel charge into the crankcase on the upstroke of the piston and compressed it into the combustion chamber on the downstroke. This engine was also water cooled, and the magneto was mounted upside down on top of the gearbox. Peak power was listed as 14 at 4400 rpm, with 4800 being maximum revs.

This blown two-stroke created quite a sensation when Toricheli first appeared at the Austrian TT, which was probably due as much to its horrendous appearance as it was to its fierce performance. Elvito won his race at 81.5 kph and came home 7th behind all of the 350- and 500-cc bikes entered. Siegfried Cmyral performed well in the other races. Puch even got brave enough to leave its home circuits and enter the German and Dutch classics, only to discover that the British

ohv Singles were much too fast for its stroker. Toricheli came home 5th in the German, and Cmyral took 5th in the Dutch.

The Puch factory found some more speed before the Austrian GP, though, and Cmyral and Toricheli demolished the fast DKW of Walfried Winkler and all of the British bikes. In the Swiss event Toricheli turned in the fastest lap for all classes, but he later retired with a broken water hose. The season's verdict was: fast, but not yet totally reliable.

During the winter the race shop toiled to improve its racer, with a foot gearshift and larger compressor being the main changes. The new engine developed 18 hp at 4400 rpm, and Toricheli clocked this model at 83 mph, a fabulous speed for 1931. Cmyral rode a special speed record model to a sizzling 87.2 mph record; this really set the British factories to work! The speed model had been shorn of its large radiator and had only a small water tank. Its record run was made on the Neunkirchner Straight in Austria.

Puch got off to a great start in 1931 when Toricheli won the Hungarian GP, and in the continental national races these Puchs easily outsped the DKWs. The marque's greatest hour came on July 5, though, when Toricheli trounced a big field at the Nurburgring in Germany to prove that the Puch was by far the fastest 250.

By then the Puch Werke was deeply involved in the racing game, so Ing. Mikina designed a totally new twin-cylinder racer that had the crankshaft at a 90-degree angle to the frame. In this design each piston had its own crankshaft, but a common combustion chamber was still used. A different setup was also used on the compressor, so that the pressure was exerted through a diaphragm valve to charge the crankcase, the same approach that DKW used. This new racer had a 23 hp output and a four-speed gearbox, so great things were expected of it.

As it transpired, the new Puch was raced only once, and it finished 3rd. Then the race shop was closed, which was an economy move in the depression years when motorcycle sales were falling quite drastically. The exotic racer saw life again during 1937 and 1938, when a privateer named Franz Novotny used it in Austrian national races for many good "places" plus a few wins. Then came the war, and the Puch race shop was totally destroyed. This is the major reason why technical data is so scarce on these unique racing machines.

In analyzing the history of Puch, it is obvious that they have never been a real giant molding history nor have they left a museum full of great classical machines. Today their emphasis in on producing good, sound, reliable bikes; aside from that there is certainly nothing spectacular about their wares. Perhaps their greatest contribution lies in the legend of some really unique designs, and for this alone they must be accorded a position of interest in motorcycle history.

The 1974 Puch 125cc moto-cross model developed 19 HP at 9000 rpm and weighed 202 pounds. A fierce contender.

The 1974 Puch 125cc moto-cross model developed 19 HP at 9000 rpm and weighed 202 pounds. A 250cc version won the 1975 World Motocross title.

ROYAL ENFIELD

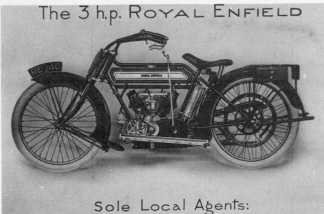

Sole Local Agents:
A. BELL & Cº Market Place, REDDITCH

The 1913 350-cc V-twin featured two-speed gearbox and chain drive. Dry sump lubrication system had glass oil tank below seat.

England is by nature a rather conservative country, yet its people often have, by the dint of sound thinking and dedication to a goal (and a paradoxical bent for creative tinkering(, achieved some noteworthy and classic results. This is especially true in the manufacturing of motorcycles, where their design innovation down through the years had been sound and progressive, while at the same time a respect for the past has been maintained that has created legends of nostalgic proportions.

Typical of this philosophy of progress tempered by tradition is Royal Enfield--a Redditch concern that has an impressive record in both design innovation and competition results. The history of Royal Enfield does not, however, contain any

dramatic successes on the world's classical road racing courses, for the company has nearly always chosen to proceed in other directions. The history does contain many splendid "firsts" in design improvement, and the marque's record in trials competition is both outstanding and colorful.

The story of this typically English business began in 1892 when the Enfield Manufacturing Company was established in Hunt End, a village near Redditch. The product at that time was bicycles, which has been a popular way for many concerns to get started in motorbike production. The name of the infant business was changed to Enfield Cycle Company in 1896, and the first motorcycle was produced in 1898.

This first motorbike was a spindly looking affair, with a tiny engine mounted on the front fork that drove the rear wheel by a belt. The engine featured the inlet-over-exhaust-valve design-- the exhaust valve was opened and closed by a cam, the inlet valve sucked open by the piston on its down stroke. This primitive engine produced about 7.5 bhp, and pedals were needed for starting and for aid on hills. There was no method of disengaging the engine on this model, since clutches were not in general use then, and neither wheel had any suspension.

It was not a particularly good design, even for those early days, so in 1902 a new model with the engine mounted centrally in the frame was introduced. This model was also less than impressive in sales volume, and for a while it looked as though the company wasn't going far in the motorcycle field. An interesting innovation was made in 1906, however, when a high-tension magneto was used. This device provided more reliable sparking than the previous battery-coil ignition, which was notoriously unreliable.

The fortunes of Royal Enfield finally turned upward in 1910 when the management really got down to the designing of a good motorcycle. With this effort came the concern's first attempt at racing, which was a popular approach in those days for the purpose of obtaining advertising prestige. The result was a 5th place in the 1911 Isle of Man Junior TT, which made the name better known to the public.

Since 1898 Royal Enfield motorcycles had used engines made by another "proprietary" company, at that time a common practice in Europe. As this approach seemed to be unsatisfactory, in 1912 the Enfield firm began building its own engines. The first was a 340-cc V-twin with a bore and stroke of 54 by 74 mm. This design proved so dependable that almost overnight the Enfield became one of the leading English makes.

The engine still featured the inlet-over-exhaust-valve design, and the power output was rated at 3 bhp--a respectable performance in 1912. This new Twin was actually quite advanced for its day; it had a two-speed countershaft gearbox, clutch, and all-chain drive in a era when the belt drive was still in vogue. Thus, Royal Enfield must be considered a pioneer of the chain drive.

Another innovation was the dry sump lubrication system, which used a mechanical pump to deliver oil to the engine and back to the oil tank. This was another area that Enfield pioneered, for in those days the hand-operated oil pump (the rider pumped a lever several times each mile) was still in common use. The oil tank, incidentally, was a glass bottle so the rider could see the oil reserve. We might point out that the idea wasn't as crazy as it sounds, since oil consumption in those days was much greater than today. We can only imagine, however, that the company must have done a booming business in selling replacements.

The Royal Enfield Twin had other interesting specifications that were far ahead of their time, such as fully enclosed valve gear that prevented oil from running down over the engine, a big selling feature. Other specifications orthodox for their day included a girder front fork with a single coil spring, caliper type of brakes on the rims, hand gearshift lever, and a rigid cradle frame.

Company sales continued to expand, and in 1915 a 225-cc single-cylinder two-stroke model was introduced to cater to the people on a tight budget. This little Single also featured chain drive and a two-speed gearbox, and a visionary idea was the footshift lever for the gearbox.

The company had a serious bash at the 1914 Junior TT with their Twin. They came home in 3rd, 8th, 15th, 18th, 20th, 21st, 23rd, and 26th positions. All told, eight of the nine entries

Almost modern looking with its clean lines, the 1935 TT single finished 8th in the Senior TT. Top speed was 110 mph.

The 1927 side-valve single had three-speed handshift gearbox and internal expanding brakes. Lights were optional equipment.

finished, which was a fine show of stamina that greatly helped the reputation of the tiny company.

Then came World War I and the RE company, like all its counterparts, was plunged into war-time production for the government. After the end of hostilities the company resumed production, dropping the little V-twin and producing only the 225-cc two-stroke and a huge 1140-cc side-valve V-twin that developed 8 bhp.

The range of machines continued to expand, and in 1924 new 350-cc Singles were offered in both overhead valve and side-valve designs. These new Enfields featured a three-speed handshift gearbox, a rigid frame, girder front fork, and a "saddle" fuel tank that went over instead of between the two top frame tubes. These Singles were very popular, mostly because of their reliability and good handling qualities.

In 1927 the company made an attempt to produce a "people's" model in their 200-cc two-stroke Single. This mount featured a three-speed gearbox and exceptionally clean lines, and proved popular as an everyday transportation machine. An interesting feature of the two-stroke was its large outside flywheel, but the rest of the machine was orthodox for its time.

During the late 1920s the company became interested in racing again, and they developed a grand prix machine that used a J.A.P. engine. The J.A.P. powerplant was a 344-cc Single with overhead valve and two exhaust ports, and the rest of the bike was modified Enfield parts. These 350s gained several good placings in the famous TT races, but they were not quite fast enough to have a chance of outright victory. The company did produce a replica racing model for sale to the private owner for a few years beginning in 1926, but then the factory once again lost interest in racing.

The next mention of Royal Enfield in the competition sphere

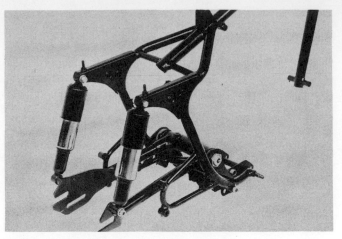

The swinging arm frame that Royal Enfield Pioneered in 1949 was well ahead of its time, particularly for trials use.

was the world speed record for sidecars set by E. Magner in 1930. The model used a 1000-cc J.A.P. engine, and it recorded 117.76 mph for the flying mile. A search in the factory archives failed to disclose any additional information about this bike. The record run was most unusual, however, in that it was set in the dead of winter on a frozen lake in Sweden.

During the early 1930s there was an effort made by several British manufacturers to produce a more refined utility model that would gain wider public acceptance. One of these was the Royal Enfield "Cycar"--a 150-cc two-stroke that featured metal paneling over the main portion of the bike. Leg shields

Bullet model was popular sports mount during late 1930s. The girder fork, rigid frame and footshift were standard practice then.

Royal Enfield

MODEL J2. "500 BULLET."
The ideal machine for really fast road work.

This Replica model was a trials classic. Alloy engine developed good low speed power. Dry weight was only 309 pounds.

In 1962 the marque produced this 250-cc trials mount. Despite its cobby appearance, it didn't perform as well as larger singles.

provided the rider with protection from the weather and wet roads, but the model never caught the public's fancy and it was soon dropped.

British motorcycles became more sophisticated during the early 1930s, with improvements in performance, appearance, and reliability. Royal Enfield designers were very progressive during those years, and a new range of Singles became very popular. These were produced in 250, 350 and 500-cc sizes, and the purchaser had the choice of side-valve or overhead valve powerplants. A new four-speed footshift gearbox was available, while the hand clutch had by then replaced the foot clutch. Another feature was the oil tank being contained in the crankcase--a move to lower the center of gravity and thus improve the handling as well as making for a cleaner looking and running bike due to the absence of oil lines.

During the middle 1930s the road racing sport developed into a magnificent international spectacle with hundreds of thousands of spectators. A good showing in these events brought a company great prestige and often an increase in sales, so it was not suprising that Royal Enfield once again became interested in the TT.

The first machines were entered in the 1934 Senior TT, and they were an interesting model as well as being a fascinating chapter in the history of the company. The powerplant was developed from the company's standard 500-cc pushrod Single, and it had a bore and stroke of 86 by 86 mm. The head, however, was totally different, being a parallel four-valve unit cast in bronze. A single 1-3/32-in. TT carburetor was used, and the engine was canted slightly forward in the frame--a common practice in the early 1930s.

An unusual feature of the TT model was the alloy con-rod with its plain floating Duralumin bushing for a big end bearing, which was used instead of the more normal roller bearing. This bearing needed a plentiful supply of oil and a large clearance. This made for ample mechanical noise and a strong smell of castor oil. The problem was eventually solved by replacing the Duralumin bushing with one of steel which was faced on both sides with white metal. This bearing could be run at a closer tolerance and proved to be eminently satisfactory.

The rest of the bike was quite conventional for 1935. A rigid cradle frame was used in conjunction with a girder front fork, and a four-speed Albion close-ratio gearbox was mounted behind the engine. The brakes were large steel drum affairs that had fins but no air scoops for cooling, and the alloy fuel tank had a long classical shape. The top end was claimed to be 110 mph, which was good but not quite good enough for 1935. C.S. Barrow brought this model into 8th place in the 1935 Senior TT, but then the company once again lost interest in racing.

During the late 1930s, observed trials developed into a leading attraction, and Royal Enfield decided to pursue this field by introducing the "Bullet" models. These were splendid

motorcycles for the fellow who needed an everyday transportation mount but who also wanted to compete in weekend trials. The 250-cc (64 by 77 mm), 350-cc (70 by 90 mm), and 500-cc Bullets used the same engine as the standard models, but modifications were made to cams and compression ratio to pep up performance. The greatest difference was in the chassis parts, with upswept exhaust, narrow fenders, wide-ratio gearboxes, quickly detachable lights, and several tire sizes and types all being available.

These Bullet models became very popular with the more sporting minded riders, and the factory even went so far as to sponsor a works team for trials events. During the 1937 and 1938 seasons the Bullet overwhelmed its opposition, and it became known as an exceptionally fine handling trials bike.

Aided by all this publicity from the trials game, the sales continued to expand during the last years before World War II. One noteworthy innovation in 1939 was the adoption of the plain con-rod big-end bearing on all the Singles, which was a benefit of the knowledge gained from the colorful TT racer.

Then came World War II and once again the Royal Enfield plant was turned over to W.D. production. After the war the company brought out a tiny 125-cc two-stroke and the 350-cc model "G." The 21-incher featured a new hydraulically dampened telescopic front fork. These utility models were continued for several years and helped get England rolling again, and the export market was exploited all over the world.

By 1949 the economy had developed to the point where more luxury could be permitted, and the factory came out with a new 500-cc Twin as well as a swinging arm frame for both the ohv models. This use of the now accepted swinging arm design was not the first, of course, but it was one of the first and was well ahead of most of the other larger British manufacturers.

The new Twin had a bore and stroke of 64 by 77 mm, and it produced 25 bhp at 5500 rpm. This Twin was subsequently developed into a 700-cc size (Meteor) and then to the 750-cc Interceptor in 1963. The Singles were also developed, with a 500-cc model added to the range in the early 1950s and the 250-cc unit-construction model in the early 1960s. The 350-cc Bullet was also changed to the unit-construction design, but then the 500-cc model was dropped. The company also produced a pair of 250-cc Twins during the 1960s, and these models had Villiers two-stroke power plants. An interesting model in 1965 was the ohv 250-cc "Continental GT"-- an 85-mph speedster set up to look much like a road racer complete with racing windscreen and five-speed gearbox. Another innovation was the availability of two streamlined fairings--a move to make the bikes more comfortable at cruising speeds.

The Singles, however, failed to maintain a brisk sales pace, so in 1967 the range was reduced to only the big 750-cc model. The Royal Enfield Company also ran into financial problems then, and the rights to production were aquired by the Enfield

Precision Ltd. concern. This passing of the Single was lamented by many, since the reputation for fine handling and stamina had gained many friends all over the world. This was true even in America, where the Enfield has won many cross-country and trials events, such as Eddie Mulder's trouncing of the Big Bear field when he was only a 16-year-old kid. The Enfield, incidentally, was imported into this country from 1955 through 1959 with "Indian" on the fuel tank. And then lastly, there is the fantastic record in flat track racing that had been racked up by Elliott Shultz and others on their 500-cc Singles.

The production of the big 750cc twin continued until 1970, at which time the financial troubles proved to be fatal. The big twin bowed out as a solid 120 mph roadburner in several stages of trim and tune, which ended yet one more name in British motorcycle history.

There are, however, two final chapters in the Royal Enfield story that hold great intrigue for aficionados of the sport. One effort was the 1964-1966 road racing model, which was promising but not overly successful; and the other chapter was the trials models, which were both colorful and fabulously successful.

The racing bike was a 250-cc two-stroke Single with an Alpha crankcase and Herman Meier-designed upper half. Operating on a 10:1 compression ratio, the engine turned to 8500 rpm and pumped out 34 bhp. This model was put into production for the 1965 and 1966 seasons, and by then it sported a huge 1.5-in. GP carburetor.

The racer's gearbox was an Albion five-speed unit, and the frame was a twin loop type with an orthodox swinging arm suspension. The front fork was a Reynolds leading-link type, and an Enfield front brake was used with an Oldani rear brake. The tire sizes were 2.75x18 and 3.25x18, and fiberglass was used for the seven-gallon fuel tank and fairing. These racers proved to be reasonably fast, but neither the works riders nor the private owners achieved any remarkable results. Many observers felt that the Single had great potential, but that not enough genuine effort was put behind the project.

The "dirt" chapter of the Enfield was more successful, and for this we must go back to 1950 when the company began producing trials and scrambles models for the private owner as well as sponsoring a works team. The 350-cc Bullet was the basis for development, and it was eminently suitable for trials use due to its low center of gravity and excellent low speed power. Operating on a 6.5:1 compression ratio, the engine developed 18 bhp at 5750 rpm.

The main changes were to the chassis parts, with 2.75 x 21-inch and 4.00 x 19-in. front and rear "tires" being used. The exhaust pipe was upswept, alloy fenders fitted, the footpegs placed higher and farther back, and handlebars were wider. With its wide ratio gearbox and swinging arm frame, this model was a superb "bog wheel," and it was thrown into competition with the best. In the early 1950's all other marques used a rigid frame for their trials bikes, since the belief was that rear springing would cause too much hopping about and handling would suffer. The Royal Enfield riders proved differently, and within a few years the others began to use spring frames on their trials bikes, especially after Johnny Brittian won the 1952 Scottish Six Days Trial.

The No. 1 Enfield rider then was a tall youngster named Johnny Brittain, and this fellow racked up a classic number of wins before he retired in 1965. Johnny first began to win the big national trials in 1953 when he came home 3rd in the championship table, and for the next few years he battled with the top AJS and BSA stars.

The great day finally arrived in 1957 when Brittain won the coveted British Trials Riders Championship, still using his trusty 350-cc Bullet that had been developed to an exceptionally fine pitch by many small but important modifications. By then the Enfield had become especially popular with the private owners, and all of the major European trials events had the beautiful Singles plonking over the hills and dales in classic trials stance.

Probably the finest achievement in the company's history

occured in May of 1957, when John won the Premier Trophy in the Scottish Six Days Trial. Many observers felt that Brittian's performance in the highlands was one of the very greatest, and it was a fitting climax to many years of outstanding performances by both Brittain and the marque in this classic of trials events. After 1957 Johnny faded from the scene a bit, which was due both to the likes of Gordon Jackson (350-cc AJS) and Sammy Miller (500 Ariel) plus having to concentrate more on the growing RE dealership he had in Bloxwich.

The company decided that this outstanding trials record justified producing a genuine Replica model for the private owner, and in 1958 it was duly offered for sale. These were magnificent trials bikes for the serious competitor, being genuine "works replicas" and not just standard production trials models.

The engine was still the basic 350-cc Bullet, but an alloy cylinder and head shed weight and improved the heat dissipation. The compression ratio was 7.25:1, and extra heavy flywheels were used to improve the low speed pulling power. Carburetion was by a small 15/16-in. Amal unit, and a special exhaust pipe was used that tucked in behind the rear frame piece. The gearbox had wide ratios of 7.56, 10.58, 16.25, and 22.68:1, and other gear sets were available. The purchaser also received extra sprockets so that he could gear the bike to suit the event.

The frame for the replica model was special, being a lightweight unit made from chrome-molybdenum tubing. Small alloy fenders were used, and a solo seat and high footpegs were fitted. The brakes were small units--7-in. rear and 6-in. front, and a narrow 2.5-gallon fuel tank was used. The ground clearance on the Single was 8-in., and the dry weight was only 309 lb. These replica models were superb trials bikes, and in the hands of private owners they established an enviable reputation.

A few years later, in 1962, the works team showed up in the Scottish event with a 250-cc model, which had been developed from the unit-construction Single. The showing by the four works riders was very good, but not quite first class. Then the interest in trials waned a bit, no doubt caused by both the trend to lightweight two-strokes and the fact that the company was experiencing financial troubles. Notable showings were made by Peter Fletcher in the 1965 and 1966 events, when he scored a 10th and an 8th place on his big 500-cc model. These performances earned Peter the award for the best "over 350-cc" performance, which was a fitting tribute to the marque that had done so much to develop the classical single-cylinder trials bike.

Something has been lost in the passing of the superb handling Singles, though, and it is in these thumpers that the real legend of the Royal Enfield lives on. For it was in the rocky highlands of the Scottish Trial that the marque carried on its quiet manner of research, and the result was a fine Single in an era when thumping exhausts were the mark of distinction.

The last Royal Enfields were produced in 1970. Developed from the 1949 500cc model, this 1966 Twin displaces 750cc.

TRIUMPH

The Triumph motorcycle, like many of its other British brothers, had its beginnings in the bicycle industry. Founded in 1885 in London, the early history of the Triumph Company is very nearly lost in the mists of time.

The founder of the company was, surprisingly, not an Englishman, but rather a German by the name of Siegfried Bettmann. Bettmann's small bicycle manufacturing business prospered, and in 1887 he was joined by a fellow German, M.J. Shulte, who was a young design engineer. Together, these two Germans were later to have a profound effect on the infant motorcycle industry.

In 1888 the company moved to new quarters in Coventry, and in 1897 the brilliant Shulte was investigating the possibilities of a motor-powered bicycle. The motor-bicycle under examination was the Hildebrand and Wolfmuller, a German machine which Shulte regarded as being far too crude to ever be a workable design. The seeds of a motor-powered bicycle were sown in Shulte's mind, though, and he was convinced that the future held great things for a motorbike.

It was in 1902 that the first motorbike was produced by the burgeoning company, when a Belgian Minerva single-cylinder engine was mounted on one of their bicycles. The original 66mm bore by 70mm stroke engine had an automatic inlet valve, battery-coil ignition, and it was mounted below the front downtube of the bicycle. For 1903 the engine was modified to standard side-valve design, and in 1904 the Triumph had a British J.A. Prestwich engine which was similar to the Belgian Minerva powerplant. The factory also produced a model that year with a larger 3 hp Belgian-made Fafnir engine mounted centrally in the frame. All these early Triumphs had belt drive and bicycle pedalgear with a single rim-brake.

Despite the early enthusiasm for the motorbike, the public had found it lacking in reliability and overall performance. With this in mind, the brilliant Shulte designed the very first all-British motorcycle in 1904 and production began the following year. The engine was a 3 hp single-cylinder side-valve, centrally mounted in a properly designed motorcycle frame. Ignition was by a reliable magneto, and the carburetor was of their own design.

To publicize this first all-British machine the company staged a demonstration run to prove its endurance. The goal was to cover 200 miles per day for six days--a really arduous test for machines of that era. The run was a success, and the new Triumph was on its way to tremendous popularity.

Production in 1905 was at the astounding rate of five machines per week, which rose to a healthy 500 machines for 1906. It was in 1906 that a front fork with a suspension spring was introduced, which made for a more comfortable ride. In 1907 the engine dimensions were enlarged to 82mm x 86mm and production increased to 1000 machines per year. In 1908 the engine was again increased to 85mm x 88mm, which made it a full 500cc; and in 1909 the production was up to 3000 units.

During those very early days Triumph became renowned on the race courses, and their trusty little singles achieved many victories. In the very first Isle of Man TT race, for instance, the marque garnered second and third places in the single-cylinder class. In 1908, Jack Marshall copped first place at 40.4 mph with a fastest lap at 42.48 mph. Other Triumphs took third, fourth and fifth places. The models featured direct belt drive at a ratio of 4.5 to 1.

A clutch in the rear hub was introduced in the 1911 models along with such niceties as adjustable tappets to set valve clearances. In 1913 a three-speed Sturmey-Archer hub gear was available, and a 225cc two-stroke was also added to the range. The company experimented with a side-valve vertical-twin engine, too, but it never did reach the production stage. This last item was a hint of what was to come in later years.

For 1914 the bore and stroke dimensions were increased to

85mm by 97mm, making it a 547cc engine. For the sporting rider a 500cc model was still available, though, as the international racing regulations limited engines to that size. The reliable Triumph single continued to make its mark in competition, such as W.F. Newsome's one-hour endurance record at 59.84 mph in 1910. The famous Isle of Man TT races continued to witness the reliability of the side-valve single as the marque garnered third in 1909, third and fourth in 1910, sixth in 1911 plus the one-hour record at 63.11 by J.R. Haswell; second, fifth and sixth in 1912; and a fifth in 1914.

Then war settled over Europe and the factory became mobilized for military production. It was, in fact, in 1915 that the model H, which proved to be such a sound design, made its

victories. Probably the most noteworthy was Victor Horsman's one-hour record of 86.52 mph. The following year he raised this to 88.21, and in May of 1925 he pushed it on up to 89.13 mph. Then he lost the record; and so in October he again made an attempt, raising the speed to 90.79 mph. This last mark was the first time a 500cc engine had pressed 90 miles into one hour. Then in 1926, Victor rode his faithful old single to a 94.15 mph mark, and that proved to be his swan-song.

During the middle 1920s the international racing scene was undergoing a great change. Previously, the machines were basically standard production models suitably prepared for racing, but by 1926 it had become necessary to build a genuine racing machine if there was to be any chance of success. It

In 1903 Triumph featured a Belgian Minerva side-valve engine mounted on bicycle frame, with pedal gear and clutchless belt drive.

debut. The 547cc side-valve engine operated through a three-speed Sturmey-Archer countershaft gearbox with a final drive by belt. Altogether about 30,000 model Hs were built for the British Army.

After the war the model H was produced for civilian use, and this was superceded in 1920 by the S.D.--a model with all chain drive and a three-speed gearbox of their own manufacture. Then chief design engineer Shulte retired and Mr. Bettmann brought in Lt. Co. C.V. Holbrook, C.B.E., to replace him. The next model L.S. was introduced which had such advanced features as unit construction and full mechanical lubrication. Previously, the lubrication was provided by a hand or foot-operated oil pump.

During the early 1920s the British switched from side-valve engines to the overhead valve design, and Triumph was right to the forefront. In 1922 the factory entered a four-valve penthouse-head engine designed by Sir Henry Ricardo in the Senior TT, and Walter Brandish took second place with it. The model had a "cast-iron" engine with a bore and stroke of 85mm x 88mm, and it was one of the very first uses of popular slipper-skirt piston. The model also hoisted the classic hour record to 76.74 mph in the hands of Major H.B. Halford.

For 1923 the factory raced a two-valve 494cc single with measurements of 80.5 x 98mm and scored some significant

was then, and still is, the policy of Truimph to race only what they sell; and so when it became evident that a "tuned" standard model had little chance of success, the interest in racing justifiably diminished. Tommy Simister did take the ohv single into a third place in the 1927 Senior TT, but other than that the name of Triumph faded away from the great racing courses.

All the knowledge gained from racing and record setting was not lost, though, and in the late twenties the company generally switched over to ohv engines. The 500cc Model P made its debut in 1925 at the modest price of 41 pounds 17 shillings (about $117) and 28,000 were produced the first year. A sporting edition called the model Q was also available in 1927, and a 277cc side-valve lightweight model W was produced.

In 1928 Triumph changed their historic grey with olive-green fuel tank colors to black with blue panels. In 1929 a 350cc ohv model was added to the range, and dry sump lubrication was adopted. In line with the general trend in the motorcycle industry, a shorter wheelbase tubular cradle-frame was used, and the fuel tank was the "saddle" type that hung over the top frame tubes instead of between them.

Then came the depression of the early 1930s and sales fell off. The whole range of Triumph machines was reorganized by A.A. Sykes, and a small, cheap two-stroke was produced along with some big singles of "sloper" design. By 1934 the company was making great strides in its automobile manufacturing, and Val Page responded by designing new vertical singles of 250cc, 350cc, and 500cc. A 650cc vertical twin was also produced which had even firing intervals with the pistons rising and falling together, unit construction, and a geared primary drive.

It was common knowledge by 1936 that the company was not doing well, though, and that their motorcycle production was going to be halted. Soon the Triumph would be a memory of the past--the only models visible would be preserved in museums.

Just at that darkest hour a man by the name of J.Y. Sangster came forward to purchase the company, and the concern's new

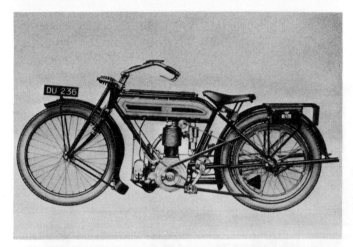

1914 side-valve Triumph single helped establish company's early reputation. Reliable machine had belt drive and wheel-rim brakes.

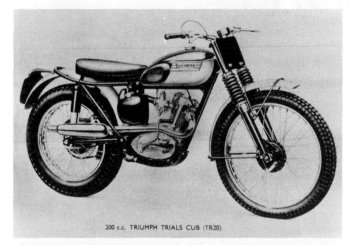

The 200-cc Cub model in trials trim. First lightweight to win famed Scottish Six Days Trial, it has great European reputation.

name became the Triumph Engineering Co. Ltd. Sangster had previously been with the Ariel Comapny, and one of his first moves was to appoint Edward Turner as chief design engineer. Turner had done a great amount of design work on the Ariel Square Four and Red Hunter single--and these models had proved eminently successful. Would this be enough to save the Triumph?

The impact of the Turner genius on the new company was immediate and positive. A new range of single-cylinder machines was marketed in 1937 that acquired a reputation of being good looking, reliable, and brisk performing. With these new thumpers, sales rapidly climbed and the future of the company was assured.

For the 1938 range another new model made its debut, and this machine can be said to have redesigned half of motorcycledom. Called the Speed Twin, the new 500cc model featured a very compact vertical twin engine with the pistons

rising and falling together but firing alternately. With the addition of the twin to the range, Triumph had a mount for just about every use except racing.

The lowest priced were the 2H and 2HC models, which were 250cc ohv singles that developed 13 hp at 5,200 rpm. The compression ratio was 6.9 to 1, and the rigid frame bike weighed 310 pounds. Both of the lightweights were popular machines.

Next were the 350cc singles, two side-valvers and one ohv model which developed 12 hp at 4,800 rpm and 17 hp at 5,200 rpm respectively. Then there were the Deluxe 5H and Deluxe 6S models in 500cc and 597cc. The 5H ohv model developed 23 hp at 5,000 rpm on a 5 to 1 compression ratio, and the 6S side-

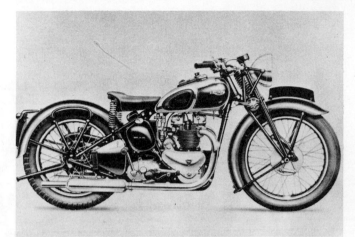

The original 1938 Speed Twin marked the beginning of the vertical twin's popularity. Top speed of this Triumph was 90 mph.

valve model produced 18 hp at 4,800 rpm. The measurements of the two engines were 84 x 89mm and 84 x 108mm. The 360-pound 6S model proved popular for sidecar use.

The pride of the range was, no doubt, the single-cylinder "Tiger" model. Produced in 250cc, 350cc and 500cc sizes, the Tiger models were "sports" machines which gave an improved performance over the standard machines. The Tiger 70 produced 16 hp at 5,800 rpm on a 7.7 to 1 compression ratio and weighed 310 pounds; the Tiger 80 developed 20 hp at 5,700 on a 7.5 ratio and weighed 320 pounds; and the Tiger 90 had 28.3 hp at 5,800 rpm on a 7.1 ratio and weighed 365 pounds. These were the 250, 350 and 500 respectively.

The star of the Tiger range was the 500cc model, and it had husky 7 in. x 1-1/8 in. brakes, narrow fenders, a 20 in. x 3 in. front tire, and a 19 in. x 3.50 in. rear tire. All the Tiger models could be ordered in competition trim, which made them suitable for trials or scrambles use. Optional extras included an upswept exhaust pipe, knobby tires, a wide ratio gearbox with ratios of 4.78, 6.93, 11.00, and 14.7 to 1, quickly detachable lights and rear wheel, and individually assembled and tuned engines. As on all Triumphs the frame was rigid and the front fork was of a girder type. The Tigers were altogether a fine mount for the Sportsman, and all this at the modest price of 77 pounds ($385).

Then, of course, there was the new Speed Twin which had measurements of 63 x 80mm and produced 28.5 hp at 6000 rpm on a 7 to 1 compression ratio. The twin weighed 365 pounds, had a 54 in. wheelbase and sold for 75 pounds ($375).

This new range of Triumph machines proved very popular, and sales of the company continued to expand. The sports singles won their share of trials and scrambles events, and the Speed Twin set an all-time Brooklands 500cc lap record at 118.02 mph. The twin was built and ridden by I.B. Wickstead, and the model featured a supercharged engine. Another Brooklands all-time lap record was also garnered by Triumph, this one in 1939 by W.F.S. Clark at 105.97 mph on his 350cc fuel burning single.

For 1939 the range of machines and optional parts offered stayed the same as for 1938 except that an exciting new Tiger

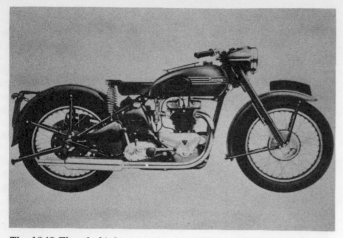

The 1949 Thunderbird set trend to big 650-cc vertical twins. Sleek 34-hp model would do 100 mph. Note rear spring hub suspension.

The 1949 Grand Prix model in all its glory. A potent racing mount with sleek lines, GP cost well below overhead-camshaft models.

100 replaced the Tiger 90 model. Based upon the Speed Twin, the new Tiger 100 was a mount to satisfy the most discriminating buyer in 1939. The engine was individually built, tuned, and tested on a dynomometer; and it was certified to produce 33 to 34 hp at 7,000 rpm on a 7.75 to 1 compression ratio. Each owner received an actual dynamometer report with his engine, signed by the works test mechanic.

The rest of the specifications whetted the appetite of the motorcycle connoisseur. The mufflers were designed to be megaphones with end caps, and by removing these caps an owner was ready to race. The front wheel had a 3.00 in. x 20 in. ribbed tire. The front brake drum was ribbed for extra cooling, and both brakes were 7 in. x 1-1/8 in. in size. A special bronze head was optionally available for the Tiger 100 which gave improved heat dissipation, and a set of tuned straight pipes were also available. With a top gear ratio of 5.0 to 1, the 7000 revs with the open megaphones gave a top speed of 106 mph. Truly, this was the machine that the British motorsportsman had dreamed of.

Then came the second war, and on a dark November night the factory was left a pile of twisted beams and smoldering rubble. To this day no one knows quite how it was done, but in ten months a new factory was built at a new location in Allesley, near Meridan. And there during the war, Triumph produced a 350cc ohv single for military use.

When peace returned Triumph immediately resumed production, and a new range of machines was fielded. Gone were the single-cylinder models, and Triumph began production of twins exclusively. A new telescopic front fork replaced the old girder fork, and in 1947 the Triumph "Spring Hub" made its debut. This Spring Hub was a rather unique method of rear suspension as it contained the coil springs within the large rear hub.

A new 350cc twin was also added to the range to supplement the Speed Twin and Tiger 100 models. In deference to the limited amount of cash available in those immediate post-war years, the Tiger 100 was not quite so sporting a mount as in the pre-war days. Horsepower was down from 34 to 7000 to 30 at 6,500 rpm, and all the hand assembled and dynamometer tested qualities were gone. The brakes were not finned, no megaphone mufflers were fitted, and few of the pre-war optional "goodies" were available.

The basic design was still very good, though, and quite naturally some sporting-minded riders turned their attention to tuning the Tiger 100 for racing. Many racing men recognized that a small-bore twin had a great advantage over a big-bore single as far as getting the highest possible compression ratio on the dreadful 72 octane "pool" petrol that was used.

It was Ernie Lyons, the Irish farmer-racer, who got the show on the road. Working with factory support, Lyons took a standard Tiger 100 and began building his racer. During the war Triumph had made an electrical generating power-unit for

Lancaster bombers using a standard 500cc twin engine which had an alloy head and cylinder with fan cooling. Ernie borrowed this alloy head and cylinder part and also obtained the experimental Spring Hub to use. With just the normal amount of speed tuning for the day, Ernie was ready to compete.

The first event for the racing Tiger was the 1946 Ulster Grand Prix. All sorts of problems were encountered that day, but the bike did show some dazzling, if rather spotty, performance. Nevertheless, Lyons was encouraged and he set about to cure all the "bugs." In September he and his Tiger appeared again, this time at the Manx Grand Prix for amateurs held over the famous Isle of Man TT course. All went well that day, despite the appalling rain, and Ernie romped home the winner at 76.73 mph.

About that time the folks at Meridan began to give some serious thought to this racing game, and so for the 1947 season a prototype racer was prepared for the Grand Prix racing season. The late David Whitworth, a top-flight racing man, was engaged to ride; and he spent the summer touring the continental events. Whitworth had a highly successful season, too, winning minor Grand Prix events at the Circuits de La Cote, du Limbourg, and George Truffant. David also captured a third place in the Dutch Grand Prix, beaten only by the factory Norton of Artie Bell and the Gilera "Saturno" single of O. Clemencich.

Encouraged by these successes, in late 1947 the factory announced that a production road racing model would be marketed for the 1948 season. Called the "Grand Prix," the racer incorporated all the knowledge that had been gained during Whitworth's campaign. The idea was certainly not to build the best racing machine available, but rather to use as many existing standard parts as was possible in an effort to keep the price down. In this manner a beginner could have a pukka racer at a price well below that of an overhead camshaft racer, and yet still have a speedy and reliable mount.

The new Grand Prix model was a beautiful machine, and it was fast. The engine was a 500cc twin with standard bore and stroke of 63 x 80mm, and an alloy cylinder and head were fitted. Megaphone exhausts were used, the standard frame had the rear spring hub, and both brakes were a massive 8 in. x 1-3/8 in. The wheel rims and fenders were of light alloy, with a 3.00 in. x 20 in. ribbed racing front tire and a 3.50 in x 19 in. studded racing rear tire.

Each engine was mirror-polished throughout, and the cams were designed to give a great amount of torque over a wide rpm range. Two Amal carburetors were used, and the float bowl was remote mounted. The engines were all hand assembled and tested on a dynamometer. On a 10.5 to 1 compression ratio the horsepower was 42 at 6800 rpm. Top gear of the four-speed close-ratio box was 4.57 to 1, and at 6800 revs this provided a maximum speed of 112 mph. On any downhill run the revs could safely soar to 7400 rpm, which gave a speed in excess of 120 mph. Another good point in the GP model's favor was its 314-lb. weight, which was well below the 370-lb. weight of a Norton Manx model.

So enthused were the Triumph folk over the new racer that they decided to set aside their policy of no direct participation in racing. In short, they fielded a genuine works team mounted on some GPs that received that little extra bit of tuning and bearing work that always helps. They also hired some of the finest riders available with such famous former TT course winners in the lineup as Bob Foster, Fred Frith and Ken Bills.

Altogether a total of nine Grand Prix Triumphs were entered in the Senior TT--but then followed a tale of disaster. One by one the riders fell by the wayside--gas tanks fractured, gearboxes disintegrated, clutches failed, and engines blew. In the end, not one GP model finished. Shaken but not yet defeated, the designers went back to the race shop and produced a new fuel tank and made minor changes in the other engine and transmission parts that had failed.

On the continent the small improvements revealed at last the excellence of the basic design. In the Dutch Grand Prix, David Whitworth took fourth; in the Ulster, Bill Beevers took fifth; and in the fast Belgian event, Foster, Whitworth, and Bills took a magnificent fourth-fifth-sixth. Then, in September, Don Crossley won the Manx Grand Prix for amateurs in the I.O.M. at a post-war record speed of 80.63 mph.

Despite the late season successes, the memory of the embarrassing Isle of Man episode brought the decision not to participate in racing anymore. The factory did produce the GP model for two more years, though, and many loyal privateers carried on with their twins. In the 1949 Senior TT they had a truly great hour, too, with Sid Jensen of New Zealand and C.A. Stephens taking fifth and sixth places, the former at 83.17 mph. These two Triumphs were the first non-works bikes to finish--a really magnificent achievement.

But then Triumph faded away from the racing scene and concentrated instead on improving their standard production machines. In 1950 the now famous Thunderbird model made its debut with a husky 650cc engine that had measurements of 71mm x 82mm. Then there followed the alloy-engined Tiger 100 and Trophy models, the later establishing a great reputation in the trials world. It was the Thunderbird that once again set a trend, though, just as the original Speed Twin did in 1937. With its beefy power it has proven exceptionally popular all over the world, and particularly so in the U.S.

Never one to sit on their laurels, the design improvement work went steadily on. In 1954 a new swinging-arm frame made its debut, and also a snarling 42 hp model called the Tiger 110. Then there was the 150cc Terrier single, a light and inexpensive mount that was later developed into a 200cc model. Then, in

1957, came the new 21 cubic inch model that featured comprehensive enclosure and provided a "gentleman's" machine.

By 1966 the range was even better, with the 200cc Cub available in road or genuine trials trim. This model was dropped in 1967, but it is historic in that the Cub was the first lightweight to win the famous Scottish Six Days Trial. Roy Peplow was the man, and he did the trick in 1959. A variation of the Trials Cub was the Mountain Cub for the American market, which had lights and a 19 in. front wheel instead of a 2.75 x 21 in. trials tire.

The company also switched over to a new "short stroke" 500cc model in 1957, which had a bore and stroke of 69 x 65.5mm. The big 650cc twin was the most popular, with the standard Thunderbird and potent 50 HP Bonneville being available. The Bonneville has been highly successful in European production racing events, with its fine handling combining with a fierce performance.

There were several models produced especially for the American market during the sixties, such as the TR-6 enduro type model and the TT Bonneville--a ready to go TT track racer. Up until the good 250 and 360cc scramblers came along, the TR6 dominated the cross country races.

During the late 1960s Triumph once again became interested in the racing game, which was first manifest with their special works racers that won Daytona in 1966 and 1967. The frame was built by the Reynolds Company, the brakes were Italian, and the engine was very much a works special. The weight was very light at around 280 pounds. The following few years the big 45 inch Harleys found more speed and the twins did not fare so well.

Triumph sprang an even bigger surprise in 1969 when they introduced their 60 HP 750cc Trident, which gained a close second at Daytona in 1970 as a works special. During these years the 650 and 750cc models were outstandingly successful in production model racing, so that the marque acquired a sporting reputation.

Triumph, however, was in financial trouble as a part of the foundering Birmingham Small Arms Company, and by 1973 it looked as though the marque was headed for extinction. Norton-Villiers then came forward to save the name with an offer of a merger, so that in 1974 a range of models was produced that included a 500cc single (the old BSA Victor), a 500cc twin in enduro trim, a 750cc Bonneville, and the 750cc Trident. The financial problems deepened, though, which resulted in a workers cooperative taking control of the factory that now produces only the 750cc Bonneville and Tiger models.

The 1965 Bonneville 650cc twin was a fast 110 mph roadburner that is still in production in 750cc form. It has been a favorite with sports minded riders for many years.

From 1956 to 1970 Triumph powered streamliners held the world speed record. This drawing reveals the details of the Dudek-Johnson rig that clocked 224.57 mph in 1962. Courtesy of Motor Cycle.

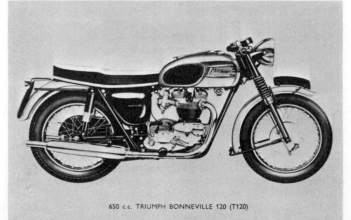

650 c.c. TRIUMPH BONNEVILLE 120 (T120)

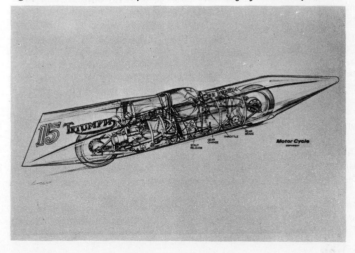

VELOCETTE

If you were to talk to European motorcyclists on their streets and ask them "which marque has the most honorable racing history?," you would possibly hear the name of Velocette mentioned more than any other. While it is true that others have gone faster, won more World Championships, and have had more exotic racing bikes, the "Velo" has still established one of the finest reputations of integrity and honesty of purpose in both their legendary racing history and their standard production roadsters.

The last true bastion of the lusty big single, the Velocette is all motorcycle. They just don't believe in gimmicks at Hall Green, Birmingham, England. Conservative to the extreme, the Velocette has always appealed to the mechanically inclined who appreciate good engineering, proven by years of racing experience, and preferably in a really good single cylinder.

One of the very greatest of pioneers in the motorcycle industry, Velocette had its beginnings way back in 1896 when Johann Gutgemann, a Prussian officer, formed the Taylor Gue Ltd. company. It was Johann's idea to join with William Gue in producing bicycles and parts. History tells us that Goodman's first business (Johann had anglicized his Prussian name) went under after they had produced their first motorbike in 1904.

Johann was not easily discouraged, though, and so in 1905 he obtained some financial backing and again went into business as Veloce Ltd. ("Veloce," incidentally, means "speed" in both French and Italian.) It was in 1910 that Goodman really got things going when he again switched from making parts to producing a complete motorcycle. The new mount was a side-valve 3½ hp single which was of a very standard design for its day.

Still a rather obscure company, Veloce Ltd. carried on in 1912 with new 276cc and 344cc singles that had an inlet-over-exhaust-valve arrangement. The new engines were designed by Percy Goodman and the tool-room work was done by Eugene Goodman, both sons of Johann, and so the business became very much a family affair. The new single gave Veloce Ltd. its first racing experience, when in 1913 it was entered in the Isle of Man TT races where it finished in 22nd (last) position at 33.27 mph.

In 1914 the company entered the two-stroke field with a 206cc single that produced a peppy 3.6 hp at 2800 rpm. The name on the gas tank was changed from V.M.C. to Velocette, and from then on Velocette it was. World War I soon interrupted activities and it was not until 1919 that Velocette resumed production with their little two-strokes. In 1921 the marque made a great hit with their model D, which had such advanced features as full mechanical oil pump lubrication, all chain drive, internal expanding brakes, a hand clutch, and a three-speed gearbox. Velocette did much better with this new two-stroke on the race courses. After the company garnered third, fifth, and seventh in the Isle of Man 250cc class, the world began to take notice and sales increased.

For 1922 the 250cc model with measurements of 63 x 80mm was improved by increasing the wheelbase and lowering the engine in the frame, adopting twin exhaust ports, fitting an aluminum head with deep finning, and using an aluminum piston in place of the cast iron sample. The three-speed gearbox had ratios of 4.9, 7.1, and 9.3 to 1. A new clutch was also introduced which was inside of the rear chain driving-sprocket- a feature retained today on Velocettes. The 250 took a third place in the TT that year, and that was about all the glory the factory garnered for a few years.

To the brilliant Percy Goodman it was apparent that the two-stroke design was about at its limit of development, and, besides, the standard of living had so increased during the middle 1920s that riders could afford the luxury of a four-stroke

Stanley Woods flat out on his Velocette at the Isle of Man. Woods won this race, the 1939 Junior Tourist Trophy.

motorbike. Hard at work at his drawing board, Percy was destined to bring forth an engine that would revolutionize engine design as well as establish the company as one of the really great leaders of the industry.

Called the model K, the new four-stroke was first announced in late 1924. It was not until 1925 that the first models were produced and these were earmarked for the June TT races. The new engine was a single-cylinder 350 with measurements of 74 x 81mm. The crankcases were very narrow and featured a full roller-bearing lower end, and the valves were operated not by pushrods, but rather by an overhead camshaft driven by a vertical shaft and bevel gears. Standard coil valve springs were used, and the head and cylinder were of cast-iron. Lubrication was provided by a dry-sump system that had a gear-type pump which forced oil through the crankshaft assembly and up the vertical shaft to lubricate the valve gear.

The frame was a "diamond" type with twin front downtubes, and the wheels had 7 in. internal expanding brakes. A three-speed gearbox was mounted in plates behind the engine, and the final drive was outside the clutch.

Performance was very good, with 5,500 revs being peak power. Two machines were entered in the 1925 Junior TT, and both failed to finish. For 1926 there were minor modifications made to correct the failures of the previous year, and a super-sports model was available which was guaranteed to do 80 mph.

With a potent 20 hp on tap, the K models were entered for the 1926 TT. Alec Bennett was engaged to ride the machine, and he won the race at the record speed of 66.7 mph, some 10 minutes ahead of the second place man. Two other Velos finished fifth and ninth, and Veloce Ltd. won the Junior team prize.

The importance and impact of this smashing victory should not be underestimated, for it had a profound effect on both the company and the entire motorcycle industry. Probably most important, at least to the company, was the tremendous public acceptance and enthusiasm for the new K model. Sales literally boomed and, from that day to this, the name Velocette was to be synonymous with good engineering and high performance.

For the motorcycle industry it brought about a wholesale rush to the overhead camshaft design, at least for racing, and within a few years all road racing machines and a great percentage of the high performance roadsters had their cams "upstairs." To Velocette went the honor of winning the first TT with an overhead camshaft engine, and for the next 26 years they were to reap the rewards of their brilliant design.

So 1926, then, is traditionally the great year for the marque, and they followed their TT success up with victories in the Brooklands and German GPs. From that year on the marque would not only be associated with racing, but they would in time aspire to the very summit--the World Championship!

It was in 1927 that the company moved to their new location at Hall Green, in Birmingham, as a much larger factory was needed to keep up with the demand for their machines. As a result, their 1927 racing successes suffered a bit, but the move did enable them to field a more comprehensive range of machines.

A newcomer joined the company that year by the name of Harold Willis--first to race and then to head up the racing department. Harold took a second in the TT that year, and Frank Longman won the French GP and also took a second in the German event.

For 1928 several new innovations came from the drawing boards of Percy and Harold--one was a success and the other a failure. The failure was an experimental spring frame that proved rather unmanageable at speed, and so it was dropped. The other idea was a positive-stop gearshift--and this was another feature that revolutionized the motorcycle industry. Previously, a rider either had to shift by hand, which was slow, or shift by foot with the chance of missing a gear. Within a few years all the other British makes had positive-stop footshifts.

In the international sporting sphere the company had a great year. Alec Bennett again won the Junior TT at the record speed of 68.65 mph and also became the first 350 to lap the Island at over 70 mph when he clocked 70.28 mph. Other Velo riders took second and fifth. The marque also captured the 350 class of the Ulster GP--and this was to be the first of many victories on the fast Irish circuit. To cap the year, the factory prepared a K model for an endurance record by upping the compression ratio from 7.5 to 1 to 10.5 to 1 and raising the gear ratio to 4.84 to 1. The attempt was entirely successful, and Velocette became the first 350 to average over the "ton" for one hour, the speed being 100.39 mph.

While the racing successes that year were good, the man-on-the-street was not forgotten, for there obviously must be profits from production to sustain a racing program. The 1928 catalogue listed six models, one a two-stroke and the rest ohc singles. The little Model U two-cycle had a 250cc engine coupled to a three-speed gearbox and it sold for a modest 37 pounds 15 shillings ($189). The lights cost an extra 6 pounds ($30), since they were considered "optional equipment" in those days.

The five K models were basically the same except for the accessories and fenders. The models KE and KES were the cheapest, and the KSS was the most expensive. The models K and KS fell in the middle. The KSS was a "super sports" model that developed 19 hp at 5,800 rpm from its 350cc engine. The compression ratio was 6 to 1 on all the models, but the KSS could be had with either 7 to 1 for petrol-benzol or 8½ to 1 for Discol PMS-2 fuel.

The ohc models all had a rigid frame with a Webb girder front-fork. A three-speed hand-shifted gearbox with ratios of 5.8, 8.4, and 14.5 to 1 was used; dry weight was only 265 lbs. An owner could obtain his KSS with an open straight pipe and a guarantee that his bike would do 80 mph. The ohc models proved fast as well as reliable, and British motorsportsmen held them in high esteem.

In 1929 the company truly took the lead when they announced that a pukka racing machine would be added to the range. Up until then a private owner had been forced to purchase a "sports" model and then modify it for racing; thus the KTT model became the very first British production racer.

Basic specifications were much the same as the KSS sports roadster, but many small changes made the KTT more reliable and faster. Although the standard frame and wheels were used, the footshift gearbox had closer ratios. The "cast-iron" engine operated on a 7.5 to 1 compression ratio and breathed through a 1-1/16 in. carburetor. Top speed was about 85 mph on a 5.25 to 1 gear ratio. The KTT had a 53-3/4 in. wheelbase

1929 350-cc KTT model, first ever British production machine. Bore and stroke measurements of 74 x 81 mm were retained until 1952.

1936 MSS 500-cc single was a rugged model with an 81 x 96-mm bore and stroke. Top speed was 80-85 mph on 4.4 to 1 gear ratio.

and weighed a light 265 lbs.

In racing that year the works team did well, with Freddie Hicks taking the Junior TT and the French and Dutch Grands Prix. Other Velo riders took third, fifth and sixth in the TT; and Hicks also brought his little 350 into sixth place in the Senior TT. In the amateur Manx Grand Prix the production KTT showed its mettle by taking first, third, fourth fifth, and seventh positions.

For 1930 there was little change in either the works racers or the production models and, as the factory was spending a great amount of time designing some new models, it was only natural that the racing program took a backseat for a few years. The 250cc GTP two-stroke was the first off the drawing boards, and it proved to be a vastly superior machine to its predecessor, the U model. About the only high note of the year was in the Manx Grand Prix where 350cc KTTs garnered the first eight places in the Junior Class, as well as a surprising second place in the Senior.

During 1931 and 1932 the economic depression slowed things down a bit, and the company produced only one new model, a 350cc side-valver that stayed in production just one year. Some design improvements were also made to the racing machines in 1932, and the works bikes featured a new engine with hairpin valve springs and a downdraft intake port. The head was cast of aluminum-bronze and the engine turned over at 6,000 rpm. The frame was also modified to carry a 3½-gallon fuel tank, and a new four-speed gearbox was used. These modifications were incorporated into the MK IV KTT, a very fine model capable of 95 mph on a fifty-fifty petrol-benzol fuel. The KTT continued to establish an enviable reputation, taking first in the 1931 Manx GP and second in 1932, plus many "places" in international classics.

In 1933 the company made another bold bid for sales with the introduction of the MOV model which had a 250cc pushrod-operated engine. The engine was square at 68 x 68mm and featured a narrow crankcase with an exceptionally rugged lower end assembly. The camshaft was located high in the timing case to keep the pushrods short and light, thus ensuring good valve control at high engine speeds. The MOV proved very popular as it was a reliable mount with a brisk performance. Subsequently, the 350cc model was produced in 1934 with measurements of 68 x 96mm, and this was followed in 1935 by the 500cc MSS with a bore and stroke of 81 x 96mm.

Meanwhile, the racing department was not sitting still. The

previous two years had not been very fruitful as the experimental work on a "long-stroke" 350 and a supercharged model had proved a failure. A new cambox was designed for both the works and KTT racers which enclosed the rockers but left the valves and springs exposed for cooling, and the twin downtube frame was replaced with a single-tube frame. The racing fortunes picked up a little with the KTTs taking fourth, fifth, and sixth in the Junior TT; first, third, fourth, and fifth in the Ulster GP, and first in the French, Brooklands, and Manx GPs.

The marque moved forward in 1934 as sales began to climb when the world moved out of the depression, and at Hall Green some brilliant engineering work was being done in Harold Willis' racing department. A new cradle frame was adopted for the works racers which had a single front down-tube. The powerful 1½ in. x 7 in. brakes were housed in massive, conical hubs which were cast from magnesium alloy, and a new alloy cylinder with a cast-iron insert was adopted. Probably the most exciting was the announcement that a new 500cc works racer would join the 350cc mount.

The new 500 made a successful debut, finishing third in the Senior TT and then winning the Ulster Grand Prix at the record speed of 88.38 mph. Walter Rusk was the rider, and in the Ulster he became the first to lap the course at over 90 when he lapped at 92.13 mph. The 350 model also did well, taking fourth through tenth places in the TT, second and fourth in the Ulster, and first in the Swedish and French events.

The MK V KTT was introduced in 1935, and it had many improvements gained from works racing experience. The new cradle frame was used and the lubrication system supplied oil to the big end, top bevel gears, and camshaft through a set of metered jets. The works racers were much the same as the year before. With the addition of Ted Mellors to the factory team, the marque's successes began the ascendancy. The Junior TT brought fourth, fifth and sixth; the Dutch GP had Velos in second and third; a second was obtained in the Spanish event; a win in the French; and then a first and second in the fast Ulster classic. The 500 did not see too much action, and a third in the Ulster was the only success.

It was apparent to the Goodman Brothers and Harold Willis that only an all-out campaign would dislodge the Nortons from their Junior and Senior class World Championships, and so for 1936 it was decided to make a great effort. Actually, the factory raced on a shoe-string budget and spent far less on racing than most of their competitors, but still they did succeed in hiring

Mainstay of Velocette racing efforts through the thirties and into the postwar era was the KTT; this is a 350cc model.

the great Stanley Woods for their works team.

In the Spring of 1936 the new works racers rolled out of the race shop. The new frame was probably the most interesting as it had a swinging-arm rear suspension that proved to be another great Velocette contribution to motorcycle engineering. The rear shock units were an oil and compressed air type, the rider pumping them up to the desired pressure. The cradle frame had a Webb girder fork at the front, and massive conical hubs were retained with an air scoop on the front brake. Two new engines were used, the 350 having a double ohc head and the 500 having a single ohc engine.

The new Velos set a trend in riding comfort and handling as most everyone else was still using either rigid frames or plunger rear suspensions. Stanley showed his worth to the team that year with a second in the Senior TT, only 18 seconds behind Jimmy Guthrie's Norton, and the record lap at 86.98 mph. In the Junior TT Stanley retired with a broken bevel gear, but Ted Mellors brought the other 350 home third. The rest of the season proved more successful with Stanley winning the 500cc Spanish GP; and Mellors taking second in the Ulster behind teammate Ernie Thomas; a second in the Swedish; and wins in the French, Swiss and Belgian classics. This splendid record gave Ted the Junior Class European Championship--the very first for Hall Green.

During the late 1930s the racing game became exceedingly competitive, so Harold Willis responded with new racers again for 1937. Both the Junior and Senior engines were single ohc as Harold came to distrust the reliability of the twin-cam unit. The new engines set a fashion in finning with a massive 11" square head that had the rockers, valves, and springs totally enclosed; and a huge "barrel" cylinder. Tappet adjustment was by eccentric mounted rocker shafts, the alloy head had inserted valve seats (another Velo first), and the metered jet lubrication system pumped oil at the rate of one gallon every

six minutes. The inlet port was downswept and the carburetor float was remote mounted on the oil tank. These were magnificent racing machines with the 350 capable of 117 mph on a 10.9 to 1 compression ratio and the 500 capable of 124 mph. Horsepower was listed as 32 at 7200 rpm on the 350 and 42 at 6700 rpm on the 500.

So into the battle they went and again Woods took second in the Senior TT, beaten by only 15 seconds. In the Junior TT Stanley had problems and finished fourth. Ted Mellors had a great year on the 350, winning the Ulster, Swiss, Swedish, French, and Italian classics, plus taking a second in the Belgian and a third in the Dutch. Velo and Mellors retained their Junior Class Championship!

Lest it be inferred here that all Velocettes did was race, let's return to the production models. The range had the GTP as a cheap utility two-stroke at the modest price of 41 pounds ($205). Next was the MOV 250 which weighed 275 lbs. and had a top speed of 65 mph. Then came the MAC 350, only 5 lbs. heavier than the MOV, and the MOV and MAC both used the same frame with a 52¼" wheelbase.

The 500 MSS was a beefy single with lots of torque, and it was very popular for sidecar work. The stars of the range were the KTS and KSS singles, the KSS being a sports version of the KTS. These ohc 350s were very popular with the sports-minded riders, and their quality of engineering and workmanship is legendary. The MSS, KTS, and KSS all used a heavier frame with a 55" wheelbase and they all weighed about 335 lbs. During 1936 and '37 a KTT model was not produced, but in 1938 the MK VII made its debut and it had all the latest refinements of the works racers except that the engine had its fins rounded off a bit and the frame was still rigid. Altogether a very fine range of quality motorcycles, and the models offered remained the same until the war.

The 1938 racing season saw a tremendous record, with

Mellors and Woods gaining many victories: Mellors took second in the Junior TT and Belgian GP, and firsts in the Ulster, Dutch, and Swiss classics. In addition, Woods won the Junior TT and set a record lap of 85.3 mph that was destined to stand for 12 years; and Stanley also took second in the Senior TT only 15 seconds behind Harold Daniell's Norton. Other Velo riders took second and third in the Senior Ulster behind Jock West's blown BMW; third, fifth, and sixth in the 350 Ulster; and second and third in the 350cc Dutch and Italian events.

It was apparent to the race shop that 1939 would be much tougher as the continental manufacturers were developing their blown racers to a tremendous level of performance. Realizing that supercharging was essential to trounce the blown BMW, NSU, Gilera, and AJS, Willis and his crew built the "Roarer" during the winter. The design was most brilliant: a vertical twin with two counter-rotating cranks, the left one driving the gearbox and the right one driving the supercharger. Full width hubs and a massive fuel tank made the Roarer one of the most potent-looking racers ever, but World War II halted all development work. The twin was given an airing in TT practice, but Harold Willis passed away just a few days before the race and it was decided to use the faithful old single. By late summer the dyno tests gave readings that would provide about 150 mph, and at 370 lbs. the twin was much lighter than some of the other supercharged speedsters of the day.

During the 1939 season the 500 singles along with their arch-rivals--the Nortons, were simply overwhelmed by the supercharged Gilera and BMW teams. Stanley came in fourth in the Senior TT and Les Archer captured third in the Ulster, and that was about it in the Senior Class. Ted Mellors and his 350 model fared better, but every race was a tremendous battle against the blown DKW two-strokes. Ted started with a fourth in the Junior TT; then took seconds in the Dutch, French and Swedish events; and then he won the Belgian to narrowly

trend to telescopic forks, the Velos all appeared in 1948 with a new air-oil fork that contained no springs. Then, in 1949, the KSS, MOV and MSS models were dropped and the model LE made its debut. The 150cc LE was an "everyman's" motorcycle with a side-valve water-cooled flat twin engine, shaft drive, and semi-enclosed for ultra-clean running.

The marque's racing successes were much the same as before the war--top dog in the 350 class and antagonist in the 500 class. Bob Foster won the 1947 Junior TT with other Velo riders in second, third, and fourth places. Peter Goodman came third in the Senior after a slow start, and Peter also turned the fastest lap of the race. On the continent the 350cc Dutch and Swiss GPs fell to Velo along with a second in the Ulster classic.

In 1948 Fred Frith led the team (he had joined Velo in 1947 but broke his collarbone in TT practice) and he won the Junior TT and Ulster events, Foster won the Belgian, Ken Bills the Dutch, and David Whitworth came second in the Swiss Grand Prix, which was the only 350cc event that they did not win that year. In the five classical events there were a total of 30 "places" giving Championship points, and Velo took 18--an altogether good year. The 500 model saw little action that season.

For 1949 the racing department brought out new 350 and 500cc models--both with dohc heads. With large GP carburetors (1-5/32" and 1-5/16"), the twin-cam racers proved very fast. Frith won every 350cc classical race, with other Velo riders gaining many second through sixth places. The 500 did not fare too well as the emphasis was then on the 350 class; a third (Ernie Lyons) in the Senior TT and a fifth (Frith) in the Swiss GP was the best obtained.

In 1950 Bob Foster carried on the winning tradition (Frith had retired) and he was crowned World Champion after great victories in the Belgian, Dutch, and Ulster classics plus a

Author Renstrom spent two years restoring this 1937 KSS 350-cc model to same trim that won 1948 Isle of Man Junior Clubman TT.

1966 Thruxton was Clubman racer with huge 1-3/8 inch GP carb and TLS front brake. 110-mph single was noted for fine handling.

retain the championship from DKW. Other 350 Velo riders took second in the Belgian (Woods), second and third in the German GP, and Stanley once again won the Junior TT.

Before leaving 1939 we must mention the MK VIII KTT which featured the swinging-arm suspension (another Velo first on production racers). With a 10.9 to 1 compression ratio, the 350 was capable of about 112 mph at 7200 rpm on a 5.0 to 1 gear ratio. These MK VIIIs were splendid racing machines, noted for their fine handling and stamina, and they garnered 25 of the first 35 positions in the 1939 Junior TT--finishing a tremendous 77% of their starters.

Then, during the War, the factory was switched over to military production. After the war the models produced were much the same as in the pre-war days, except that in 1947 the GTP model was dropped. In line with the industry-wide post-war

second in the Swiss event. Bob had tough luck in the Junior TT when he was forced to retire with a broken rear brake rod after becoming the first to break Stanley Woods' 1938 lap record. The big 500 saw little action, with only a sixth place by Reg Armstrong in the Senior TT.

In 1951 the factory surprised all by adding a new dohc 250cc model to the works team and by dropping the venerable old 500. Velos ridden by Foster, Bill Lomas, Cecil Sanford, Tommy Wood, and Les Graham carried on the battle, but the old enthusiasm for racing was slowly slipping away. Lomas and Foster took fifth and sixth in the Junior TT, Wood won the Spanish with Graham second, Lomas and Sanford took third and fourth in the Belgian, Graham won the Swiss event with Sanford second, private owners took fifth and sixth in the Dutch; and Norton regained the 350cc World Championship.

The little 250 took fifths in the IOM, Swiss, French, and Ulster events, plus a third in the Ulster. Then, at the end of the year, it was announced that the KTT was no longer to be produced. The factory made one last feeble effort in 1952 with Les Graham taking a fourth in the 250cc TT plus a few "places" in the 350 class. Then, it was all over--a great chapter in motorsport was ended.

But if the racing game was all finished at Hall Green it was apparent that the standard production range was not--for the Velo has shown a vigorous growth in quality since then. In 1951 the MAC was improved by using a telescopic front fork of their own manufacture. In 1952 an alloy head and cylinder were fitted, and the swing-arm frame was adopted in 1953. Then, in 1954, the "alloy" MSS was re-introduced with engine dimensions of 86 x 86mm. The scrambler model was added in 1955, and in 1956 the Viper and Venom high performance sports roadsters made their debut--one of these becoming the first motorcycles to average 100 mph for 24 hours. Then lastly there was the Valiant, a 200cc ohv sports version of the gentlemanly 200cc LE model.

This range of machines was continued through 1970 with the only change being to a battery and coil ignition in place of the Lucas magneto. Late in 1970 the sad news floated out of the factory that production was going to cease, despite the fact that the company was still selling all they could produce.

The reason given was that the Goodman family wished to concentrate on their other engineering interests, and it would have required outside capital to re-tool for a more modern Velocette. The family did not wish to lose control of their company, so they have decided to halt the production of Velos. A truly great name thus passes from the scene.

During its last ten years the Velo did exceptionally well in European production machine racing, generally dominating the 500cc class, so for 1965 a "Thruxton" model was added to the range to satisfy the demand for a sports-racing machine. The Thruxton established a splendid reputation, and is noted for its reliability at speed over long distances, powerful brakes, and super-fine handling.

So this, then, is the story of the "Velo," a marque that has a worldwide reputation for integrity of engineering based upon many glorious years on the world's great race courses. Long may we see the loyal riders of these magnificent singles--it's the last of the breed, really.

The famous "Roarer" supercharged twin that was never raced due to World War II and then a change of rules. Full-width hubs, a speed of 145 mph, shaft drive, and counter rotating crankshafts were featured.

The silent LE model of 1967 featured a 200cc side-valve engine, water cooling, and shaft drive. For smooth and quiet transportation it was hard to beat.

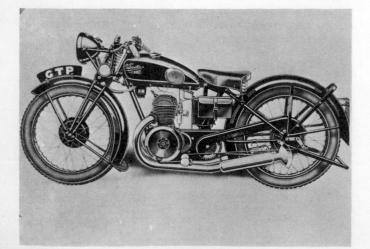

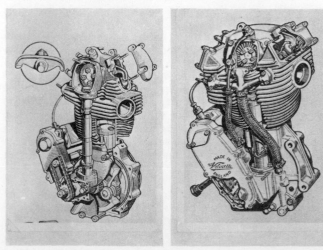

The 1939 GTP model was a 250cc two-stroke that featured an oil pump to deliver oil under pressure to the crankshaft. Last produced in 1947.

Left: The 1936 KSS engine — one of England's best. The valve clearance was set by eccentric rocker arms. Right: The 1939-51 Mk VIII KTT 350cc engine — one of the great classics in motorcycles. The 350cc engine developed 32 HP at 7200 rpm.